Coming Together,
Coming Apart

Also by Daniel Gordis

God Was Not in the Fire:
The Search for a Spiritual Judaism

Does the World Need the Jews?:
Rethinking Chosenness and American Jewish Identity

Becoming a Jewish Parent:
How to Explore Spirituality and Tradition with Your Children

If a Place Can Make You Cry:
Dispatches from an Anxious State

Home to Stay:
One American Family's Chronicle of Miracles
and Struggles in Contemporary Israel

Coming Together, Coming Apart

A MEMOIR OF HEARTBREAK AND PROMISE IN ISRAEL

Daniel Gordis

WILEY

John Wiley & Sons, Inc.

Published by John Wiley & Sons, Inc., Hoboken, New Jersey
Published simultaneously in Canada

Design and composition by Navta Associates, Inc.

For general information about our other products and services, please contact our Customer Care Department within the United States at (800) 762-2974, outside the United States at (317) 572-3993 or fax (317) 572-4002.

Wiley also publishes its books in a variety of electronic formats. Some content that appears in print may not be available in electronic books. For more information about Wiley products, visit our web site at www.wiley.com.

Library of Congress Cataloging-in-Publication Data:

Gordis, Daniel.
    Coming together, coming apart : a memoir of heartbreak and promise in Israel / Daniel Gordis.
        p. cm.
    ISBN-13: 978-0-471-78961-1 (cloth)
    ISBN-10: 0-471-78961-5 (cloth)
    1. Jews, American—Israel—Biography. 2. Jews—Israel—Social life and customs. 3. Israel—Social conditions—21st century. 4. Arab-Israeli conflict—1993– —Influence. I. Title.
    DS113.8.A4G665 2006
    956.9405092—dc22
    [B]

                                                                                    2005033576

Printed in the United States of America

10 9 8 7 6 5 4 3 2 1

For Elisheva's parents

Bernard Waxman, ז"ל
Eleanore Waxman

With admiration and with gratitude

באר ץ זרה אתה צריך לאהוב
נערה שהיא תלמידת היסטוריה...
היא מספרת לך מה שקרה בעבר
"אהבה היא עניין רציני"

(יהודה עמיחי, "בארץ זרה")

And in memory of
Limor Ben Shoham, הי"ד

רחל מבכה על בניה מאנה להנחם

ונתתי רוחי בכם וחייתם
והנחתי אתכם על אדמתכם

יחזקאל לז:יד

I will put My breath into you

And you shall live again

And I will set you upon your own soil

Ezekiel 37:14

Contents

Prologue

Our house, toward the southern edge of Jerusalem, is about two miles from the very end of the city and the neighborhood of Gilo, right across the valley from Beit Jala, a Christian Arab town that was overtaken by Muslim gunmen in the fall of 2000, in the early days of the second Intifada. Each night, as my wife and I put our kids to sleep during those first months of the renewed conflict, we could hear the rat-a-tat-tat of Palestinian gunfire from Beit Jala onto Gilo. Occasionally, it was only a few shots. But more often, what we heard were streams of machine-gun fire, bullets that we knew could not hit us, but the sounds of which still ricocheted across our house as our kids were trying to fall asleep.

Then it would be quiet for a few moments, and, rubbing the kids' backs as they lay in their beds, we could feel them beginning to relax, drifting off to sleep. Another shot or two, and the children would stir. I'd rub their backs a bit more, sometimes noticing the way they were clinging to their stuffed animals, with a desperate grip that I'd never seen before. And again they'd relax and begin to float off to sleep.

And then an Israeli tank or two would fire back. Our house would shake, and an enormous boom would bounce off the walls of their bedrooms as if the tank were just downstairs. Now they'd be awake all over again, unable to fall asleep.

This went on for days, for weeks, and then for months. They were exhausted, and we were beyond stressed. But we tried to make life as normal as possible. We went to work, and we sent the kids to school. And we promised them that on nights when there was shooting, my wife and I wouldn't go out. They weren't in any physical danger, but still, it's not a terribly comfortable feeling to be sitting in your living room, or trying to fall asleep in your bed, when your house suddenly shakes from the firing of a tank. So for week after week, month after month, Elisheva and I scarcely left the house at night.

Until one night, when there was no shooting, and everything was quiet. Why not? We had no idea. But Elisheva and I were suffering from a serious case of cabin fever, and this was our big chance. So we quickly looked in the paper to see what was going on. The community center down the street was having a celebration of its fiftieth anniversary, with food, music, fireworks, and dancing. But we weren't much in the mood. So we checked the movie section and found something decent at the closest theater. We told our kids we'd be available on our cell phones, and walked down the road to the movie.

When we got home a few hours later, there was still no shooting. Except for the sounds of the celebration at the community center, our neighborhood was quiet. As we walked down the street toward our building, though, we saw that our bedroom light was on. Not a big deal, but unusual. Who was awake? And why?

When I got to our room, I found our son, Avi, who was then about ten, craning his neck to see out our bedroom window.

"Hey, buddy, what are you doing up?" I asked him.

"What is that?" he asked nervously, still looking outside.

"What's what?"

"That!"

I had no idea what he was talking about, so I looked. And saw nothing.

"That, Abba, *that*!" he said again. "Listen!"

I listened, and got it. Louder than I'd realized, crackling as if they were just over our heads, were the sounds of the fireworks from the community center's celebration down the street. And I understood. There's not much of a difference between the sounds of fireworks on your street and the sounds of gunfire a mile or two away. And Avi, barely ten years old, thought that despite our promise that we'd never go out when there was shooting, we'd left him alone during another gun battle.

"Sweetie," I said, holding him now, "that's nothing. It's just the fireworks from the *matnas*."

"Are you sure?" he asked, a pleading in his voice that was quickly breaking my heart.

"I'm positive."

"Are you really sure?" he asked, burying his not-so-little head in my chest.

"I'm sure, Av. It's just fireworks."

Holding him, I could feel him shivering. It was a warm spring night in Jerusalem, not even a chill in the air. He was wearing boxers and a T-shirt, and there was no reason for him to be quivering like that. But he was shaking, shuddering in my embrace, so I held him tighter, hoping I could get the shaking to stop.

"It's just fireworks, Av, just fireworks. I promise."

He looked up at me, his big blue eyes staring right into mine. "Good," he said, gripping my shirt tight, with fingers that suddenly seemed very small. "Because I can't do this anymore."

I doubt I'll ever forget that night—the sounds of the fireworks, my son shaking in my arms. But most of all, I remember Avi's looking up at me and telling me the unabashed truth in a way that kids can muster and that grown-ups often can't: "Abba, I can't do this anymore." I want to be able to fall asleep without the sounds of shooting. I'm tired of being scared all the time. And, I assumed, the implicit question that he never actually asked, "Why did you bring me here? Why are you and Ema making us live this way?"

We'd come two years earlier from Los Angeles, where I was teaching at a small university and where our kids had had a pretty typical American childhood. Two cars in the driveway, soccer league on Sundays, and a quiet tree-lined neighborhood with its own private security patrol. A wonderful Jewish community, lots of friends in the neighborhood.

It was a great place to live. A place where nothing ever happened. Where my kids didn't know any adults who didn't either like them or love them. And where it never, ever occurred to them that someone would actually try to kill them.

But then in the summer of 1998, my wife, our three children, and I came to Israel on what was supposed to be a one-year sabbatical. In the middle of that year, though, we decided to stay. We'd always loved being in Israel, and when I got a job offer to work with an outstanding foundation, the combination of the work and our love of Israel seemed too much to turn down. And the timing, we thought, couldn't have been better.

That year, Ehud Barak had defeated Binyamin Netanyahu in the race for prime minister. Most Israelis assumed that the region was now headed toward peace. They argued, day and night, about the concessions that Barak seemed to be making to the Palestinians, but most agreed about one thing—peace was getting closer. So we moved from Los Angeles to Jerusalem, sold one house and bought another, shipped all our worldly possessions by boat to Haifa, and dared to hope—maybe our kids would be the first generation of Israeli kids not to have to go to war.

But the Camp David talks collapsed in the summer of 2000, and soon after came the beginning of the second Intifada. War followed, a war fought on a front not thousands of miles away from home, like America's wars in Iraq or Afghanistan, but playing out on our streets and in our restaurants, our buses, and our schools. It was a war in which our children were also targets, not because we wanted them to be, but simply because we lived in Israel. It was a war in which, at least in Jerusalem, there were no demilitarized zones and no civilians. We were, as far as the suicide bombers were concerned, all legitimate targets, and little by little, the city we'd fallen in love with descended into fear and paralysis. Restaurants emptied and businesses began to fail. Hotels were dark at night, and unemployment skyrocketed. Day after day, bombings shattered one city or another, and before we even realized what had happened, a country that had believed it was on the cusp of peace found itself at war.

It was a war that has yet to be named. Some people, believing it's over, now call it the Five-Year War. Others call it the Terror War. But whatever we will eventually call it, it was a war not about Israel's borders, but about her survival. It was a war that Israel had to endure just after we were convinced that the last war had already been fought, a war that meant we'd lied to our kids when we'd told them that by the time they were old enough to go into the army, there would be peace. It was a war that taught us that no matter how much we might like to believe otherwise, peace might not come in our lifetime, and therefore, we had better be prepared to explain to ourselves—and to our children—why there was still no place we'd rather be, no other place we'd rather call home.

In the past five years, we've gone from hope to worry to despair. And then to hope again. We've gone from a sense of helplessness in the face of bombings we couldn't stop to renewed faith in our army's ability to protect the one country where Jews imagined that they would have the power to defend themselves. We've become a smaller country. And we've been reminded of why this country matters.

As our kids have grown, Elisheva and I have gone from having three little children to having a daughter in the army and a son on his way to the army. And another son will get drafted after that. Throughout this war, we've tried to teach our kids why we're here, what we hope they'll grow up to believe in. But in the end, they've taught us infinitely more than we've taught them. They've taught us with their courage, with their calm. And they've taught us as we've watched Israel go from being a foreign country in which they were living to a home they love with every fiber of their being.

Thus, on one level, this book is a memoir of the Terror War, tracking Israel and its society through the lens of one family living in Jerusalem, struggling to raise children with a sense of security and purpose, even in the face of the violence, the divisiveness, and the despair of the war. It begins with the depths of the war in 2003 and, through vignettes and memories that I recorded during these years, tracks Israel through the completion of the unilateral withdrawal from Gaza in the summer of 2005 and, at least as of this writing, to the budding of the possibility of peace.

But more than a memoir, this is a love story. It's an account of how a family can fall in love with a place, with an idea, with a dream. It's about why love can inspire people to make a war-torn city their home, and how, at the end of the day, the most gratifying moments are those in which we realize that our children have inherited that love and made it their own.

. . .

When the Terror War first started, Talia, our daughter, was fourteen years old and in ninth grade, just starting high school. Avi was eleven, in sixth grade, and Micha, our seven-year-old, was in second grade. The kids now spoke Hebrew and felt completely at home here, so the following years would, we thought, be years of newfound confidence for all of them.

But as the war became increasingly violent and drew closer and closer to home, Jerusalem became a city in which you could take nothing for granted. Too many people died every week, too many buses and restaurants exploded with regularity, and there were too many shootings on too many roads to allow us to let our guard down.

One morning I was running a few minutes late for my first meeting of the day. The kids were still in the kitchen, packing their backpacks and their lunches before heading off to school.

"Bye, guys, I'm late," I said to them. "Have a great day—I'll see you for dinner." And I walked out the door and headed to work.

For some strange reason, though, I suddenly thought of the evening news the night before, and of the image of the mother of one of the most recent victims of a suicide attack, somewhere in the north of the country. "I didn't say good-bye," the mother was sobbing into the camera. "She went to school and I never got to say good-bye."

I stopped in my tracks, and turned around. As I walked back into the house, Elisheva looked up in surprise.

"Everything OK?"

"Everything's fine," I lied, a lump in my throat making it hard even to speak. For nothing was really OK.

"Love you guys," I whispered to the kids. I gave them each a hug and a kiss. "Be careful out there," I told them. "And I'll see you for dinner, OK?"

They nodded, apparently surprised by the unexpected recapitulation. I blew my wife a kiss, walked out the door, and headed to the office.

No matter what happened, I told myself as I headed up the street, at least I'd know that I'd said good-bye.

A HAVEN,
A BATTLEGROUND

January 2003~April 2003

What Did You Learn
in School Today?

What did you learn in school today?" A pretty typical question, and one that rarely generates an interesting answer. But Jerusalem isn't a typical place. And this isn't a typical time.

It's January 2003, sixteen months since the attacks on the Pentagon and the World Trade Center, and the drums of war are beating. The first twenty-five thousand American troops are getting ready to leave for Iraq, and Hans Blix is warning Saddam Hussein that time is running out. Though France is telling President George W. Bush that it will not support the war, people here in Israel are pretty convinced that Bush will go ahead, and that when Saddam realizes the end is at hand, he may well follow through on his threat to attack Israel with missiles.

So the Ministry of Education is getting our kids ready, teaching them all how to use the gas masks that have now been distributed across the country.

Micha, our youngest son, walked in from school, fresh from another day in fourth grade, and Elisheva, my wife, asked him how his day was. "Fine." And what did you learn? "We learned that there's going to be a war. America is going to attack Iraq, and Iraq won't be able to fight back against America, so instead, they're going to drop bombs on us. And then we're all going to die."

He said it with the same intonation that he might have used to say, "Oh, we did an art project about tigers." No irony. No exaggeration. He just told us what he'd learned: There's going to be a war. We're going to get attacked, and we're all going to die. It's really that simple. One has to wonder if that is the official Ministry of Education prediction.

Obviously, Elisheva and I both tried to assure him that that wasn't entirely true. But that's not as simple as it sounds. We've got to be very careful what we say to him. It's tempting, of course, to say, "Don't worry, there won't be a war." That would probably enable him to fall asleep a bit easier tonight.

But it's not true. There probably *is* going to be a war. And if there is in fact a war, he and the other kids will remember that we promised them that there wouldn't be. And then they won't believe us when we really need them to. If we're stuck with them in sealed rooms with gas masks, we need to be able to comfort them. They need to believe us. So we can't tell Micha that there won't be a war. We're telling him more or less the truth. Yes, there's probably going to be a war between the United States and Iraq. And there's some chance that Saddam, as he senses that the end is near, will unleash something on us. And yes, he may try to use chemical weapons on us, but we have gas masks and sealed rooms. So, no, we're not going to die. We'll be OK. How convincing does *that* sound?

If there's any good news in this, it's that we're not doing any worse a job about reassuring our kids than the country's leadership is doing in reassuring the rest of us. A couple of days ago, Deputy Minister Efi Eitam told the public to start amassing water. But there's no reason to panic, he says. Right.

Each family, he said, should have twelve liters of water per person, assuming that if the water supply is harmed, it will take the country three days to restore it. Another highly plausible claim. Anyone who's watched the Municipality of Jerusalem take months to repair a small pipe under a street knows that either we won't need the water at all, or we're going to need a lot more than twelve liters per person. I'm assuming that we won't need it at all. Elisheva, on the other hand, is coping by preparing for the worst. She's redecorating the house so that it looks like a modern art museum exhibition made of bottled water.

The next day, more governmental reassurances. The gas mask distribution centers are working at full capacity, the newspapers report, and everything is going smoothly. Of course, the government can't agree about whether or not to inoculate the entire population, and the medical establishment doesn't agree as to whether there's enough serum stock to inoculate everyone should the government or army decide we need it.

But at least the gas mask distribution is going well. The distribution, that is. Because, by the way, the paper noted, it seems that there's a little problem with 1.7 million of the masks that have already been distributed. No, they're not exactly defective, but neither were they designed to protect against what we're likely to get hit with. But again, we're told, everything is being evaluated. There is no reason for the public to panic.

Amazingly, people actually seem not to be panicking. True, thousands have booked flights out of the country for a "vacation" in February in a moving demonstration of Zionist commitment, but the resilient majority who plan to remain in the country are not noticeably panicked. Instead, some are just trying to laugh.

Gidi Gov, Israel's answer to Jay Leno, devoted his opening monologue to a "war drill" with his studio audience on Wednesday night. He divided the studio into different segments, just as the army has divided the country into different lettered zones so instructions can be given on a regional basis. He then assigned different codes (like the ones that are broadcast here on the radio to tell you what the nature of the attack is and what to do) representing biological, chemical, or nuclear attack. Then he drilled the audience to see if each region could do what they were supposed to as they were given the signal (stand up, sit down, put your hands on your head, and other such made-up gestures). You can figure out the rest. He made the signals so impossible to follow that everyone was hopelessly confused, standing up when they were supposed to be sitting down, arms in the air when they were supposed to be doing something else, until he looked at them, and declared them all dead. Everyone in the audience was laughing.

But if you looked at them carefully, they didn't seem to be having very much fun.

Then on Thursday evening, Ariel Sharon, our beleaguered prime minister, went on national TV. The event was described as a press conference in which he would respond to allegations he had received illegal loans. But poor Mr. Sharon got so worked up during this "press conference" that he actually said nothing about the issue he was supposed to be addressing and instead launched into a tirade against his chief opponent in the election. Not a terribly big deal, except that's illegal, too, since Israeli law doesn't allow campaigning on television within thirty days of an election, and we were scheduled to have elections at the end of the month, on January 28. So in the middle of his press conference, a member of the Supreme Court ordered the TV and radio stations to cut the prime minister off the air, and they did.

No one seemed terribly disappointed not to have to hear the rest of whatever it was he was going to say. *Chaval al ha-zeman*, Israelis say. Rough translation: Life is short. Save your time.

So, we're stocking water, learning how to use gas masks, being told that the gas masks may not work anyway, and watching our prime minister get yanked off the air by the Supreme Court. It would be nice if Shabbat, at least, was a bit more restful, no?

No chance of that. Just as we were about to leave the house midday on Shabbat to go to the home of some friends for lunch, Micha said to me, "Abba, what does this cartoon mean?" He was holding the newspaper's weekly TV and movie guide, and handed it to me. The cover illustration showed three "people" (though one was a mouse) running down the street. One was wearing a gas mask, one was busy injecting his arm with something, and the other had his fingers in his ears to block out some deafening sound. "Abba, what's it trying to say?"

I really, really didn't want to go there, so I feigned a bit of confusion. "I don't know. That mouse is doing something silly, but I can't tell what."

"Abba, he's wearing a gas mask. That's simple. But why's the other guy giving himself a shot?"

It seemed that his classroom instruction on the use of gas masks hadn't covered the use of the atropine syringe (an antidote to nerve gas) that comes with each person's kit. "I don't know," I told him. "It must be about some television show I haven't seen. It looks pretty stupid to me— I don't think we'll watch it." And I took the TV guide, flipped it upside down and put it on the coffee table. "OK, let's go to lunch."

Talia and Avi had heard this little exchange, but knew better than to offer their own explanations of the cartoon. Instead, we all filed out the door and headed to our friends. But lunch was a couple of neighborhoods away, so we had a twenty-minute walk. What were the chances that this little exchange would not be pursued? Not good, it turns out.

We'd been walking about five minutes, when Talia suddenly asked,

"Why do some people think America shouldn't attack Iraq?" This was clearly becoming the theme of the day.

"Why do you ask?" I wanted to know.

"Because we were working on this issue in my debating club, and I don't get it."

So I explained why some people think it's a bad idea. Saddam had nothing to do with the World Trade Center, they say. Or maybe he doesn't really have weapons of mass destruction. Or, bringing democracy to a place like Iraq is impossible, and the United States will never get out. It will be Vietnam all over again. And then I added, "And of course, some people here hope Bush won't attack because they're worried that then we'll get attacked."

Now it was Avi's turn. "I know everyone says that, but it doesn't make sense. Why would Iraq attack us if America attacks them? Why don't they just use their missiles to attack the American soldiers, if that's who they're mad at?"

Talia quickly launched into an explanation of what ground-to-ground missiles can and cannot do, making the point that Saddam wouldn't be able to hit U.S. forces, but he might be able to hit us. While Avi was pondering that one, she added, "and besides, this is Israel, and we're Jews. And every country in this part of the world would like to destroy us, whether they have an excuse or not."

Not a heck of a lot of nuance there, but when you think about it, it's pretty true. Being a sixteen-year-old in this part of the world is different than in suburban America. My daughter is living a life very different from that of the friends she left behind in Los Angeles. Even 9/11 hasn't changed that.

Lunch was nice, with all the laughing and singing normally thereunto appertaining. Eventually, the conversation turned to Pesach, and what everyone was doing for the Seder and for vacation. Finally, we were talking about something other than the war. Until one woman at the table said, "Isn't it strange that we can plan for April, but we can't plan for February?" And sure enough, the floodgates opened up.

"What room are you turning into your sealed room?" became the question of the hour. This might seem a simple matter, but it's not. Our house, relatively new, actually has a "bomb-shelter/sealed room" (*mamad* is the Hebrew acronym) built in, but we're not going to use it for that purpose. Why? Because it's small to begin with, and when we bought the apartment, the need for a sealed room seemed like a relic from the ancient past. Israelis and Palestinians were on their way to Camp David and to peace—who needed a sealed room? So like virtually everyone else, we filled it up with lots of stuff, including a washer and a dryer, and then paid a fortune to have the contractor violate the building code and drill holes through the reinforced concrete and steel walls so we could vent the dryer and get water and drainage for the washing machine. So now we have a tiny, and no-longer-sealed, room. And now we may need a *mamad*. Oops.

Elisheva has decided we'll use the study, instead. It has only one window, which should be easy to seal, and one door. Admittedly, the door is a regular wooden door, unlike the steel door with the hermetic seal on the *mamad*, but we'll seal that, too, she figures. She'd rather be in a room with a TV, a computer with access to the Internet, and a pullout bed than in a small closet-sized room that's not so sealed anymore anyway.

I've decided not to point out to her that if missiles come raining down on Jerusalem, the likelihood that our cable and DSL Internet line are going to continue to work flawlessly is not too great. Besides, I'm banking on the fact that because we live about a mile or two from the Al Aksa Mosque on the Temple Mount, Saddam can't afford to aim at us and just barely miss. If he misses us and hits Islam's third-most-sacred site, he'd be in even worse shape than he is now. So we'll use whatever room Elisheva wants.

Sealed rooms, though, weren't the only subjects of conjecture at lunch. Our hostess said, "The kids had the whole drill in school and were told that if you give yourself the injection that comes in the kit, you keep your knee at a ninety-degree angle, and just jab yourself in the thigh. Then, you pin the empty syringe to your shirt, so that rescue teams who find you will know that you gave yourself the injection."

"But when do you give yourself the injection?"

"If you start to feel the symptoms of a nerve gas attack."

"What are the symptoms?"

Again, no one really knew. One person hazarded a guess. "I think it's difficulty breathing." Probably as good a guess as any, though in this situation, I'd much prefer something better than a guess.

"But if I'm wearing a gas mask," one of the adults pressed on, "and I'm in a sealed room with my kids, scared out of my mind, won't I almost definitely have difficulty breathing?" Not a bad question, so we cleared the table and moved on to dessert.

Coffee, tea, and cake seemed to herald a break in the war-suffused conversation, for which I was appreciative. After all, I was getting on a plane to the States that night, and I didn't want to leave Elisheva not only alone, but a nervous wreck to boot. But there wasn't much talk. The clatter of silverware on the plates, the sounds of coffee being sipped. And the silence of a group of adults pondering an uncertain future.

Our hostess broke the silence. "You know, if I thought they would leave us alone if we just left this place and moved to Hawaii, I'd go." Really? No one at the table said much, but she could tell, I think, that people were surprised to hear her talking about giving up, packing it in, as if this were the first time that Israel had faced the threat of attack.

So she tried to explain. "I mean, I'd like us to be here, and I think we deserve to be here, but maybe it's just not possible. I mean, can you believe this? It's 2003, and here we are, talking about the Jews getting gassed again. Whoever would have thought that this is what we would come to? But then again, there's not exactly room for five million Jews in Hawaii. And it wouldn't be ours anyway. And we do need one place that's ours, don't we? And there's not exactly an empty space on the planet waiting for us to come and live there, is there? Oh, well. Forget it."

She's not alone. For the first time that I can recall since we moved here, you hear people talking in similar stream-of-consciousness modes about the whole experiment called the Jewish state just falling apart. For some, it's Saddam, and the combination of the possibility that we might be attacked and the fact that there's nothing we can do about it. This is no June 1967, when a preemptive strike on Egypt's air force could save us. George W. Bush has made it clear he wants us on the sidelines. He's got bigger fish to fry than the safety of a tiny little Jewish state.

Other people think that Saddam is the least of our problems, that the real issue is the conflict with the Palestinians, a conflict that shows no real signs of subsiding. *Ha-Aretz Magazine*, the weekend magazine of Israel's most sophisticated daily paper, ran a long interview with Amos Oz and David Grossman, two of Israel's most prestigious writers, reflecting on their sadness at the possibility that the whole thing could fail. A society calloused by conflict. No solution with the Palestinians. And who wants to live at war forever?

Whenever I read articles like that, I try to console myself that perhaps those are just the hyperintellectual musings of the elite, that maybe most Israelis think nothing of the sort. But then you go around the city, and you're bombarded with the new ad from Ikea (yes, we too have discount, self-assembled Scandinavian furniture all over the place). It's on Israeli Web sites and plastered all over the city. It's for Ikea's big sale.

The ad gives the dates of the sale, and then, urging the population to hurry to the store, asks, *"Ki mi yodea mah yisha'er po machar?"*— "Because who knows what will be left here tomorrow?" The double entendre is obvious—to everyone, not just to the elite. There may be no furniture left after the sale.

And there may be no country left after the war.

I Wonder If This Is What Peace Is Like?

It snowed the other day in Jerusalem. Not a blizzard by American standards, but a lot of snow for Israel. Inches of it. So in a city where no one has snow tires or chains, where there are virtually no plows and no salt machines, everything came to a halt. A beautiful, white-encrusted quiet descended over a city that desperately needed it.

In the afternoon, we took a family walk. Boots and parkas, gloves and scarves, and a few accessories (a carrot and an extra scarf) for making a snowman. And after a while, just enjoying the streets that were as deserted as they are here on Yom Kippur, we walked up the small hill toward Bethlehem Road. The old Arab houses on the sides of the street, like the newer Jewish buildings, were covered with a white lining. Here and there a couple or two walked by, arm in arm or holding hands. Smiles on everyone's faces, and a calm we haven't seen in a long time.

As we walked up the road, Elisheva and the boys were trailing behind, looking at something or another. Tali, though, was next to me. She took my hand (unusual in her current sixteen-year-old mode), and said, "This is so great. Look how happy everyone is. I wonder if this is what peace is like."

For a few seconds, I just couldn't move. Just sixteen, and she doesn't remember what peace is like. She doesn't remember what it's like not to have a guard in front of every store, every restaurant. What it's like not to be searched everywhere you go. What it's like not to dread the news. What the paper's like without the pictures of dead people on the front page. She doesn't remember what it's like not to be afraid every day. She doesn't remember any of that.

"I wonder if this is what peace is like." There are times your kids just break your heart.

And when our children say things like that, there's nothing I want to do more than to talk to Elisheva, to tell her what one of them just said. And this time I know that I can't. It's one thing for our kids to break our hearts. But it's another entirely for me to break Elisheva's.

Elisheva is the one who's always wanted to live here. The night I proposed to her, in a trendy Jerusalem bar when we were here for our junior year abroad, she said, sort of, "Yes, on condition that we can live in Israel." Deal breaker, I sort of said to her, more than twenty-five years ago. But she was patient, and here we are. She got what she wanted all along.

Sort of. We live where she's always wanted to live, but we're living in a war. And though I suspect that she, like me, never has a moment's regret, we actually don't talk very much about what this war may be doing to our kids. The war has drawn us closer to each other than we've ever been, and our kids seem to be doing OK. But you never know for sure, and I know that she's as worried as I am.

So when I realize that Tali doesn't even remember what peace is like, there's nothing I want more than to find a quiet moment with Elisheva on our walk in the snow, and to say, "Guess what your daughter just said."

But I can't. I won't. Part of living in this mess is learning to shield each other from the hurt and the sting that have become part of our daily lives. There is, after all, a limit to how much heartbreak any of us can take.

So this one, I keep to myself. I hold my daughter's hand, not knowing exactly how to explain what peace is. And not apologizing for our having brought her here when she was twelve years old, though I wonder for a moment if that's what I should do.

Instead, I find myself wondering what she's thinking. And knowing that we can't let this war go on. That this has to change. That somewhere, somehow—someone has to figure a way out of this.

We keep telling ourselves that our kids are OK. But they don't even remember what peace is like. And we call that OK?

On Reentries

Sometimes you just know it's going to be a long flight. We were all seated and ready for takeoff at JFK ready to come back home when the flight attendant asked the guy sitting next to me to please fold his footrest for takeoff. He ignored her. She asked again, relatively nicely I thought, but he refused. His logic wasn't bad—we were in the very first row of the plane (the only advantage of flying this often is that you occasionally get the coveted upgrade to first class), he had the window seat, and all the exits were behind us. His footrest wasn't going to impede anyone's exit, so he wasn't going to fold it. Exasperated, she gave up and walked away. Satisfied that he'd won, he looked behind us to make sure that she wasn't watching, and then folded his footrest.

Welcome back to Israel, I thought. A classic moment. That macho need to transform everything into a confrontation is one of the things about Israeli society that I really detest. So, rather than staying awake and having to acknowledge his existence, I went to sleep and slept almost the entire flight back. But, alas, you do have to wake up to get off the plane.

They ushered the first-class passengers out of the plane first, but when we got into the arrivals hall, the lines at passport inspection were incredibly long because another 747 had landed just moments before us. The twelve of us first-class folk were ushered to the side, where we were told to wait in the "Crew" line, which was very short. We were waiting rather patiently, and the line was actually moving, when a young guy in jeans, a T-shirt seemingly painted onto his pecs and those ubiquitous curved sunglasses perched atop his crew-cut head, approached and proceeded right to the head of the line. The flight attendant who was still attending to our welfare told him to wait at the end of the line. He refused. She asked who he was, anyway. Like a peacock in mating season, he puffed up his chest and announced, "I'm a pilot. This line's for me, not for them, and I'm not going to wait."

I was about to tell him to take a hike, but this is Israel, where pilots are demigods, and I realized there was no point. As I expected, he got his way.

I always worry about these reentries to Israeli life. After a few days in Manhattan, with the array of offerings at Barnes and Noble and the decent service even at Starbucks (to say nothing of the veritable fawning at Banana Republic), I dread those first bumps that inevitably remind me that we live in the rough-and-tumble Middle East, not the long-since-civilized North American continent. On the ride home from the airport, I thought about that second little demonstration of Israeli ego-strutting and that rather disheartening (to put things mildly) pilot syndrome. And then, thinking about pilots, I remembered Ilan Ramon, Israel's first astronaut. How different he was. How self-effacing he was. And how tragic it was—for so many reasons—that he was gone.

We'd met at a cocktail party in Philadelphia, when Ramon was still stationed in Houston, training with NASA for the Columbia's takeoff just months later, and we hit it off. An intense e-mail correspondence ensued, covering everything from Zionism to his requests for help getting his story published once he'd returned to Earth. But never in our conversations or in the e-mails we'd exchanged had Ramon ever mentioned to me that he had been one of the pilots in the raid on the Iraqi reactor in 1981. (Amazingly, I learned that only when I read it in the paper after he died.) Even when we'd talked about the book he wanted to write when he returned from his mission, he mentioned Houston and the shuttle, the Holocaust and Israel, but not the Air Force. And as our e-mail correspondence moved from his book idea to discussions of *aliyah* (Hebrew for "going up," commonly a reference to moving to Israel) to the future of Zionism (something he'd begun to think about quite a bit after four years of living and training in the States), one thing remained consistent: the discussions were never about him. They were always about ideas, about Israel, about the future.

I wondered, as my taxi meandered through the hills that separate Tel Aviv from Jerusalem, what we might do to create more people like that.

What would it take for this country to produce more people like Ilan Ramon, rather than the guy next to me on the plane, or the pilot who was too important to wait in line with mere mortals? And what, I wondered, could we do to have our kids remember Ilan Ramon, to remind them that he embodied much of what we want for them?

He was very different from us in many ways, of course. But we cared about many of the same things. His life wasn't about the Shoah (a biblical word that means "utter destruction," and the word that in modern Hebrew refers to the Holocaust), but neither did he deny that the Shoah made Israel ever more necessary. He believed in Israel. He believed that Judaism wasn't just for the religious. He was enormously talented. He was accomplished. He was bright. He was modest. How do you get your kids to focus on those kinds of values when they're surrounded by the footrest revolutionaries and pilot egos of the world?

As the taxi began the long climb up the last set of hills to Jerusalem, I remembered the three envelopes Ramon had given me for the kids. It was at the end of our conversation during that cocktail party in Philadelphia. The formal part of the dinner was about to begin, and we'd been assigned to different tables. As we were about to part, he reached into his jacket pocket and took out some "date of issue" envelopes with stamps that the Israeli government had printed in honor of his mission, and asked for our kids' names. I told him, and he inscribed an envelope to each of them. They were all simple. "To Micha, *be-hatzalachah* [best of luck], Ilan Ramon." And so on.

I showed the kids the envelopes when I got home, but to say that they weren't terribly impressed would be to put it mildly. At that point, in November 2002, no one was thinking about the space shuttle, and the kids had never heard of Ramon. "Cool, but what do we do with them?" Somewhat annoyed by their being so blasé about the whole thing, I nonchalantly tossed the envelopes into a drawer in the study and forgot about them.

And then he died, on February 1, 2003. I was on Long Island that weekend. While we were still at synagogue that Shabbat morning, we began to hear the first rumors that something had gone terribly wrong with the space shuttle Columbia. Because it was Shabbat, I couldn't listen to the news. By the afternoon, we'd heard enough rumors to know that it was over, that there was no hope.

As soon as Shabbat was over, I turned on the laptop and checked the Web, and then my e-mail. The Web had only bad news. In the e-mail was a message from Avi. "Dear Abba: I don't know if you've heard what happened to the shuttle, but it exploded and all the astronauts were killed. Ema's really depressed about it, so I'm trying to be especially good while you're gone. It's so sad. After all the *pigu'im* [terrorist attacks], you'd think that a person would at least be safe if they left Earth and were in space. Don't you think? Love, Avi."

You'd also think that a thirteen-year-old kid wouldn't have to see the world that way. A kid who's barely a teenager shouldn't have to think that the only way to be safe is to leave the planet. Don't you think?

I was musing on that little note, and the childhood innocence and goodness that it bespoke, as the taxi idled at one of the traffic lights at the entrance to Jerusalem. I asked the driver, the same guy who always picks me up from the airport, if anything was new in the country. "Nothing that you don't know. The shuttle broke apart, and the war continues. And we idiots risk our kids to save their buildings."

He was referring to the events of February 6, when Israeli demolitions experts detonated an explosive belt found in a Taibeh mosque, shortly after they arrested two Islamic Jihad militants on their way to carry out a suicide bombing in Israel. The police found the belt, and its fifteen kilograms of explosives, in the mosque's toilet. Two Israeli sappers worked for hours to remove the belt from the mosque, to avoid any damage to the building. "What do you think they'd do if it was our holy place and they were the ones in charge?" my driver wanted to know.

We didn't have to wait long to find out. A few days later, an item appeared in the Israeli press (and not surprisingly, has not been mentioned much outside of Israel) about what's happened to Joseph's Tomb since the shooting there at the very beginning of the war. After one of our soldiers bled to death there on the very first day of the Intifada, the site was abandoned by the Israel Defense Forces and was subsequently taken over the by Palestinians. Jews are forbidden entry, blocked by both the Palestinians and the Israeli security forces, but Bratslav Hassidim (an ultra-Orthodox sect known for its intensity of prayer and its focus on joy and sincerity) continue to enter illegally.

The grave has since been reduced to rubble. It's been pounded with hammers, there are used car parts strewn above, trash all over, and a huge hole has been smashed into the dome.

I understand my driver's frustration, and if it were my kid who was the sapper, risking his life so that the mosque didn't get destroyed, I'd undoubtedly have second thoughts, too. But I'm still glad that we asked those kids (because that's who many of our soldiers are—they're really just kids who, if they lived in the States, would be gallivanting around some college campus somewhere) to do what they do. I'm glad that in the face of everything, there are still forces in this society that are about goodness, about being better. About not letting the frustrations not only of this war, but of five decades of war, erode our sense of what's right and what's wrong, what's honorable and what's not.

I don't think we're idiots. I want my kids to grow up worried about being decent, not about getting even. Worried about being good, not about the possibility that someone might be getting the better of them.

And even though they meet people like Mr. Footrest and Captain Ego every day, something about this country still seems to be working. They read the newspaper accounts of what those sappers did, and they're mystified but still proud. They read about what's happened to Joseph's Tomb, and they conclude—I think correctly—that the people who did that are barbarians. They sense that they're different. That they're supposed to be different. I just hope that they don't lose that take on the world.

Which is why I finally fished Ilan Ramon's envelopes out of the drawer. I took them to Michael, our favorite framer near the Russian compound, and had them matted and framed, so that they'd last. So our kids would remember, whatever the future may bring, that there are people who grow up here who stand for all the right things, who manage to withstand the cynicism, who fiercely protect this country without growing callous or ugly.

A few days later, we gave the kids their framed envelopes. This time, they knew who Ilan Ramon was. And this time, they weren't nonchalant. They knew what he represented, and they understood why we want them to remember him.

We hung the frames in their rooms. And in the months and years to come, I hope that they'll be reminded that with all its traumas and with all its pain, this place still produces real heroes. Real people who remember what the dream is all about—real people, like Ilan Ramon, who with all they've accomplished, could choose to be anywhere, but chose to be here. Real people for whom decency, modesty, goodness, Jewishness, and Zionism were all fully compatible. Can one simple framed envelope remind them of all that? Probably not, but I hope it's a start.

The next few weeks in this country are likely to be tense. Colin Powell has made his case for war at the UN. American personnel and materiel are pouring into the Persian Gulf region. The date's getting closer. War is going to start, and what that means for us, no one knows. Which is all the more reason to think about Ilan Ramon, and what this place is all about.

Yehi zikhro barukh—may his memory be a blessing. To his kids, to our kids, and to the generations of kids who, we pray, will follow.

The Masks We Wear

The costumes have been put away, for Purim's over, but mask season isn't. American cruise missiles and bombs started raining down on Baghdad yesterday, and the Israel Defense Forces now believe that Saddam is going to go down fast. If he's going to try to get us, apparently, now's the time. So the command has come across the radio, the TV, the newspapers: Those gas mask boxes we've been told for weeks not to touch, and certainly not to open? It's time to open them, and to get our kids suited up for school.

There's not really much you can say to your nine-year-old kid to camouflage what you're doing. He knows what the masks are, and he knows why we might need them. So we just did it. When Micha came downstairs in the morning, we told him that he didn't have to wear his mask, and that he probably wouldn't have to, but that he had to take it to school and keep it with him at all times.

"During recess?" he wanted to know. Yes, we told him. "And if I go out of school to the kiosk to buy a snack?"

"All the time," Elisheva told him, with an edge to her voice that I knew she didn't intend. "You don't go anywhere without this mask." And starting to cry, and not wanting him to see her crying, she sat down on the stairs he'd just descended and left the assembly of the mask to me.

There's not much to it, it turns out. I broke the paper seals on the box, took the plastic seal off the filter, and screwed it into the face of the mask. Then, the harder part. We helped Micha fit the mask to his face and tightened the straps behind his head. I placed my palm over the filter so no air could enter, and told him, "Breathe in a bit." He did. As it was supposed to, the mask stuck to his face, and no air got in around the sides. Sealed.

"I can't see," he said, a barely perceptible quiver in his voice. I looked at the mask, which was now all fogged up. Having no idea what to do about that, we took the mask off. "If you need it, the fog will go away," I told him. Would it? I had no idea. "Anyway, you won't need it. Just keep it in the box. And don't take it out unless a grown-up tells you. OK? It's not a toy. It's really important. And don't forget it anywhere."

He nods. Breakfast, and then it's his school bus time. Up he hops, a backpack, a water bottle, and his gas mask draped over his shoulder with its black plastic strap. I walk him out of the house to wait for the van to pick him up. A few minutes later, the van arrives. Right on time, as if nothing's different.

"Bye, Abba."

"Have a good day, buddy."

"Abba? Don't forget your mask. OK?"

Not the way we'd thought we'd send him off to school when he was born, or when we were living on the West Side of Los Angeles. Not even close.

Outside on the sidewalk, there's no sense of imminent war. People are coming and going. Some are going to work, getting in their cars or walking to the bus, while others are pushing a stroller or chatting with friends. And they all have their boxes, slung over their shoulder. One or two have decorated their boxes with colored markers, as if the mask is now an apparel accessory.

There's something surreal about it. A city functioning pretty normally, waiting to get gassed.

I go back in the house and put Elisheva's mask together.

"Put it on," I tell her. "I'll adjust the straps."

She doesn't want to. "I'll do it myself if we need them," she says.

"No, you won't. If the siren goes off, everyone's going to be nervous. That's not the time to be fiddling around with this thing." She's still not convinced.

"If the big kids see you not getting yours ready," I tell her, playing my trump card, "they won't do it either." She slumps back onto the couch and lets me get her mask adjusted.

The big kids come downstairs, and we do theirs, too. And off to school they go.

"What about yours?" Elisheva asks me when they're gone.

"Yeah. I'll do it in a minute."

But I don't. I take the box, with its seal still intact, and try to fit it in my briefcase. But it's much too big. I yell good-bye to Elisheva, who's now upstairs, and make my way out the door to work, my untouched mask slung over my shoulder.

At the office a colleague knocks on my office door. He's a few minutes late for a meeting we'd scheduled. "Sorry," he says, "rough morning."

"Everyone OK?"

"Meltdown," he says, and mentions his daughter, exactly Micha's age. "She got hysterical when I put the mask on her." And he can't say any more. He can't speak at all. He stands in the doorway, not moving, not speaking. Paralyzed.

"I'm around all morning," I tell him. "Pop in when you've got time." And he disappears down the hall.

Later in the day I realize that I've left a file at home, and I need it. It's only about a five-minute walk home, so I figure I'll just go and get it. On my way out the door, my secretary says to me, "You forgot your mask."

"I'm only going to the fourth floor," I lie.

Out the door I go, and walk the few blocks to the house. The streets are sparsely populated but not deserted. And everyone else has a box, a mask. As far as I can tell, I'm the only person without one.

For a moment the thought that I've done something very stupid gives me pause, and I actually stop, wondering whether I should go back to the office to get it. But I'm halfway home by now, and it doesn't seem worth it. Anyway, I tell myself, I'm not that far from my office. If the siren goes off, I can sprint and be back to my mask in a couple of minutes. We've got to get at least a few minutes warning, no?

I actually have no idea.

I get the file, and start back to work. And wonder why it was that I left work without my mask.

It doesn't take me long to realize that I'm not going to carry that mask. Not today, not tomorrow. I'm just not going to do it. This sitting-duck exercise, waiting for Saddam to gas us, just wasn't what I bargained for. So I'm not going to play.

The fairy-tale Israel I grew up with didn't sit back hoping it wouldn't get gassed. Growing up in a Zionist family in Baltimore, I was raised on the stories of the plucky soldiers in the War of Independence, who fought off Arab invaders and dramatically improved Israel's borders. The soldiers who used the Davidka mortars, which, though hopelessly ineffective, made a cacophonous racket and scared the enemy into retreat. Or the pilots of the 1948 war, who, having no bombs, dropped glass seltzer bottles to create confusion among the enemy. And scared them off.

And the 1956 Sinai campaign in which Israel captured the Sinai Desert. The Six-Day War and its preemptive strike against the Egyptian air force. Entebbe, and the July 1976 raid in which Israel sent two hundred commandos more than twenty-five hundred miles to rescue the hostages from an Air France flight that had been diverted to Uganda.

That was the image of Israel that my parents raised me on. It may have been naïve and overly mythologized, but it's in my blood.

And now, something's changing. For years now, the "right" has been saying that we didn't leave Lebanon, we fled. With our tails between our legs, they say, we let Hezbollah fire and fire until we couldn't take it. And then we retreated, convincing the terrorists that if they kill more of us, we'll leave other places, too. That, they say, is why we have this Intifada in the first place. We got weak and invited this terror. It's actually *our* fault.

I don't know whether I fully believe that, but now, watching people across this city carry their masks around, suspecting that the sealed rooms and plastic over the windows and flimsy masks probably won't work anyway, I'm beginning to wonder. The Sinai's gone back to Egypt. We left (fled?) Lebanon. Then we got a war of suicidal bombers that we have no idea how to stop. And less than sixty years after the chimneys of Europe stopped spewing the ash of Jews into the air, we're going about our business, pretending that life can be normal, even if we're about to get gassed.

For the first time since we got here, the long term doesn't look any better than the short term. And in an absurd and useless one-man protest against a fate that none of us can control, I take my mask when I get home, the seal still unbroken, and put it up on a high shelf in the *mamad*. And I never take it out again.

No Other Land

There's a look on people's faces. Eyes not so much vacant as staring out toward something none of us can actually see. It's been a hard week, but we've made it through. Purim and gas masks. And waiting. And nothing.

The city is beginning to slow down for Shabbat. There's less traffic. And even with the attendant danger, there are the customary flower vendors, sitting by the side of the road with fresh flowers in old white buckets, because even today, people know, you don't start Shabbat without flowers.

But after days with tension so thick that it was often hard to breathe, it's hard to articulate what it is that I'm feeling, and what I suspect that everyone else is feeling, too, until a disc jockey somewhere gets it just right.

It's Ehud Manor's song, written in 1982 during the War of Attrition, during which his younger brother was killed. It's as if Manor has an answer to our unspoken question. It was a week during which it was often too painful to look at our kids' eyes as they packed up their masks for school, or to wonder, as we watched them head off to the van, what it would be like for them if the siren went off when we were nowhere near them. It was a week when it was impossible not to wonder, at least for a fleeting moment, why we would possibly put them through this, whether it's really worth it, whether we might not be serving our kids better if we raised them elsewhere.

And to answer that unasked question, Manor's song echoes across our neighborhood, from porches and open windows, and even from the occasional car driving by:

Ein li eretz acheret
gam im admati bo'eret . . .

I have no other place to go
Even if my land is burning
One Hebrew word burrows
into my veins, into my soul
with an aching body
a hungry heart,
This is my home.

It's All about Questions

It's unusual, I imagine, to associate Yom Ha-Shoah (Holocaust Memorial Day) with the image of dogs. But when I think back to Yom Ha-Shoah 2003, there are two dogs that will probably come to mind.

To start the day, we brought Haim Gouri, perhaps Israel's preeminent poet of the Shoah, to speak at the Mandel Leadership Institute, where I work. The institute brings top educators from Israel and Jewish communities around the world to Jerusalem for a two-year midcareer fellowship, and over the course of their time with us, we try to expose these Fellows to the very best minds in Israel and beyond.

Gouri's a perfect fit. He's not young anymore, beyond eighty, but the morning with him was still a tour de force. What I remember most were the questions he dropped here and there. Who, he wondered aloud, looking at us—all born after the end of the war, and inclined to think we have the big questions figured out—was a greater hero? Those who fled to the forest and joined the Partisans, or those who stayed with their wives and children, accompanying them on the long, last road to a certain death?

Because this is a country often committed to a certain form of macho heroism, Gouri's question cut right to the core. And I heard people chatting about it throughout the day.

Gouri left us with more than questions. I doubt that anyone who was there will ever forget the moment at the end of his speech, when this elderly but still extraordinarily compelling man, who has spent his entire adult life reading, thinking, and writing about the Shoah, tried to read a poem by Natan Alterman, another of Israel's greats, about the losses of the Shoah. Gouri, old but by no means frail, sitting behind a table in the front of the room, began to tremble. We could see him struggling to hold the book steady so that he could at least read the words, but to no avail. And then, without warning, he began to sob, as if he couldn't catch his breath, and he simply stopped.

He sat in front of us, Israelis and foreigners, Jews and Arabs, faculty and Fellows, unable to speak, unable to cry. Frozen, stonelike. For what seemed like an eternity. So many years later, the pain is still too palpable. The sheer magnitude of the event is so awesome that it defies words. Even from a poet.

He eventually got through the lecture somehow, and more questions followed. One of the Fellows asked what sounded at first like a strange one. "I'm interested in how much you believe our consciousness of the Shoah ought to color how we behave here. I'll give you an example. I was a soldier in Lebanon in the early eighties, when it was terrible there. We were losing soldiers almost every day. There was simply no way to protect the entire perimeter of the area we were in. So I suggested to my commanding officer that we bring in guard dogs. I knew that guard dogs would cover the ground better than we, and that they'd save lives. But my officer refused. He said, 'No Jewish soldier under my command is going to walk around with a dog.'"

The implied reference, of course, was to the Nazis' use of dogs to control their prisoners, in death camps and in other places. Given all the museums Israeli kids get taken to, the image of a soldier with guard dogs inevitably conjures up the image of the shiny black boots and the Nazi soldier holding the leash.

So, this student summarized, his commanding officer simply wouldn't consider the idea. The dog idea was declined, and, according to this Fellow, soldiers kept dying.

Gouri didn't have much to say about the specific incident (though he did, amazingly, recite from memory most of Natan Alterman's lengthy poem "From the Notes of a Dog," published in August 1946 about dogs that the British were using to sniff out the weapons that Jewish military groups were stashing on the kibbutzim of Sedot Yam and Dorot). But I heard more than one person during the rest of the day comment on that question. It was a question that may sound mundane, but that you nonetheless can't get out of your head. The more you think about it, the more complex it becomes. The more you try to solve it, the more you realize you're trapped. Do we let Israeli soldiers die because we're still paralyzed by the photos in those museums we saw as kids, or because of the stories many Israeli kids have heard from their grandparents? What kind of a society are we trying to build here? What do we really want this place to be? How much do we owe the memories of those photos, those years, those Jews who never got out to tell their stories, those Jews whose names we don't even know?

Can we allow what the Nazis did to color what we do? Dare we not?

Haim Gouri, dogs, and the Shoah aren't the only questions hovering around this hurting place. Not by a long shot. Though on the surface, there was nothing terribly interesting about the news last Friday afternoon, one of the stories was another indication of how, just beneath the surface, this society is still trying to figure out who's in and who's out, and what values we want to place at the core of the country we're still building.

A few days earlier, a terrorist bombing at the Kfar Sabba train station had broken a string of a few quiet weeks. But the damage was slight, and the number of dead relatively small. It should have been an outrage, of course, someone blowing himself up at a train station. But here it takes a lot more than that to get people outraged. The strange thing about Israel is that when a suicidal maniac walks into a train station and blows himself to high heaven, people are mostly relieved that he didn't kill more people than he did.

So the incident would ordinarily have passed from the Israeli news relatively quickly (just as last night's bombing of the Tel Aviv pub undoubtedly will, because "only" three people were killed), except for the fact that one funeral became a national story.

In a country as small as this, funerals are always national news. After each attack or army mishap, the national news announces—every hour on the hour—specific information about funerals for each of the dead, including the day, the name of the cemetery, and the time. If the funeral is taking place at the time that the news is broadcast, that's the top story, no matter what else is happening.

But the funeral of Alexi Kostyov, the twenty-two-year-old security guard who asked the bomber for ID at the entrance to the train station (thus preventing a much more grisly disaster) at the cost of his own life, was different. The radio announced that his family had decided to return his body to Russia, near Odessa, and that he would be buried there.

It's strange that a simple fact like that would become a national story, but it did. In a country that prides itself on having absorbed millions of immigrants, from northern Africa to France to the United States, the idea that Alexi might be buried outside the country he died defending struck many people as horrifying. Not exactly because he'd be buried somewhere else, but because of the reason why.

And again, the questions about what kind of a country Israel is becoming. Why didn't his parents, who had followed him here after he made *aliyah* on his own, want him buried here? Was it that Russian immigrants still do not feel welcome here? Are we that closed a society?

There's another reason, which no one wants to talk about very much. Alexi's father is Jewish, but his mother is not, so according to Jewish law, Alexi is not Jewish. Therefore, according to the Israeli rabbinate and standard Jewish religious practice, he is not eligible to be buried in a Jewish cemetery.

When Israel's Law of Return was created in the first years of the State, the Knesset decided to "strike back" at the Nazis and offered immediate citizenship to anyone who would have been persecuted as a Jew by the Nazis. If you had one Jewish grandparent, the Nazis would murder you. So the Knesset said that if you have one Jewish grandparent, you're Jewish enough for automatic Israeli citizenship. More fallout from the Nazi legacy.

In the 1950s, that decision had little more than symbolic impact. Almost everyone who made *aliyah* had a Jewish mother. But the Russian *aliyah* changed all that. Somewhere between a third and a half of the million Russian immigrants (some say it's even more) aren't Jewish according to Jewish law, because they have a Jewish grandparent, but not a Jewish mother. So Alexi's funeral raised all sorts of fundamental questions about this society that no one's had the time or the energy to think about for a long time. What does it mean that you can be Jewish enough to serve in the IDF, or Jewish enough to die defending Israel, but still not Jewish enough to be buried as a Jew?

As if that weren't enough of a conundrum, Alexi's situation raises other questions that no one feels comfortable asking out loud. In hushed tones, knowing that it's politically very incorrect, people are asking about these Russian immigrants, or at least good numbers of them. How committed to Israel are these Russians? Do they really care about a Jewish state, or were they simply looking for an easy way out of Russia to what was then a thriving economy? Is there some sort of fifth column budding in that one-fifth of Israeli society? After all, people said, Alexi's family didn't say much about the issue of where he would be buried. They just wanted him buried at "home," which isn't here.

Because of all these questions, a sense of national crisis surrounded the simple question of where Alexi would be buried. And the news covered it incessantly. First it was reported that he would be buried in Odessa, following which his parents would return here. Then an update. His parents were also leaving Israel. A flurry of activity and more reports. Then the minister of absorption wanted to meet with the family. Then, a solution. The government would fly members of his family now living in the States and others in the former Soviet Union to Israel for the funeral; he would be buried in Israel at a site acceptable to the rabbinate and to his family, and his parents will remain in Israel.

And then the story disappeared from the news just as quickly as it appeared. All's well that's buried well.

Except that in typical Israeli fashion, nothing's resolved. All those questions still lurk just beneath the news, waiting to be awakened the next time something like this happens. Once the immediate crisis has been averted, Israelis lurch on to the next one. And leave the big questions unanswered. For fear, perhaps, that facing them head-on, in not-so-hushed tones, could expose the fissures in this tenuously bound-together society.

Back to the news. After the story of Alexi's funeral, the news cut to the emerging government headed by Mahmoud Abbas (commonly known in Israel as Abu Mazen, his more informal Arabic name), which was now ratified and official. Again, mostly in hushed tones, people are trying to figure out what this all means. Could this guy be for real when he says that it's time to end the armed conflict against Israel? Would Arafat actually let Abbas do anything? Dare we trust Abbas? Dare we not?

Some on the left, as one would expect, desperately want to believe he's for real. But understandably, many are nervous. They were caught holding the Oslo bag after being warned by the right years ago. So people are tiptoeing around the issue, asking a few questions, not saying much. If you listen carefully, it's clear. People are afraid to hope, but they're equally afraid that they've lost the ability to hope.

The right, of course, is not tiptoeing. They know for sure that Abu Mazen is bad news. They point to his Ph.D. dissertation, written for some Russian university, in which he apparently claimed that "only" several hundred thousand Jews were killed by the Nazis, and those only because of a "deal" arranged between the Zionists and the Nazis. Again, the long shadow the Nazis still cast over this place.

Now the right is pointing to Abu Mazen's suddenly "revealed" role in funding the 1972 Munich Olympics Massacre, an accusation making its way all over e-mail lists here, but so far not picked up by any reputable press that I've seen. But it's clear what's really going on. If, by some small chance, Abu Mazen is for real, he's going to do to us what Alexi Kostyov did—he'll make us ask ourselves all over again how much we're willing to rethink what being Israeli means, what we're committed to without question, and on what we might be willing to compromise. What happens when your mortal enemy (or part of it) all of a sudden seems willing to have a different sort of conversation? What would we be willing to give up in order to forge some deal that would put a stop to this endless conflict? How much might we be willing to give away (Gaza? the West Bank? more?) if doing so meant that our kids might have a shot at living in peace? What shape (literally and figuratively) do we want this country to take?

But, on the other hand, what happens if this fledgling peace is a pipe dream, and there's no putting a stop to conflict, to the constant upsurges in carnage? We've grown used to the idea that our children will grow up with this fear, the constant dread. But our grandchildren, too? And their children? With no end? Could a country this small actually imagine surviving that way?

So it's easier just to point to Abu Mazen's ugly past and to say that of course we want to deal with the Palestinians. It's just him we won't deal with. We don't like his past. (As if the Palestinians are ever going to elect a Zionist with a lifelong record of commitment to the Jewish National Fund as their leader.) That takes all the pressure off of us. Because if we insist on their electing a leader who's been a lifelong pacifist with impeccable Zionist credentials, they'll never be ready for peace. We'll never have to contemplate giving anything up. We'll never have to engage in the soul-searching that shifting gears always requires. We'll simply avoid all the questions. A much better solution, no?

Which brings us back to the news last Friday. It started with Alexi and cut to Mahmoud Abbas's new government. Then a brief word about Defense Minister Shaul Mofaz's insistence that he's serious when he says he's going to remove all the illegal outposts. More dreaded questions. What will happen when the army comes to remove those armed (and often radical, and sometimes not too stable) illegal settlers? Are they going to simply pack up and thank the soldiers for their help? That doesn't seem terribly likely, does it? Could this turn ugly? Could this become the long-dreaded civil violence that we've all known was possible as soon as things with the Palestinians cooled down? Could it be that there are some fringe Israelis who, like Arafat, don't want to conceive of a world in which they're not at war? Simply because they wouldn't know what else to be, how else to be? Could it be that there are parts of our society that don't *want* anything else? Are the scars of the war so permanent that we can't imagine ourselves not being at war?

Which brings us back to Yom Ha-Shoah. Haim Gouri was in the middle of his lecture when, at precisely 10:00 A.M., the two-minute siren went off as it does each year, sounded in memory of the Six Million. The instant the siren started its low, hollow wail, everyone stood in perfect silence. Except for the siren piercing the air, not a sound could be heard.

We stood, immobile. Americans and Israelis. People who were alive during the war and those too young to remember it. Ethiopian Jews and French Jews. Right wingers and left. Silent, except for the siren. Because in the face of the Nazi legacy, words never suffice. The haunting moan of the air-raid siren says everything that can be said, as does our silence. And stillness.

In the midst of the ossified moment, I happened to look out the window. Cars had come to a complete standstill on what would normally have been a busy thoroughfare. Drivers opened their doors and stood outside their cars. Pedestrians stopped in their tracks. Buses froze where they were. The lights at the main intersection outside our building turned green, and then red, and then green again, but nothing moved. A perfectly still landscape.

Except for one white mutt. The dog crossed the street once, and then back, and then back again, seemingly confused that the cars didn't move, that it didn't have to hurry. It was a strange sight. A city frozen, motionless. And a little dog scampering around the middle of the avenue.

The oddity of the dog somehow made all the people seem utterly identical. And that, strangely enough, was a reassuring contrast to the contentiousness and divisiveness boiling just below the surface. For a few seconds, with the haunting siren wailing in the background, that strange little dog provided a fleeting sense that despite the battles over who's Jewish and who's not, who belongs here and who doesn't, what the shape of the country ought to be, whom we should trust and whom we shouldn't, we still have enough in common to believe that, just perhaps, we'll really be OK.

The next day, at the end of the workday, I started home, and on Hebron Road, the same avenue that just the day before had been so still during the siren, the traffic was rushing by. And amidst the cars and trucks, Jewish and Arab, some military vehicles, and a UN jeep or two, a truck with a tall cherry picker was stopping at each light pole, hanging Israeli flags in preparation for next week's Yom Ha-Atzma'ut (Independence Day) celebration.

That's it, in a nutshell, it struck me: those who still want to hang the flags versus those who've given up and can't wait to get out of here.

I'm still betting on the flag hangers. I'm betting that most of us are willing to do what it takes to keep this experiment going, no matter how painful the steps. I think that most of us celebrate the questions, not despite the fact that they're hard, but precisely because of that. Because, in the end, figuring out the tough stuff is exactly why we're here. Not all of us, maybe, but most.

At least so I think. Or, more honestly, so I hope. Or pray.

AN ENDING,
A BEGINNING

May 2003~December 2003

Nine Things Worth Remembering

I t hasn't been that hot outside, but the temperature in Jerusalem has risen considerably. After a brief respite, it has all started again, and things are blowing up left and right. This country is on edge in a way we haven't seen for a long time.

On April 30, 2003, a suicide bomber tried to get into Mike's Place, the seafront coffeehouse in Tel Aviv that's a popular hangout. He didn't get in, but he blew himself up outside, killing three people and wounding fifty. Less than a week later, Gideon Lichtman of Shiloh was killed, and his daughter seriously injured, when he was shot by terrorists as he was driving to work. A few days later, Zion David, a father of six, was killed in another shooting in the same area. And then, a couple in Kiryat Arba (near Hebron) was murdered when a suicide bomber blew himself up next to them as they were walking outside on a Saturday night. The next day, a bomber on the #6 bus in north Jerusalem killed seven passengers and wounded twenty others, four seriously. And now the suicide bombing (a nineteen-year-old woman bomber this time) in the Afula mall, killing three and wounding seventy. The war is back.

The other day, Avi, now thirteen years old and an eighth grader, was having some cereal and reading the morning paper's report about the latest attack. He looked up at me and said, "This is all our fault, you know."

Our fault? For a moment, I was stumped. How is this our fault? But then I assumed that I understood. He was referring, I figured, to the "occupation," the occasional brutality of the soldiers, or the absence of a Palestinian state, suggesting that if matters were otherwise, we'd be spared this kind of violence. But I figured that it was still worth a conversation, and asked him, "How so?"

"It's our fault because when they started this crap two and a half years ago, we didn't show them that we wouldn't take it. We responded a little here and a little there, and then everyone got used to this. If we had smashed them hard when they started, this would never have happened. Serves us right." And he got up, took his bike off the porch, and rode to school.

You've got to love breakfast in the Middle East.

I thought about that brief exchange a lot that day. I wondered what it must be like to be a thirteen-year-old kid who's so sick of this that he's just decided that "they" are right—that the way to win this is with brute force. So let's win it, he's apparently decided. There are nuances he's missing, obviously—he's only in eighth grade. But who can blame him for thinking that it's time to put a stop to this? Who can blame him for wanting to believe that there's a solution, any solution?

Like Tali, who wonders what peace is like, he's had more than enough.

It seems that even our kids' schools sense that the kids are stretched to the breaking point. A couple of nights ago, we went to a parent-teacher night at the Hartman Institute, where Avi is finishing up middle school. Cooling our heels while we waited for one of his teachers to become available, I wandered down the hallway to see what was on the various bulletin boards, and came across what I thought was a very interesting poster.

It was put out a while back by an educational project called Tzav Piyyus. *Tzav Piyyus* literally means "An Order to Get Along," but what's clever about it is that it's a play on the frequently heard phrase *Tzav Giyyus*, which means "Draft Notice." The poster was entitled "Nine Things Worth Remembering." An unauthorized but fairly literal translation of the poster reads as follows:

Nine Things Worth Remembering (and Doing):

1. This is not an easy time (but we got through Pharaoh, too).
2. We have shared objectives (even if it sometimes doesn't seem that way).

3. We all share responsibility (even though we like to cast it on others).

4. Each of us has a view on every subject (and also an opposite view).

5. Everyone has a right to express his viewpoint (that's democracy).

6. Everyone is obliged to obey the law (that's also democracy).

7. Verbal violence leads to physical violence (we've been there).

8. We should engage in dialogue with each other (we'll always discover things we didn't know).

9. We have no other land (!).

Tzav Piyyus—We Have No Other Land

It was, I thought, a very telling poster to find in a middle school, a window into what these kids—and their parents and everyone else—are feeling. There's no need to reflect on all nine items, but with some, there's just no way not to reflect on what our kids are dealing with.

1. This is not an easy time (but we got through Pharaoh, too).

This is not an easy time. Kind of the understatement of the year, no? The list of things that are wrong with this place grows by the day. The security situation, which wasn't good before, has gotten much worse in the past two weeks. Bush's "road map" is a (bad) joke, but just to make sure that Bush has no chance of making peace, Palestinian radicals have gone on a full offensive, blowing this place up night and day.

The economy is in tatters, and Bibi Netanyahu (now minister of the treasury) says that there is no choice but to undergo serious cost-cutting measures. He's probably right. But those about to take the brunt of it won't take it sitting down, and as of last Thursday, we were in the midst of our second national strike in just about as many weeks, with garbage piling up outside and then being blown about by the wind, making this city (and much of the rest of the country) a stinking, disgusting mess. Walking down the sidewalk has become, quite literally, a nauseating experience.

In the past few days, the papers have carried several stories about indigent couples who committed suicide because of their mounting debts, and one about a teenager who took his life because he didn't want to be a financial burden to his parents. When you do think of the human anguish at every level of that story, it's almost more than one can bear.

At first, many people respond to stories like that by reinforcing their commitment to what's left of the socialist underpinnings of Israel. If that's what privatization and capitalism will bring us, the unspoken line goes, we'll stick with socialism, or whatever's left of it.

But that sentiment doesn't last too long. For then, the Histadrut (our version of the AFL-CIO, more or less) declares strike after strike, piling the streets with garbage and shutting down the only international airport we have so no one can get in or out (they shut down the seaports, too). People here feel like they live in Cuba, locked in, and they are mortified about how we look to the rest of the world. So everyone gets sick of the unions, too, and they forget about the indigent people who've become despondent.

Let's see, what else? Well, there was the recent poll (more on this below) about the low level of commitment to democracy in the country, or the recent announcement (now that summer is just about here) that Israel has the world's second-highest skin cancer rate. (Australia wins.)

One could go on. We've got a newly appointed chief Ashkenazi rabbi who, as a Haredi (ultra-Orthodox, in common parlance), is basically not a Zionist. He's been accused of taking bribes and, now, of pedophilia. He denies it all, of course, but the press is out to skewer him. Jerusalem's mayoral elections are just days away, and the current incumbent (and a leading candidate) is a very nice guy who's also not much of a Zionist and thus refused to attend the annual Greeting Ceremony on Independence Day. The mayor of Israel's capital is uncommitted to the notion of a Jewish sovereign state? You can get dizzy here. Not only from the stench on the sidewalks.

So yes, kids, it's not an easy time, the poster admits to these eighth-graders. As if they didn't know that already.

2. We have shared objectives (even if it sometimes doesn't seem that way).

We have shared objectives? The poster, of course, is talking about Israelis, but foremost on everyone's mind these days are the Palestinians. As Bush insists that the road map is the only way, and Colin Powell asserts that it won't be revised, the Palestinians are accepting it, and Sharon is insisting that he wants elements clarified. Of course, the Palestinians can safely adopt the road map, because if they ever want or need an out, they can rely on extremists to bomb the road map to smithereens no matter what they've said. So Israelis feel themselves sliding into an untenable diplomatic position. We're saying "Let's see," and they're saying "Yes." But they blow us up day and night, and the world thinks we're the obstacles to peace.

So much for shared objectives.

4. Each of us has a view on every subject (and also an opposite view).

The irony is that beyond all the histrionics, most people are conflicted. Sometimes I think that the reason Israelis yell so much is that they're actually trying to convince themselves of something, in a place where no one is sure what to believe anymore. Sure, it's the ones on the fringe who capture the most attention, but the average person on the street (if you can find him or her in the piles of garbage) is deeply torn.

Behind every conversation looms the virtual inevitability of our having to give back significant chunks of land. Most people fear that some plan, the road map or its successor, will eventually be forced on the region, and Israel will have to make significant territorial concessions. And that leads to each of us having two views.

On the one hand, we should be happy to get out because we want to believe that it's a shot at peace. And the vast majority of Israelis don't want to control or occupy another resentful population. We hate what it's doing to our kids to have to man those checkpoints, to have to search Palestinian homes in the middle of the night. We do not want to keep pouring millions of dollars that we don't have into infrastructure there only to be forced to eventually hand it over to the Palestinians.

And if we care about democracy, we know that there's something terribly wrong with occupying millions of Palestinians who can't vote in Israel and who are citizens of no country. Those who care about the Jewish quality of the country (which is not everyone) know that we have to maintain a distinct Jewish majority here. So, these people say, if we're going to redraw the borders, maybe we should give back not only big chunks of Gaza and the West Bank, but portions of the heavily

Arab-populated parts of the Galilee, within Israel proper, too. Once we're redoing the map, the argument goes, let's buy ourselves a couple of decades before we're a Jewish minority here.

But on the other hand, why should anyone believe that those concessions would lead to peace? Dare we forget that the entire Intifada erupted when Arafat was pushed to make concrete steps for peace at Camp David in the summer of 2000? Nor has he changed. When has Arafat ever said, in Arabic, to his own people, that Israel has a right to exist?

And what do we do with the fact that it was actually Sharon's meeting with Mahmoud Abbas that unleashed this latest round of violence (the Muslim radicals wanting to show that no negotiations with Israel will be tolerated)? It may be an internal Palestinian conflict about who's in control, but we're the ones dying.

And what do we do with the obvious pattern that as soon as our forces leave some Palestinian areas, in an attempt to make life easier for Palestinian civilians, we get rewarded with more attacks, and more bombs exploding? Are we really going to leave our own security interests in the hands of Arafat and Abbas (who has no power anyway)? And what will we do if the West Bank becomes a sovereign foreign state, but terrorists are still infiltrating us from there? Then what? Do we still send in the tanks, and receive even more of the world's opprobrium?

And as for the idea of safeguarding the Jewish majority in Israel by giving an emerging Palestine even *more* territory than they expect by including part of the Galilee: do we really imagine that the Galilean Arabs would be willingly handed over to Palestine? This is a region with no shortage of ironies. Israel's Arabs would much rather live in the Jewish state than the Palestinian one. They'll protest all day (sometimes with justification) about our abuses of their rights, but they still have no interest in being citizens of Palestine. This probably has to do with something about basic liberties and human rights, not a high priority in the Palestinian Authority.

So Tzav Piyyus isn't really kidding when it says that we all hold both an opinion and its opposite. It's the hallmark, I guess, of a society that simply sees no way out. Of a society that believes everything. And nothing.

5. Everyone has a right to express his viewpoint (that's democracy)
and
6. Everyone is obliged to obey the law (that's also democracy).

Why mention democracy? Because anyone who watches and listens here knows that there may be a democratic edifice in this country, but there's not much of a democratic culture.

A few basic stats released by the Israel Democracy Institute's 2003 survey give the fundamental picture. The survey showed, for example, a twenty-year low in the level of support for the statement that democracy is the best form of government. Only 77 percent of the Jewish population thought it was. In the previous survey a few years ago, the figure was 90 percent. What will the next one say?

Not depressed enough? Of thirty-two countries for which there was data, Israel and Poland ranked lowest in the percentage of citizens (for Israel, that included both Arabs and Jews) who agreed with the statement that democracy is a desirable form of government. Israel (together with Mexico, India, and Romania) is only one of four countries out of thirty-one in which the population is of the opinion that "strong leaders can be more useful to the state than all the deliberations and laws."

Then there's the more subtle stuff. In 2003, more than half (53 percent) of Israeli Jews stated explicitly that they were opposed to full equality for the Arabs; 77 percent said there should be a Jewish majority required for crucial political decisions; less than a third (31 percent) supported having Arab political parties in the government; and the majority (57 percent) felt that the Arabs should be encouraged to emigrate. On all issues there was a dramatic decline in support for democratic norms, compared to 1999.

Today's kids don't remember peace. And we expect them to be desperately concerned about democracy when they grow up? One expects them to worry about the rights of Israeli Arabs, when they see Israeli Arabs lending at least vocal support to the terrorists seeking to destroy this country?

Elisheva and I were raised and educated in a different reality, in a place where no one was trying to kill us. So we had almost forty years to internalize liberal sensibilities before we got here. Our kids didn't. *That's* the difference. Which makes you wonder how much good a poster will do, no?

9. *We have no other land (!).*

The good news, if there is any, is that our kids really do get this one. We went to bed Saturday night to the news of the suicide bombing in Hebron. We woke up Sunday morning to the news of the bus bombing in north Jerusalem. Monday morning the radio reported that the police had foiled a plot to hijack a bus, drive it into the territories, and use the passengers and hostages to obtain the release of terrorist leaders the IDF has captured. Tuesday was the bombing of the Afula mall, which was followed by the comment by Hamas spokesman Abdel Aziz Rantisi that the attack showed that "our fighters are capable of reaching them [Israelis] in every corner of our occupied land. . . . As long as the occupation remains on our land and as long as the occupation soldiers are breathing."

"Every corner of our occupied land." Where, exactly, is that "occupied land"? Afula, as Abdel knows well, is well within the Green Line. It's not the territory that Israel captured in 1967 and that the world now wants us to return so that the Palestinians can have a state. Afula has been part of Israel since 1948. So which part of this land is "occupied"? All of it?!

There's not much accounting for that attitude in the road map, is there? It makes you wonder why any rational country would consider giving up anything at all, doesn't it? What, after all, would be the point?

Which brings us back to #9. On Yom Ha-Atzma'ut, we all took a hike to celebrate Independence Day. We were climbing a pretty steep hill, and Avi and I ended up out in front. Huffing and puffing our way up the rocky incline, Avi suddenly said, "Abba, I've decided I'm not going to be in the navy."

I wondered why an eighth-grade kid has to be thinking—while he's on a family hike, and years before he'll get his *Tzav Giyyus* in the mail— about what branch of the army he wants to be in, but I decided, instead, to ask him why he'd decided against the navy.

"Because I'm healthy," Avi said. "And I think that if you're healthy, you owe it to Israel to do *keravi* [be in a combat unit]." Trying to catch my breath (in more ways than one), and grateful beyond words that his mother was out of earshot, I said something like, "Well, we'll support you no matter what you want to do." But he wouldn't let it rest. "No, Abba, that's the point. It's not about what I want to do. It's about what I should do. I just think that it's only right for me to do *keravi*."

I have no idea what he'll do in the army, and neither does he, really. Nor did it matter at that moment that the navy *is* a combat position and plays a very important role in Israel's security. He has time to figure all that out.

But one thing is already clear: He doesn't need that poster to remind him that we've got no other place. He knows that as clearly as he knows anything. And he knows that this war is not about the edges, but about the middle. About the heart. And for that heart, young as he is, he's decided he's going to fight.

When Magical Thinking
Will Not Suffice

A possible bright light, a glimmer of hope. For over a year now, sixty leading Israeli philosophers and educators have gathered in an attempt to produce a statement about the values that they believe should lie at the core of the state. Right and left, religious and secular, yuppies and settlers, they have worked diligently to demonstrate that they could agree on a foundation for the future.

The result is a document called the Kinneret Covenant. Not bad, not bad at all. A civil, thoughtful, intelligent piece of work, it's been produced by the sorts of people who are so different from each other that they normally never even meet, much less agree on Israel's future.

But the more I read it, the less good I'm feeling. This is the eleventh hour for Israel. And the time for deluding ourselves has long since passed. So how, then, do the highly intelligent authors of the document propose to implement three of the principles to which they say they're absolutely committed: (1) Israel as a Jewish state, (2) the equality of Israel's growing Arab minority, and (3) Israel's democratic underpinnings? I just don't see how they can all coexist. And I'm getting alarmed by the wishful, magical thinking that lies at the heart of all Israeli planning.

We would all like a state that is Jewish, democratic, and deeply respectful of its Arab minority. But that's not the question. The question is whether it's possible.

The agreement states that Israel is, by definition, a Jewish state. The Jewish character of the state is to be reflected in a profound commitment to Jewish history and culture, in its connection with the Jewish communities of the Diaspora, and in the Law of Return (which grants all Jews the automatic right to settle in Israel), the encouragement of *aliyah* (Jewish immigration), the Hebrew language as the primary language of the state, the centrality of the Jewish calendar to the rhythms of state life, and the primacy of Jewish symbols in its culture, among others.

At the same time, the covenant insists that Israel must respect the rights of its Arab minority. But does the thick Jewish culture described in the covenant really leave room for a culturally thriving Arab minority? Why should Israeli Arabs feel any commitment to a society that not only gives primacy to a culture not their own, but was actually created *for the sake* of that other culture? When Pat Buchanan claims that the United States is a Christian country, despite the plethora of evidence to the contrary, American Jews feel threatened and disenfranchised.

But in Israel, the situation is very different; Israel *is* a Jewish state. It is, to paraphrase Lincoln's Gettysburg Address, of the Jews, by the Jews, and for the Jews. (That, obviously, is why many of us chose to live here.)

In what meaningful ways, then, can Israeli Arabs truly be equal? They can (and should) be given equal access to housing, and equal budgets can (and should) be spent on their schooling and health care. But will they ever really be full partners in this society? Could we ever expect them to be part of what Jean-Jacques Rousseau called the "general will" that lies at the core of liberal, democratic society? The very nature of the Zionist enterprise suggests not, but no one here is willing to admit that. As a friend said to me not long ago, we're sailing at full speed, and that's an iceberg ahead, not a snow cone. What are we going to do?

I get a call from the American Jewish Committee. They're publishing a small volume about the Kinneret Covenant and want to know if I'd write a reaction. "Are you open to something that's going to be controversial?" I ask them. Fine, they say.

So I give it a shot. Though the Kinneret Covenant notes that the Israeli Arab population is growing, I note, it underplays the real demographic threat facing Israel. In fact, the Israeli Arab population is growing at a much faster rate than the Jewish Israeli population. Israel faces a virtually certain future in which this marginalized and increasingly radicalized minority will become so large that it could influence the fundamental nature of the state and perhaps even undermine its basic Jewish character.

Were Israel not a democracy, the growth of the Arab population would be of less concern. But Israel *is* a democracy, and that, the Kinneret authors say (and I agree) has to be nonnegotiable. How, precisely, did the signatories of the agreement imagine that, as this intrinsically disenfranchised Arab population grows, Israel will be able to preserve its Jewish *and* its democratic aspects? Not even an attempt at a solution.

Of course it's hard. But is that a reason to avoid facing critical issues, or to shy away from suggesting possibilities that we might at least debate? The authors of the covenant say that a substantial Jewish majority in Israel will have to be preserved, but "only by moral means." What does that mean? What are our options?

Classical Zionism, of course, would suggest fostering increased Jewish immigration to Israel to safeguard the Jewish majority. But let's get real. There has never, ever been a substantial immigration to Israel from countries where Jews feel secure, and for all intents and purposes, everyone else has already come. Barring an unforeseen (and hard to imagine) catastrophe in North America, there will be no significant *aliyah* from the United States. Therefore, one has to conclude that significant Jewish immigration to Israel is over.

Some Israelis prefer fascism, of course. If dramatically increasing the number of Jews in Israel is not a viable option, and if lowering the Israeli Arab birthrate is possible only in the long term, simple logic dictates that the only other possibility is the reduction in the number of Arabs residing in Israel. That conclusion is what has led to the distressing discussion of "transfer" in right-wing Israeli society.

But it's an absurd, and sickening, proposal. Even if Israel's Arabs were willing to be moved, there's no place that wants them. But much more important, because they would never leave willingly, "transfer" is a euphemism for "ethnic cleansing," which is itself a euphemism. Even if the world would abide this (which it wouldn't, and the response would be infinitely faster than it was in the former Yugoslavia), is *that* what we want to become? The people who barely survived Nazism can actually even *discuss* rooting out another population? What's become of us?

Enter post-Zionism. Some Israelis propose a dramatic step in the opposite direction, namely, that Israel become a *medinat kol ezrakheha*, a "state of all her citizens." But this is shorthand for admitting defeat, for giving up on the Jewish character of the state, something that the agreement itself says is unacceptable. Of the three equally nonnegotiable principles in question, the Jewishness of the state is, with apologies to Orwell, more equal. It is the point of the entire enterprise. Wholesale liberal democracy, therefore, is also not the solution.

What, then, are we to do? One option is to recognize that the likely redrawing of Israel's borders in the next few years presents an opportunity for public discourse not only about what land to keep, but about what land to yield. Painful though the thought is, perhaps Israel needs to consider giving up not only territories that were captured in 1967, but other lands inside the Green Line, which Israel has had since 1949. For example, if Israel gave away the Galilean Triangle, where a large proportion of Israel's Arabs live, it would substantially reduce the number of Israeli Arabs for the time being. According to some estimates, the population of this area consists of approximately 350,000 Arabs and 50,000 Jews. Giving the Triangle to an emerging Palestinian state, therefore, would reduce the Arab population in Israel by approximately one-third, and the projected growth in the number of Israeli Arabs by at least that percentage.

Without question, this choice would be exceedingly painful for many Israelis, and particularly so for the Arab inhabitants of the area. But while borders would be redrawn, no Arab families would be uprooted. This is not a population transfer. (Indeed, if anyone would have to be moved, it would be Jews who live in the area and would have to be moved back inside the newly drawn borders.) The primary thing that would actually be moved is the border, something that happened countless times across Europe during the twentieth century.

Undoubtedly, the Israeli Arabs who would be "given away" to a Palestinian homeland—and presumably lose their Israeli citizenship—would cry foul. We know why they'd rather be Israeli citizens, and they'll fight. So we'd better be prepared. Let's get the best international lawyers, the leading Jewish ethicists, and ask them. Can this be done? Legally? Morally? Jewishly?

Perhaps. Perhaps not. But let's not pretend that we don't have a crisis, I wrote. And let's put this on the table, so at least we can have a conversation about it. For given the brutal choices that Israel faces, this one *might* be the only way we can maintain the Jewishness of the Jewish state.

. . .

I send the article off to the American Jewish Committee but keep a copy in my briefcase just to review it one more time before it goes to press. Later that afternoon I meet a friend for coffee. She and I are toying with the idea of writing something together. A colleague from work, she's become a good friend. Elisheva and I were at her wedding. She and her husband have been to our house on more than one occasion. And she's an Israeli Arab.

We order our drinks, and I reach into my bag to pull out my notes. But the wrong file comes out. It's the AJC draft. "No, this isn't it," I mumble.

"What's that?" she wants to know.

"An article I'm finishing up."

"What's it about?"

I look up at her, and I know I'm going to lie. There's no way I'm going to tell her what I've just written. I still think I'm right to propose the idea, but at the same time, I'm mortified.

And I wonder, rummaging through the briefcase, what does the fact that I'm too embarrassed to show her the article mean? How serious am I about exploring that proposal, if I can't even tell my friend about it? And how real can our friendship be?

Who, it now strikes me, is the one hiding behind magical thinking?

A Place Where Life
Goes through You

A friend wrote me recently, telling me that she had written to the mother of a child who was killed in a recent attack. She asked this mother if she ever thought of leaving, now that she'd paid such a high price for being here.

That mother wrote her back and, in reflecting on why she still lives in Israel and has never once thought of leaving, told her that in America, she and her family had had a wonderful life but had always felt that there, they essentially watched life go by. Here, she wrote, life doesn't go by you—it goes through you.

It does. Tonight Israel will be on the evening news, so Americans can gawk at our burnt-out bus, the line of a dozen body bags neatly laid out on Jaffa Road in the center of the capital. It will confirm everyone's impression of what life is like here, and it will fortify those supporters of Israel who are secretly thrilled to have confirmation that they're right not to want to come, even for a visit.

But that is not the stuff of which life here is made, and especially on a day like today, it's important to remember that. Life here is not about body bags or the charred remains of buses. For us, to live here is to live in a place where very little gets taken for granted, where even the simplest things are often seen for the miracles they are.

My parents were recently here for a brief visit. When they arrived, my father told me about their flight over. They were flying El Al, and as the plane began its descent into Tel Aviv, the pilot made an announcement and said in English, "Ladies and gentlemen, we will shortly be landing in Tel Aviv. Tomorrow is my sixty-fifth birthday, and thus I'll be retiring.

This, therefore, is my last flight as an El Al pilot, and I wanted to thank you and wish you the very best." Then, the same announcement in Hebrew, to which he added, "I chose to make this announcement in English first, in a departure from general El Al practice, because I wanted my last words as a pilot to be in Hebrew. *Shalom u-le-hitra'ot.*"

Even the language we speak strikes many of us as a miracle. True, Hebrew was never quite a dead language, but a hundred years ago, virtually no one on the planet spoke it. That's why to me, just waking up in the morning to a radio broadcast that tells us the news and the weather in Hebrew is miraculous. Sure, it would be nice if the news were different, and we already know that tomorrow's news will be brutal. But at least its language reminds us that the horrors of the news aside, there's a miracle unfolding here.

A couple of days after my parents arrived, we took them to an outdoor Yom Yerushalayim (Jerusalem Reunification Day) concert that was being held in memory of two American students who were murdered last year in the bombing of the cafeteria on the Mount Scopus campus of the Hebrew University. A couple of good bands were scheduled to perform, and it sounded like a nice way both to honor their memories and to celebrate Yom Yerushalayim without getting caught up in the annual debate over whether it's good to celebrate the "conquest" or the "liberation" or the "unification" of the city. If nothing else, I figured, we'd get a great view of the city—from West Jerusalem to the Old City to Mount Scopus and then Jordan beyond—on Jerusalem Day.

It was a very mixed crowd, and big (about thirty-five hundred, according to the press). Young and old, from preteens to senior citizens, from a few Haredim (ultra-Orthodox) to lots of "national religious" and secular, from the dreadlocks crowd to the yeshiva dress code of black pants and white shirts. People without kippot (skullcaps), with knitted kippot, with the now funky Bucharian kippot. People who were there to dance up a storm, and those who were content to listen and watch. People who had known Ben and Marla and were there to honor their memories, people who didn't know them but still felt it important to go, and people who were there to honor and celebrate a city that much of the world still says we're going to have to split, or share, or return, if we ever want peace.

An amazing thing—thousands of people out to celebrate a city. When, I asked myself, did we ever think that Baltimore, or New York, or Los Angeles, as much as we liked them, were miracles to be celebrated? People celebrating a city, and mourning the deaths of two young people who died because they loved it, dancing and singing, swaying to the music, connecting with friends, marveling at the still flickering lights of this ancient city.

And it struck me. This country is an unmitigated success. It's an achievement of cosmic proportions.

True, we've got an economy in tatters with unemployment, poverty, and hunger. True, we're still light-years away from a workable peace agreement, and too many people have died in the past three years, and will continue to die. True, the roads are far too dangerous and the streets way too dirty. The public education system is a catastrophe. Israeli Arabs don't get nearly their fair share, and neither do Jews of North African extraction. And the democratic tradition here is a bit wobbly and needs a lot of bolstering. The army has to be more careful, more disciplined. Those are all critical issues, and we have to address them.

But tonight, the music and the dancing remind us that those are minor issues. Really. Because they can be fixed.

Not long ago, though, there were things we couldn't change. Without our own country, there was nothing we could do to help ourselves, to save ourselves. I watched the hundreds of kids at this concert (Tali and Avi, who had come with us, had long since disappeared into the crowd, having found friends, assuring us that they'd eventually make their way home and we shouldn't even bother looking for them), swaying and dancing to music almost exclusively about peace, totally at home and relaxed in a city that to many is synonymous with terror, conducting their evening in a language that not long ago people didn't even speak.

And I thought for a fleeting moment about where the Jews were sixty years ago, which to my kids is an eternity but isn't—my parents were the age of our youngest child then. Where were the Jews? Going up smokestacks, barred by FDR from U.S. shores, blocked by the British from entering Palestine and imprisoned if they persisted in trying, thoroughly vulnerable to violence even here as the British watched (helped?) the local populations terrorize each other.

And look where we are today. Today's problems—yes, even with today's violence—seem minor in comparison. You can't survive here without some historical perspective. But with perspective, you can't help but see how much better off we are.

The first of the two bands ended their set and played their best-known song, "Od Yavo Shalom Aleinu" (roughly translated, "Peace Will Come Someday"), a song in which the refrain is one Arabic word, "Salaam." The crowd went wild, cheering and singing with the band. I could scarcely believe my ears. Ringed by hundreds of security personnel, because there really are people out there who would like to kill them, these kids were still singing and clapping to songs about peace.

It would have been good if the leaders of Hamas and Islamic Jihad could have been there for a few moments to witness this. For if they did, maybe they'd get it. They'll never, ever win. No matter how many buses they blow up, no matter how many people they kill. This is not a population or a generation that will be scared into leaving or into despair. The hope of this place runs too deep. Despite the wet blood still on the streets of our downtown, there's a pulse to life here that they simply cannot kill.

"Why would one stay here?" people sometimes ask us. I think it's the wrong question. How could one leave? With even a thin, cursory sense of the tapestry of Jewish history, how could one not want to be here? Who wouldn't want to live in a place where even concerts are miracles?

Who, for that matter, wouldn't want to live in a place where even the neighborhoods are miracles? Where on a Friday morning the shops are packed, as everyone is getting ready for Shabbat. Where the fruit market is jammed with people, and the sounds of Hebrew, Arabic, English, and some French flow through the air. Or the flower shop down the street, always busy, but with an especially long line on Fridays. And all this just a block or two from one of the side streets, where there's a memorial to a nineteen-year-old soldier, Iris Azoulai, who was killed right there, in the middle of the neighborhood. Where people remember and honor, but go on living with an appreciation for the mere miracle of being.

A few nights after the concert, we went a Bar Mitzvah party for the son of friends. This was one of those classy, creative affairs that you don't forget. We were told to meet at Liberty Bell Park in Jerusalem, and then we were bused to an unknown destination. Eventually, we arrived—all two hundred of us on four different buses—at Beit Guvrin, about an hour west of Jerusalem, for dinner and dancing. More or less the standard works, except that the dance floor was enormous, and they had the very best band that I've ever heard in Israel. They were outrageously good, and after a couple of sets of standard "Jewish stuff," they turned to the Beatles and onward, all the music that the parents' generation had grown up with. And this crowd, with many Anglo immigrants, partied, and partied hard.

They danced, drank, and sang late into the night, but this was more than a party. It was a chance to celebrate, to let loose after almost three years of far too much stress, too much fear, too many tears. It was the perfect night for people desperate to feel joy, to forget the rest. Because we're tired, and hurting, but not despondent.

I looked around the crowd. Lawyers (lots of them!), venture capitalists, educators, therapists, a generous smattering of high tech folks, some academics. A couple of government types. Different professions, a full spectrum of religious orientations, a reasonably wide socioeconomic spread. Huge gaps between their political viewpoints, particularly on the subject of how to achieve peace, or how to live if you're resigned to peace never coming.

But most had one thing in common. They were immigrants. Mostly from the States and England, but from Russia and other places as well. And as such, it was a group of people who had chosen this life, who had elected to be here, and who thought that being here was just about the greatest blessing life can offer. No despair. Just a sense that out in the open, celebrating a Bar Mitzvah surrounded by hundreds of other people who wouldn't want to live anywhere else, life just doesn't get better.

Toward midnight, it was clear that the party had to come to an end. After all, we had to leave as a group, and most people had to work the next morning. But the band wouldn't stop playing, and the people wouldn't stop dancing. Finally, the father of the Bar Mitzvah went to the bandleader and whispered something in his ear, and the band started to play "Ha-Tikvah," Israel's national anthem.

For a split second, I was worried. I'm not a big fan of singing "Ha-Tikvah" at every turn, and all too often, it strikes me as kitschy, or forced.

But there was nothing to worry about here. At the very first strains of "Ha-Tikvah," two hundred people who only a minute or two earlier had been drenched in sweat, wildly singing and dancing up a storm, stood perfectly still. Standing almost at attention, everyone sang. Staring out at the desert hills, or up at the star-filled sky, or straight ahead at nothing in particular, we stood, singing words we understood and an anthem in which we deeply believed. This was no Star-Spangled-Banner-before-the-ballgame moment. It was one of those existential moments in which, when you least expect it, you're reminded of what your life is all about.

> *Od lo avdah tikvateinu*
> *Ha-tikvah bat shenot alpayim*
> *Lih'yot am chofshi be-artzeinu*
> *Eretz tziyyon vi-yerushalayim.*

> Our hope is not lost
> That two-thousand-year-old dream
> To be a free people in our land
> The Land of Zion and Jerusalem.

It was one of those moments when, surrounded by people you knew and people you didn't, the power of this place overwhelms you. One of those moments when life doesn't just pass you by, but in ways that words can hardly attest, a moment in which life goes through you.

It's hard to know what the future will be here. Though I hope the country will make it, some of us know that there's a chance that it won't. But I don't think that anyone there at that moment had any doubt that doing our small share to give it a chance was worth it. Given where we were sixty years ago, can there be any greater gift than to have been born at this moment in Jewish history and to be part of creating a different future for our kids?

Why would one stay? Because even out there, in the desert, miles away from our apartments, everyone standing and singing "Ha-Tikvah" knew and felt exactly the same thing. That two-thousand-year-old dream has already come true. And from dreams, you don't just walk away.

The Bearable Lightness
of Peace

Walking to the office this morning, on a calm, midsummer day, I passed the little French bakery in our neighborhood where elderly men sit outside on the sidewalk, sip their Turkish coffee, and read the newspaper. Two of them were looking at this morning's headline about Corporal Oleg Shaichat, a soldier who disappeared a few days ago and was found yesterday, buried in a shallow grave. One said to the other, "*Rak tzarot yesh lanu*" [Nothing but troubles for us]. To which his companion replied, "*Nachon, aval yoter tov, lo?*" [True, but it's better, no?].

That little interchange pretty much summed up how people are doing with this little *hudna* (Arabic for "cease-fire") we're having. Small incidents of terror continue almost every day, and some rather large plots are still being thwarted. But the pace has undeniably lessened, and everything has changed. Life is unquestionably more comfortable, infinitely more relaxed. At restaurants, some of the guards are gone, but even where they remain, the security check is cursory. A glance, a quick electronic wand over your back, and you're through. None of the careful rummaging through your briefcase, or the wand covering every inch of your chest and legs, front and back, each time you go into the bank or a store or an office building. There's a "time-out" in effect, and while some people believe it will last and others believe it won't, most of the people we know are enjoying it as much as they can.

The sidewalk tables at many cafés, spots that used to be unoccupied because most people wanted to be inside (beyond the security guard) are now full. Everyone is more relaxed, and no one dreads the news quite as much as they did just a bit more than a month ago. On Shabbat afternoon, just outside our kitchen window, kids from the building next door sat outside on the grass and sang all afternoon. If I hadn't seen it and heard it, I wouldn't have believed it. But there they were, for hours, just sitting on the grass and the stone wall around the yard, laughing and playing, singing the whole day. Was it because they know about the *hudna*, or because it was just a pretty day? Or because their parents are probably less stressed out? Or because everyone's taking a deep breath? Hard to know, but it was certainly welcome. It's nice to hear the kids singing again.

We've only got one kid at home this summer, but he's ecstatic. Without his even knowing why, he's singing in the shower. Add to that the kids singing next door. . . . It doesn't get much better than that.

For three years, every time we thought that things had hit rock bottom, they got worse. But now, this city is coming alive again. Elisheva and I went to the summer outdoor Jerusalem fair last Thursday night. Tight security, to be sure, but packed. Unlike last year, though, when security was even tighter, no one seemed nervous this time. There were clowns and jugglers and tons of kids. Lots of music. Thousands of people. And a lot of people busy being happy.

We got tired of the fair and decided to grab a bite to eat. We left the secured downtown area, walked past the guards into the unprotected part of town and began to roam. Still, even outside the guarded area, the streets were filled with people everywhere. We passed Machaneh Yehudah, the outdoor market that is always packed on Thursday nights, and this time it was a virtual Mardi Gras. There were guards, to be sure, but the place was relaxed. People shopping, eating, tasting, even laughing. There would have been no way to know that that same market has been on the front page—for horrible reasons—far too many times in the past three years. Most everyone here has decided to live, even if only for the ninety days of quiet that we've been "promised."

The big question, of course, is whether it will last that long, or beyond that. No one here is naïve enough to imagine that Hamas, or the Al Aksa Brigades, or the Islamic Jihad are using the "time off" to read Bialik, or to perfect their Hebrew grammar. We know that many of them are using this period to rearm, to retrain, and to prepare for the next round. Some Israelis are busy reminding everyone that *hudna* is a complex term. It's used to refer to the treaty that Mohammad made in 628 C.E., which he used as an opportunity to regroup after he failed to capture Mecca, so that he could once again march on the city and capture it. That kind of a *hudna*, these Israelis remind us, we don't need.

The settlers are nervous, too. Because on the off chance that this "peace" sticks, they're going to have to move. Peace will come—now, or in the years to come—only if there's a Palestinian state. And that can't happen with the settlers living in Gaza and on the West Bank. So, they, too, have a vested interest in assuring us that this is just a ploy, that it will never endure.

But others focus on the fact that *hudna* in everyday Arabic also means just plain old "truce." What we don't know, obviously, is which form of *hudna* we've got. If it's the former, we could be in trouble. But if it's the latter, life here could get much better.

The strange thing about this region is that working for peace can be dangerous. We ignored the right when they warned us about the Oslo Accords of 1993, and we are still paying the price. But if you believe the right and their warnings, then you don't take any risks for peace. And if that's what happens, you might look back one day and realize that there may have been a chance to build something different here, but it's too late now, and you've squandered what might have been the last opportunity.

So people here live in a kind of surrealistic world of hope and fear, optimism and petrified caution, fueled by the memory of the last time that their sanguineness led to heartbreak, and then to a lot of death.

Even the press can't decide what to make of all this. On *Ha-Aretz*'s English Web site today, I saw a headline so complex that I had to read it several times. It read (and this is a precise quote):

SECURITY OFFICIAL: SAFE TO PREDICT TRUCE WILL LAST
MORE THAN THREE MONTHS
Says Abbas believes it possible to dismantle
terror groups without bloodshed
IDF Chief Ya'alon braces for next wave of violence

Talk about surreal. What, exactly, does that headline mean? Which *hudna* do we have? It depends, apparently, on whether you believe the (unnamed) "security official" (who believes that the peace might last) or Ya'alon (who's getting ready for the next round of violence). The incomprehensible headline is a commentary on the times.

Add to this convoluted headline the statement by Egyptian president Mubarak two days ago that "only Sharon can bring peace," because Sharon was the one who oversaw the evacuation of Jewish settlements when the Sinai went back to Egypt. Mubarak is uttering a sentence with the words "peace" and "Sharon" in it? What's going on? Is there something new about Sharon that we don't know?

And what's with the restoration of diplomatic relations between Israel and Austria, as (tentatively) announced today? And cozying up, finally, with Pakistan, also as announced today? Or Jordan and Egypt talking publicly about sending their consular staffs back to Israel? And then, tonight on the news, Sharon and Bush at the White House, without any mention of the "fence" that was supposedly going to be such a bone of contention. How good would things have to get for people here to actually believe that they'll be OK?

The problem, of course, the cynics will tell you, is that things were good before. And then it all dissolved into horror. But still, when does one say that things are good enough to at least merit some hope?

Talia, our daughter, who's away for the summer at a program at Brandeis University, called a few days ago, and as we were chatting, she asked, "So what's in the news?"

"Nothing," I told her.

"Nothing at all?" she asked.

"Nothing."

She was quiet for a second and then said, "That's amazing. It's really amazing."

We hung up a few minutes later, and I found myself trying to calculate how long the *hudna* was scheduled to last, and whether she'd be home for any of it.

And then I wondered which would be better. To experience some of this, only to risk the devastation that we'll all feel if it ends? Or would it be preferable for her not to have to face the disappointment, but not to see some peace, either?

She'll be home in time, I calculated, and I'm glad. This peace may not last, and if it doesn't, we'll be devastated. No question. But I want her to see it, at least a little bit of it. I want her to open the paper, every morning, day after day, at least for a couple of weeks, and see that there don't have to be pictures of blown-up buses, destroyed restaurants, mug shots of the people to be buried that day. I want her to see that this place, too, yes, even this place, can be normal. I want her to see the laughter, the lightheartedness, the sloppy security. I want her to hear the singing of the kids next door, to see the cafés full again, to go downtown without being afraid.

Remember that snowy day when she wondered what peace was like? Wouldn't it be great if she could see for herself? Wouldn't it be great if she could see this place as we thought it would be, when we brought her here in 1998?

Will it last? I don't know. But I, for one, am going to hold out hope, even though I know that the "right" may be right. My kid's coming home in a couple of weeks, and she doesn't remember what peace is like. I'd risk a lot for her to find out.

Shattered

What do you say to your teenage daughter who's still awake at 11:15 P.M. when the bomb is so loud and so close that the house shakes and the windows rattle? And when you turn on the news (because a noise like that in a place like this can only mean one thing), and it turns out that they just blew up the main street that's a five-minute walk from here, and on the TV she sees her favorite café shredded and flowing with blood. What do you say?

What, you wonder as you try to figure out what to say, is going through her mind? Is it occurring to her that this sort of thing never happens in Waltham, near Boston, where she just spent the summer? Is she wondering, now that it's September and school's started again, whether the whole year is going to be like this?

And how do you wake your younger kids the next morning? What do you tell them before they head off to school? When it's this close, there's no lying. They're going to find out anyway, and the news that they hear during the day could be so bad that it would be unthinkable not to prepare them. So what do you say? That the war's come back? That the people (if that term is even applicable to anyone who would do something like this) who want to kill them are closing in? That we don't yet know the names of the dead and wounded, but it's not unlikely that we'll know someone, or know of someone? That Café Hillel is gone? That the block where our kids rent their videos, buy their falafel, and go shopping for school supplies is now undeniably what we've long known it is—a place where they might be blown to bits?

I'd figured that we'd talk to the kids when they got dressed and came down for breakfast, so I didn't give much thought to how we'd wake them up. But Elisheva had a different idea. She wasn't taking any chances. I happened to glance into Micha's room to make sure that he was getting up and dressed for the second week of fifth grade, and I saw her sitting on the side of the bed, rubbing his back, talking to him. I didn't hear any of the conversation, but I knew what it was about. And then I heard him asking questions. I didn't hear those either, and I was glad. What in the world would I have said? What do you tell a ten-year-old when the evil has gotten so close that now there's no denying what he knows—they could get him, too?

At the end of the day—a long, angry, nausea-filled day of work while anxiously reading the Web, waiting for the names to appear—I headed home from the office to make dinner and to eat with the kids. But Elisheva, training to become a tour guide, was in class, Talia was in the middle of something, and Avi had a friend over, so when I called everyone for dinner, only Micha showed up. We sat down, but he didn't want to eat too much. Mostly, he had questions. And things to tell me.

"How was your day at work?"

"Pretty good," I told him. "It's sweet of you to ask."

"Were people at your work sad?"

"Everybody was sad. Were you sad?"

"My teacher was crying today when she was teaching us."

"Do you know why she was crying?"

"Because she was supposed to go to the wedding tonight of that girl who was killed with her father. But she left school to go to the funeral instead. She was crying the whole time she was teaching us."

"Did that make you sad?"

"Yeah, but other kids in my class were sadder."

"Why?"

"Yoel was sad because his doctor was killed."

"The doctor who was the father of the girl who was supposed to get married?"

"Yeah. And another boy was sad because his sister's gymnastics teacher was killed."

Seemed like a lot for a ten-year-old to process during the day. I thought maybe it would be a good idea to walk over there, so he could actually see the place and remove some of the mystery. "Would you like to walk over there after dinner? At eight o'clock, there are going to be people saying *Tehillim* [Psalms] there. Would you like to come?"

"OK. Ema took me there when I got home from school."

"What did you see?"

"It's all boarded up, and there are lots of police surrounding it, because there's really no way that they can lock it up. All the walls are gone. The bomb blew them up. And there were lots of candles lit. It was pretty, but it made me sad."

Not much you can say to that, it seemed to me. If this doesn't make you sad, not much will. So we ate dinner and chatted, and eventually, Tali and Avi joined us. The conversation turned to the guard at the café. There were two guards, they said.

"Did he get by the first guard?" one of the kids asked.

"I don't know," I told them. The papers were full of conflicting accounts (not surprising, given the pandemonium at the scene and the fact that many of the witnesses were either dead or unconscious). And besides, I didn't see the point of the conversation. What difference did it make?

"I think that the first guard tried to block him, but he pushed through, and the second guard stopped him from getting further into the restaurant," one of the kids said.

And then I got it. This was no idle chatter. They were trying to figure something out. If we have guards in front of every restaurant, office building, bank, and other public establishment, but we're still not safe, what can we possibly do? Where can they go and feel secure, they were trying to figure out. But they knew the answer already, so I didn't have to say much. They're not safe. They know it. Now they really get it.

I asked Talia and Avi, too, if they wanted to come with us at eight, and they did. We finished dinner, cleaned up, and just before eight, headed out to Emek Refa'im Street. On the way we passed a couple of people in civilian clothes carrying loaded submachine guns. Talia was a bit taken aback.

"This is quite the place."

Trying to reassure her that Jerusalem isn't turning into Liberia, I pretended not to know what she was referring to. "What?"

"Did you see that guy with the loaded M-16 and those other huge pistols stuck into his jeans, just walking around?"

"Yeah, but I assume he's just Shin Bet (Israel's much-vaunted General Security Service) or something." Total lie, as I also had no idea what he was doing walking around like a one-man arms depot, but I figured I'd try to calm her down.

"Well, even if he is, doesn't it strike you as interesting that no one on the street is paying him any attention?"

Touché. Nothing to say to that. So we kept walking. The café was, as Micha had reported, all boarded up, surrounded by dozens of police. We crossed the street, brazenly jaywalking in front of about fifty policemen, who clearly understood that a family illegally crossing the street is the least of this country's problems. They didn't even look at us. We walked up to the table where the candles were flickering, and Tali lit one.

We knew dozens of people there. Quiet hellos, some handshakes. Some hugs. A couple of Tali's friends came over and hugged her. And we waited around for someone to start the Psalms.

Behind us there were two secular men in their forties or fifties having a heated conversation. You couldn't help but listen, as they were just shy of shouting at each other.

"Thirty years, and there won't be an Israel."

"Of course there will be."

"Well, it might be called Israel, but it won't be a Jewish state."

"Yes, it will."

"No, it won't. You know what the problem is? We're too good to live in this neighborhood. If we'd take the bomber's family and kill them, bombers might think twice in the future. Or we could just exile their families. But we've got to do something more than blowing up their empty houses. That doesn't work. We're not willing to be the monsters that you have to be to live in this part of the world. They actually live better after their sons blow themselves up. And they don't care when their kids die. They're proud.

"So we hang around here and cry, and they're one step closer to victory. Why would all these young kids [and he pointed to the dozens of teenagers who were hanging out with their books of Psalms] stay here? Why in the world should they raise their kids in this? They won't, they're going to leave. They don't know it yet, but they will. We've lost this war, and just don't want to admit it."

"That won't happen so fast. And it would be wrong to do that to the families."

"Why's it wrong? Why's it OK for Bush but not for us? But wrong or not, if we don't do it, we're never going to make it here. You live in France, you act like the French. You live in America, you act like the Americans. You want to live in the Middle East, you have to act like you live in the Middle East. But we're paralyzed by our fear of what the world will think of us. So we're losing this war. This country is finished. Maybe not thirty years. I'll give you forty. But the end is getting closer. We gave it a try, this bit of having a country, but it was just the wrong time in the wrong place. *Chaval* [a pity], no?"

"Maybe. I don't know. Yes, *chaval*."

And they walked away. Tali looked at me. She didn't say anything, but I knew what she was asking me. "Tell me that they're wrong," her eyes said. But I couldn't. I didn't have anything to say. He's right in some ways. We're just not willing to be the animals that one has to be to make it here. And he could be right about the outcome, too. My daughter, I suspect, desperately wanted me to tell her it would be all right. But I wasn't in the mood to lie anymore. So in a moment of gross parental incompetence, I didn't say anything at all. I suspect she got the point.

The whole thing reminded me of a conversation we'd had just the weekend before at home. It was Shabbat, and we were having a rare dinner by ourselves after having been apart for various trips all summer long, when Elisheva said something about "when there's peace." Avi looked at her as if she'd gone mad. "What in the world are you talking about?" he wanted to know, in that tone that only a kid in the prime of adolescence can muster. "You don't get it, do you? There's never going to be peace here. They hate us. They want us out of here completely, and they won't stop this until we're gone altogether. They're proud when their kids blow themselves up. You can't make peace with that, no matter what."

It's a theme you now hear in many quarters. We live in a part of the world drowning in an ethic that is incomprehensible to me, that has nothing to do with the alleged occupation since 1967. It has to do with our being here at all, in any part of this land. For the terrorists, it's all or nothing. They will sink to depths to which we will not sink, and they know that time is on their side.

Back to Emek Refa'im Street. By the time the reading of Psalms and the recitation of Ma'ariv were over, Micha was getting tired, and he had school the next morning. So we started the walk home, Avi, Micha, and I. Tali stayed behind with friends, who were now singing those slow, mournful songs in minor keys that Israelis have raised to an art form.

This time it was Avi's turn to pipe up.

"You know, Abba, I wanted to go to Emek Refa'im last night, but Ema wouldn't let me."

It wasn't really a question, but it was more than a mere statement of fact. It was a musing on the Russian roulette that life here has become. He knew full well that if Ema had let him go out with friends that night, things could have turned out very differently for us. And he knows that the guards don't always work. And that the savages have now discovered our neighborhood. And he's read the reports that Hamas says that they're now going to blow up multistory apartment buildings instead. He gets it. He didn't even need to ask a question. He just knows.

We got home three minutes later, and it was time for Micha to go to bed. He got undressed, brushed his teeth, and hopped into bed. It was too late for a story, so I just sang to him. After the Shema and the other things we say with him each night, at which point he usually just grabs his pillow with both arms and goes to sleep, he suddenly turned onto his side, and looked at me.

"Abba, why do the suicide bombers blow themselves up?"

Why, I wanted to know, is your mother not here for this conversation? But it turns out she'd already had it. Because he continued.

"Ema says that it's because they believe that after they do that, they're going to be treated extra nicely." I suppose that's the euphemism for the whole seventy-virgins bit. Thank God he didn't ask about that. "Do you believe that?" he wanted to know.

"No," I told him. "I think that they're wrong. They're not going to get anything special. They're just killing themselves and lots of other innocent people. What they do is evil, and they're being taught terrible things by their teachers."

"That's what Ema said, too." So far so good.

He turned onto his stomach, grabbed his pillow, and closed his eyes. But I couldn't leave him, not with that. So I sat back down next to him, rubbed his back, and told him I was sorry. "I'm sorry that you have to think about that kind of stuff," I told him. "Kids your age shouldn't even know about this."

"It's OK," he said. He paused for a minute, and then he said, "I still like it here. I'm still glad we live here."

I gave him a kiss on the head, told him I loved him, and walked out of the room. I figured that the last thing he needed at the end of a day like that was to see me crying. What would I have told him? That the world is falling apart and no one knows how to stop it? That exactly two years after 9/11, the day on which everything supposedly changed, Osama bin Laden is still making home videos, Saddam is still alive, and we're still being blown to bits? And that no one has any idea what to do?

Micha had asked me if people at work were sad. Of course people were sad. Who wouldn't be? Toward the end of the day at the Mandel Institute, we had a lecture from someone on our faculty, a well-known Israeli man of letters, who is far to the left, often far too left for my particular taste. But he's smart, very smart, and you can't easily ignore anything that he says. Yesterday, though, it was clear he was in no less pain, and feeling no less fury, than anyone else. He'd scrapped what he'd planned, he told us, and did something different.

It was a brilliant presentation. He ended with a passage from Yosef Hayyim Brenner (1881–1921), perhaps the greatest writer of the Second Aliyah, who was murdered by Arab rioters in May 1921. In 1911 Brenner wrote a novella called *Mikan U-mi-kan* ("From Here and From Here") in which he penned the following lines:

> *Efshar, efshar me'od, she-kan i efshar lichyot*
>
> *Aval kan tzarich le-hisha'er*
>
> *Kan tzarich lamut, lishon*
>
> *Ein makom acher*

It's possible, it's very possible, that here, it's not possible to live
But here one must stay
Here must one die, and sleep
There is no other place.

That pretty much sums it up. I still pray for peace, but I know I won't live to see it. I suspect that my children won't either. Sure, there will be *hudnas*, and other celebrated cease-fires will come and go, but there won't be peace. Not in my generation, and not in the next. And yet I can't imagine the Jewish people without a state, and I can't imagine how I'd be able to look myself in the mirror if we left. So we stay, try to raise decent Jewish kids who are both passionate Zionists and moral human beings, and try to learn to live with what I believe will not change.

If I don't hope for peace anymore, what *do* I hope for? I hope that Micha will also put his kids to sleep here, and not somewhere else. And I hope that somehow we'll survive here, and that despite everything, we'll build the kind of society here that will lead his kids to tell him, a few decades from now, on some dark, oppressively sad, tear-stained night, "I'm still glad I live here."

In That Split Second

We're back to Jerusalem of old. People are eyeing packages, and each other, nervously, wondering, now that the *hudna* has been blown apart, when the next bombing will be. The skittish anxiety from which we'd temporarily escaped has returned.

Given the proximity of our house to my office, I walk to work each morning, and walk back home at the end of the day. (With Jerusalem traffic, it's no exaggeration to say that it would take more time to drive.) A few days after the Café Hillel bombing, I pass a small apartment building on Bethlehem Road. In front of the building stands a large, green plastic garbage dumpster, about four feet high and several feet wide, with a couple of cats pacing back and forth across the top, seeking a way in.

They are ubiquitous in Jerusalem, these dumpsters, and in the years that we've lived in this house, I've walked this route many hundreds of times. But I've never really noticed the dumpsters before. Today, though, I see the dumpster looming ahead of me, and it occurs to me that it could have a bomb in it. And I ask myself, "Should I cross to the other side of the street?"

I don't cross. It's obvious, even immediately, that that's a place you can't go here, dodging dumpsters in a city where they dot virtually every street. Go there, and you lose your mind. So I walk straight ahead, right toward the dumpster.

And then I wonder, still walking. "What's it actually like when one of those things blows up? If you get hit, do you know that you're dying? Is there a split second between the time that you realize it's all over, and the moment you don't think anymore? And if there is, what would I think in that split second?"

I imagine that I'd be sad. I'd like to watch my kids grow up, to see in full bloom the people they're already becoming, to live to see them have their own kids. I'd like to spend a few more decades with Elisheva, reading, walking, laughing. And I'd like to see my country in a very different condition.

I also sense that I'd have no regrets. If that split second does exist, I imagine, I'd feel sadness, but not regret. In that last moment of thinking, before I thought no more, I'd feel fortunate. Fortunate to have been born during that slender window in time when the Jews were trying, for the first time in thousands of years, to build something of their own. Fortunate to have been alive at this critical juncture in Jewish history, and to be part of this experiment. And fortunate to have been born into a family that raised me to want to come here and to have been lucky enough to be able to make it happen.

When you come right down to it, does anything at all matter more than being part of something like this? How many of us get to live our lives as players (even if insignificant ones) in the unfolding of something majestic, historic, and transformative? Very few of us do, very few.

No, I tell myself as I walk right alongside the dumpster, no matter what happens, it doesn't get better than being here. Even now, with the city hurtling back to the frightening days of last year, there's no place else I'd rather be. There's just no other place.

What's a Disengagement?

There was a time, when Micha was a little boy, when he used to ask about the army incessantly. At the beginning of the Intifada, as he was trying to fall sleep to the sounds of gunfire and tank shells, bundled under his quilt, his tiny little hands desperately gripping his favorite blanket, he'd sometimes say, "When I get older, am I going to go to a war?" Elisheva and I would try to assure him, without lying. "Well," we'd say, "you're going to go to the army, but hopefully, by then there will be peace, and you won't have to go to war."

"That's good," he replied more than once. And then, after a pause, "Because I know that if I go to a war, I'm going to die."

Now he's older. His formulations have become more sophisticated. He and I were sitting at the dining room table a couple of days ago. He was doing some homework, and I was reading. Out of the blue, he looked up at me and asked, "Do you think I'll still have asthma when I'm a grown-up?"

For the life of me, I couldn't figure out why in the world he was asking me that. "I don't know. You might. But I'm sure it's going to get a lot better. Why do you ask?"

"Ema says that the army won't take me if I have asthma."

Now I couldn't imagine why his mother would say something like that, given the fact that first, it's not true (there are plenty of noncombat jobs he could do even if he did have serious asthma) and, second, the mild form of asthma he has would probably not get him out of very much.

"Did it make you sad when Ema told you that?" (If she even did, which I suddenly doubted.)

No answer. And then, after a minute, "Do you think that I'll go to the army?"

OK, now we're getting somewhere. I'm beginning to see where all this is headed. "Well, I assume that you'll go to the army, but you know what? I think that there's a very good chance that by the time you have to go to the army, there'll be peace and being in the army will be very different than it is now."

He looked at me with that ten-year-old "How stupid do you think I am?" look and just said, "Right." And he went back to his homework.

I watched him for a while, working on his math homework and then memorizing some Arabic vocabulary, and felt bad for him. You shouldn't have to spend your life at the age of ten wondering if you're going to have to go to the army. You shouldn't have to believe, at the age of ten, that peace is just the stuff of fairy tales. Or a joke. At ten, shouldn't you be able to do your Arabic homework without having to worry about being killed a few years down the road?

You should, of course. But the question is how do we get there? How do we break through this stalemate, with its occasional *hudnas* followed by its inevitable flare-ups? We've tried it all before, haven't we? Oslo, first. Then Camp David. And nothing much has changed. The road map is dead, Arafat is not. Something has to give.

Well, Yossi Beilin and his Palestinian partner, Yasser Abd-Rabbo, have decided to give it all another whirl. Unauthorized by the Israeli government, Beilin, a highly intelligent if (for my taste) wildly optimistic Israeli left-leaning intellectual and politician, has sat down with Palestinian counterparts, and they've come up with a new plan. The Geneva Accords. They're going whole hog. Once and for all, a final settlement with the Palestinians. Peace. Mutual recognition.

Yossi promised all of us our very own copy in the mail, and sure enough, it arrives. It's a pretty thing, this brochure. Lots of blue and white. That's clever. The same with his Web site. The maps are pretty also. They're also a bit incomprehensible, so it's not entirely clear what exactly we're giving back (though it's clearly a lot). But the basic formula is clear—we give back lots of land, and they promise to play nicely.

They even promise to recognize our right to exist. That would be nice. But Arafat wasn't part of the negotiating process. So what good is it, I'm wondering. Seems that I've heard all this before. Indeed, Yossi has, too. Even the opening paragraphs of the accord make it clear that, as

Israelis say, *"Ba-seret ha-zeh kevar hayinu"*—"We've seen this movie already." Been there, done that. Almost incredulous that Beilin and Yasser Abd-Rabbo think this can work, I reread that section of the Preamble, over and over:

> Confirming that this Agreement is concluded within the framework of the Middle East peace process initiated in Madrid in October 1991, the Declaration of Principles of September 13, 1993, the subsequent agreements including the Interim Agreement of September 1995, the Wye River Memorandum of October 1998 and the Sharm El-Sheikh Memorandum of September 4, 1999, and the permanent status negotiations including the Camp David Summit of July 2000, the Clinton Ideas of December 2000, and the Taba Negotiations of January 2001.

That's the rub, isn't it? The very preamble of the accords essentially demonstrates that this cannot work. We've talked. We've negotiated. We've signed. And we've been burned each time. Arafat didn't want Camp David to succeed. Because if he'd wanted a deal but thought that Barak hadn't offered enough, the solution would have been easy. Instead of starting the second Intifada, he could have pushed Barak to wherever he wanted him, in a matter of days. All he had to do was to tell the thousands of Palestinians who were then coming into Israel to work every day just to sit on the highway between Jerusalem and Tel Aviv, and further north, to block the highway between Tel Aviv and Haifa. Nothing violent. Just a Martin Luther King–like sit-in that would have paralyzed the country. And he could have invited CNN to film the whole thing, thus ensuring that any fears of violence on the part of the Israeli security forces would have been mitigated. And finally, he could have used a few hundred thousand dollars of the many millions he's stolen to buy the back page of the front section of the *New York Times*, put the maps there, and shown the world, "This is why we can't take Barak's offer, and here's what we need."

How long would it have taken before the country's paralysis and the world's opprobrium forced Barak to capitulate? Arafat could have had anything that he wanted.

But he didn't *want* a deal. He didn't want to make the transition from revolutionary to statesman, and he didn't want to acknowledge our right to exist. Or our right to not have our kids get killed. So why would Yossi Beilin think that Arafat would want anything different now? Madrid, Oslo, Wye River, Sharm El-Sheikh, Camp David, Taba—Arafat was around for all of them. And Yossi just thinks, well, this time he really means it?

Come on, Yossi. We've buried a lot of people in the last couple of years because we wanted to believe that so badly. How many more are going to die?

So, despite all the hoopla, the Geneva Accords disappear off the Israeli radar screen almost as suddenly as they'd arrived. A few days of intense debate, and then they're gone. Yossi hasn't given up, but everyone else has stopped listening. "Yossi," they're saying, "We've tried all that." It's time for something new.

Others throw their hats into the ring. Ami Ayalon (a former director of the Shin Bet) and Sari Nuseibeh (a moderate Palestinian) have cooked up their own plan. Doesn't seem that different. And a group of religious Zionists (yes, religious ones) have started a Web site calling for a return to the 1967 borders so that we can begin to focus on the kind of society we want to build here. *Religious* Zionists, these days commonly among the most uncompromising, are now calling for a withdrawal? Now, *that*'s new. But these are kids, for the most part. The idea's interesting (and troubling, at the same time), but why would they think that anyone in government would give them a second's notice?

And then, it's December 18. Ariel Sharon gives a speech, and drops a bit of a bombshell. He says that "if in a few months the Palestinians still continue to disregard their part in implementing the road map, then Israel will initiate the unilateral security step of disengagement from the Palestinians." The road map, Sharon seems to be saying, is dead. But his intention to end the stalemate isn't.

What does he mean? How do you get disengaged? Is Ariel Sharon, of all people, talking about pulling back? In exchange for nothing? Ariel Sharon, commonly known as the "bulldozer," is going to withdraw under fire?

"Do you think he means it?" Elisheva asks me one night, seconds after I've fallen asleep.

"Who? What?"

"Sharon."

Somewhat incredulous that Ariel Sharon has now occupied my bedroom as well, I struggle to wake up. I'm exhausted and am having trouble keeping my eyes open. But it's a conversation Elisheva obviously wants to have.

"Do what?"

"Do you think he'll really just pull out from some places, unilaterally? With nothing negotiated?"

"It sounds like that's what he's saying."

"I know. But do you think he'll do it?"

"It's hard to imagine," I say. "But I'll tell you, I kind of think that he might. I don't know why. But I think he might just be serious."

I give her kiss on her forehead and say, "And I seriously need to get some sleep." And almost before I've finished the sentence, I'm asleep again.

"I'm glad you think he's serious." I hear a voice, but it takes a few seconds to register.

"What?"

"I'm glad you think that Sharon might actually do it."

"You think it's a *good* idea?!" Elisheva's become the more hawkish of the two of us in the years since the war started, and I'd have expected her to think Sharon was off-base. Or faking.

"I don't know if it's a good idea. But I like the fact that someone's trying to figure a way out of this. And I trust him not to compromise security."

"I hear you. Well, my money's on the possibility that he's serious. We'll see, I guess."

Seconds later, I'm fast asleep again.

"Remember sophomore year, and the argument we had about a Palestinian state?"

I don't. All I can remember right now, frankly, is that if I don't get some sleep, I'm going to die.

"No."

"We were in your dorm room, sophomore year. A whole bunch of us.

Lewis, Marcy, Adina, you, and me. And you said that there would be a Palestinian state, and we all thought you were nuts."

"Maybe I was wrong. After all, there still isn't one."

"No, you weren't wrong. That was 1978, before anyone in our crowd was talking about it seriously. But you said that without one, the conflict would never, ever end."

"And?"

"Maybe that's what Sharon gets. Maybe he's just realized that if they don't have what it takes to make themselves a state, we just have to create it for them."

It sounds a bit magnanimous for Ariel Sharon, but who knows. Maybe even the bulldozer has decided to leave the state a different legacy. What I'm wondering, as I finally fall asleep, is whether people can really change that much. Whether Sharon has. Whether the Palestinians can.

And I'm not sure.

LOST, AND FOUND

January 2004~May 2004

Plus Ça Change,
N'est-Ce Pas?

I'd thought, packing for Paris, that it would be nice to get out of the country for a few days. A bit of Parisian chic, some good museums, and a brief parole from the Israeli pressure cooker, I imagined, would be good for the soul. Even as the terror seems to have calmed a bit, for now, the country is heating up with discussion of Sharon's plan to leave unilaterally some of the land captured in 1967. The country is a cauldron of debate and no small amount of vitriol, with no end in sight. A bit of European calm will be a much-needed reprieve.

But things are rarely as simple as we imagine they'll be. We're a small group from work, studying the French Jewish community for a couple of weeks. It's a busy trip, so I'm stealing one of the precious few free hours to just hang in a cute little bistro, to blend in to the scene. And blending in is the operative term. We were told by the Israeli Foreign Ministry before leaving that we should not speak Hebrew in public, if possible. We should not carry bags or wear clothing with clear Jewish markings on them. No kippot should be exposed. Not alone, and not in groups. Even the chief rabbi of France has said that Jews should wear hats, and not kippot, in public.

So here I sit, sipping some ridiculously expensive bottled water, typing away at the table in this outdoor café, wearing my Yosemite National Park hat, suddenly missing the pressure cooker, where I never have to pretend to be something that I'm not. Where all the arguing is precisely about telling others what we think, not about trying to disappear.

With each passing day, we're learning more and more about the French Jewish community. Americans would be astonished to discover the degree to which anti-Jewish sentiment now pervades French society, even in its upper echelons. Jewish kids regularly get beaten up in the French public schools, and principals have acknowledged that there's nothing that they can (will?) do to protect them from the violence that has now become endemic there. So Jewish kids are fleeing the public schools, and private Jewish day schools are full beyond capacity, with long waiting lists.

On Shabbat a few of us were invited to a lunch at the home of a French family. In a stunning apartment on Rue Saint Georges in a beautiful section of Paris, where the meal was served on china and crystal, the maid came and went silently, evoking, at least for me, a different era of European Jewry, an era when Jews had lived like this in Vienna, or in Berlin. And speaking of Berlin, what was the topic of conversation at lunch, for several hours? Is it really as bad in Paris as people are saying, or is it not?

"It's unpleasant, yes," the gentleman of the house suggested, "But it will all pass."

"That's exactly what the Jews of Berlin said," I thought of saying, but decided not to.

His wife, of Moroccan descent, insisted that matters really were as bad as everyone was saying, and to make her point irrefutable, she pointed out that just days earlier, a Jewish school had been burned to the ground.

"Oui, ma cherie," he replied, undaunted, they burned down a school, "mais c'était pendant la nuit"—but it was at night.

They burned down a school, but no one was hurt, he proffered, a sense of calm in his voice. What's to be worried about? And I tried to imagine our friends in Los Angeles, or my brother's crowd in Manhattan, and their reactions, if their kids' day school had been burned down, even at night, and even if no one was hurt. It's staggering, the things you get used to. And it's frightening, how myopic we can be.

The couple's daughter is a lawyer, and she told us of an interesting case. Recently, a French Muslim accused of some crime was sentenced by a Jewish judge. The defendant appealed, though, claiming that he could not get a fair hearing from a Jewish judge.

The case went up the ladder of the French legal system, until a high court ruled that the sentence stood. But why did it stand? Because, the court says, the defendant had no way of knowing with certainty that the judge was actually Jewish. It wasn't that Jewish judges could be trusted to judge Muslims fairly. It was that Parisians cannot be certain who is Jewish and who is not.

I looked at the gentleman to see what he thought about *that*, but he smiled, as if to say, "Those silly French courts."

Was the Vichy government silly, too? At what point precisely did a polite smile over lunch no longer work back then?

When we asked people what they were doing to combat all this, the answer was, not much. Because the French at large feel very vulnerable now, and the last thing that the Jews want to do is to call attention to themselves. Because there really is an unspoken rule that while Jewish institutions can be burned, they can only be burned at night, when no one will be hurt. And no one wants to provoke a change in the rules.

And besides, what else could they really do, except leave?

My friend Pierre takes me to meet the principal of a Jewish school, a school that has kids from kindergarten through twelfth grade. I spend some time chatting with the principal, who describes the school. It sounds a lot like my kids' schools in America in some ways. Modern Orthodox, open, serious. And I ask him what he's done to equip the kids, especially the older ones, to live as Jews in a France that is changing so rapidly, and so dramatically.

"Nothing," he says.

I can scarcely contain my surprise. France is getting more difficult for Jews day by day, and he's doing nothing? What kind of education is *that*? So I ask him.

"We're teaching exactly what we've always taught them," he responds. "The parents here know our position. There's no future for Jewish kids in France. Today it's more clear. But we've known it for a long time. So we teach what we've always taught: graduate high school, and go to Israel. Study. Join the army. Whatever. But get out of here. And go there. It's your only chance for a future."

And suddenly, I desperately want to get home. Back to the cacophony, to the endless debate. But back to the place where we don't have to pretend, to the place where we say what we think without worrying that we'll annoy the majority population. To the place, the only place, where we, and no one else, will determine our future.

On the way to the airport in Paris, I really want to take off my hat. I'm sick of wearing that Yosemite cap. But it's not a good idea, I'm told. Just wait until you're through security, and passport control.

It feels like I'm escaping from France, as though I have to sneak out.

"What did you think of France?" the soldier asks me at the passport control.

I smile, and don't say what I really want to. That I love the Musée d'Orsay, but that I can't wait to be out of here. That, all our hopes to the contrary notwithstanding, Europe still feels poisoned to me. "Plus ça change, plus c'est la même chose. N'est-ce pas?"

When we landed at Tel Aviv's Ben Gurion airport, we collected our baggage and made our way through customs. Just as we were passing the customs officials, not exactly the place to start being cute, Rafi, a member of our group muttered, "Finally, a normal country."

You had to be there, but it was incredibly funny, given how not normal that airport is. No Jetways, so you have to get bused from the plane to the terminal. Baggage belts that often break down, where people stand smoking right under the "No Smoking" signs. And public bathrooms that look more or less as I imagine they do in the main airport of Mozambique.

At the suggestion that Israel is "a normal country," a few of us started laughing, not because Rafi was wrong, but because he was so right. Given Paris, with all its glory, its wide boulevards, museums, culture, and even stability, or this place, where stability is nowhere in sight, I'll take this place. Every time. Any day.

We laughed because we were relieved to be out of Paris, relieved to be in a place where we don't have to hide. We were relieved to be able to speak Hebrew again, to have our hats off, our kippot (those of us who wear them) on, and most important, our future squarely in our very own hands.

Difficult Choices,
Irreparable Losses

I t's surprising to me that the great British philosopher Isaiah Berlin didn't think very much of our first prime minister, David Ben Gurion. When the two met in December 1950, Berlin's biographer Michael Ignatieff reports, Berlin thought Ben Gurion a "peasant leader—rough, ruthless, and cunning."

It's true that Ben Gurion went to some great lengths, not all of them pretty, to get this country started. But I would have thought that Berlin would have understood that. After all, it was Berlin himself who pointed to the fact that in "real life," ideology and practice cannot always come together neatly. In Berlin's own words, "Some of the Great Goods cannot live together. That is a conceptual truth. We are doomed to choose, and every choice may entail an irreparable loss." Real life is messy.

Israelis are now coming to terms with the sorts of losses that Berlin wrote about. If in 2000 many of us were convinced that we could have Israeli security without employing harsh measures in certain Palestinian areas, we know now that we were sadly wrong. If we believed that we could both stay alive and conduct ourselves according to the moral standards advocated in the rarefied halls of America's liberal universities, we acknowledge today that that was probably naïve. If we dreamt that we'd earned the Gaza Strip and the West Bank honestly, after we were attacked, and that therefore we could keep them forever, we're now recognizing that the world is a very different place from what it was in June 1967.

But aside from the loss of life and limb, the greatest losses of the past few years have been the losses of our dreams.

The war is calming down, at least for now. Deaths from terror were down 50 percent in 2003 from 2002 (due in no small measure to the much-maligned security fence). They haven't ceased, and there will undoubtedly be worse periods, but we've proven to the Palestinians and to the world that terror is not going to uproot this society. We've persevered. In many respects, we've won. A horrible price has been paid on both sides, in a conflict that we, at least, didn't want, but we've won. For now.

But only for now. For it's clear that Israel is now getting ready for the next showdown—a showdown not with the Palestinians, or even the Arab world, but with ourselves. And in that showdown, what will win the day will not be force. Or classic battlefield bravery. What will ultimately enable us to survive is the recognition that even though Berlin was wrong about some of his appraisals of Israel, he was right when he reminded us that not all the "Great Goods" can coexist. We're going to have to give up some of them and accept the pain of knowing what we've lost.

Ariel Sharon, whatever other faults he may have, gets it. Sharon was pivotal in recapturing the Sinai during the 1973 Yom Kippur War, even when the high command thought it impossible and too dangerous. But that same Sharon has now decided that the present boundaries are simply unsustainable. So he has said, very publicly, that if the Palestinians don't rein in terror and start a real peace process, he, Sharon, will pull back the army, unilaterally establish new borders, and redeploy the army along more effective lines.

Israel's political right, of course, is accusing Sharon of caving in to the left. And the left is busy accusing him of harming the Palestinians by putting up the fence. What Sharon has done, though, I think, is declare a willingness to live with tough decisions and irreparable loss. The right's ideology that the land can never be forsaken, Sharon has effectively said, endangers the very survival of the country. It must be compromised, he has declared. And the left's desire to pretend that we border Canada, not the Palestinian Authority, Sharon says, is myopic. That myopia, Sharon is saying, cannot be allowed to determine policy. The one ideology that we need to hang on to for now is . . . survival. Because survival in the current state of affairs is by no means guaranteed.

Maybe it's something in the air, but Sharon's not the only one who seems to be willing to live with a loss of ideological neatness. Another recent example is Professor Benny Morris of the Ben Gurion University. Morris is famous as one of the leading Israeli "new historians," long associated (incorrectly, Morris insists) in most people's minds with the radical left. The author of *The Birth of the Palestinian Refugee Problem, 1947–1949*, Morris has been regularly excoriated by the right as being just short of a traitor for having argued (most would say proved) the untruth of Israel's claim that all the Palestinians who fled in 1948 did so of their own accord, and that Israel played no role in it. Not so, Morris has shown. Some fled. But there were, in fact, expulsions. There was, in fact, murder. (Though not nearly as much as some suspected.) There were, in fact, rapes. (Though unforgivable, they were extraordinarily few, he notes, compared to the behavior of other armies.)

Morris recently gave an interview to *Ha-Aretz* that was published a week ago. The picture, Morris claims, wasn't simple. Real life rarely is. But what does he think about the fact that, as he claims, Palestinians were forced out? That's where his interview got interesting. "In certain conditions," he said, "expulsion is not a war crime. I don't think that the expulsions of 1948 were war crimes. . . . A society that aims to kill you forces you to destroy it. When the choice is between destroying or being destroyed, it's better to destroy."

Morris continues, "A Jewish state would not have come into being without the uprooting of 700,000 Palestinians. Therefore, it was necessary to uproot them. There was no choice but to expel that population. . . . It was necessary to cleanse the villages from which our convoys and our settlements were fired on."

So is he "right" or "left"? Not so simple anymore.

And what about the Palestinians who suffered? "I feel sympathy for the Palestinian people, which truly underwent a hard tragedy. . . . But if the desire to establish a Jewish state here is legitimate, there was no other choice. It was impossible to leave a large fifth column in the country. From the moment the Yishuv [pre-1948 Jewish community in Palestine] was attacked by the Palestinians and afterward by the Arab states, there was no choice but to expel the Palestinian population. To uproot it in the course of war."

And finally, perhaps the most quoted segment of the much longer interview: "I think [Ben Gurion] made a serious historical mistake in

1948. Even though he understood the demographic issue and the need to establish a Jewish state without a large Arab minority, he got cold feet during the war. In the end, he faltered. . . . I assert that a mistake was made here. . . . The non-completion of the transfer was a mistake."

The interview, as one might expect, rocked much of Israeli intellectual society. The left, predictably, was outraged and disgusted. Some of the right is now willing to "forgive" him for suggesting that Israel helped create the Palestinian refugee problem. But the debate about whether he is right or wrong misses the point completely. Morris (who was jailed in 1988 for refusing to do military duty in the territories) has done something very important. He has brought Isaiah Berlin home to roost. Morris is asking us to think about the most important question Israel has to face: "What ideological convictions are you willing to give up on in order to survive?" Or: Beyond a commitment to human rights (the left) and the love of the land (the right), does the survival of the Jewish state also count as one of your core values? Because if it does, you'd better wake up. You can't have American-Canadian foreign policy here and survive, and you can't keep all the land and survive. We're going to have to pick our losses, and they are going to be painful.

But even now, it's clear that those ideologies will die hard, and long before they die, Israelis will. The right (or some of it, to be fair) loves this land so much that they're willing to lose the whole country to keep the land. They won't leave, they insist. Send in the army. Do what you want. But we're not budging.

Hmm, some Israelis say. Now that's going to be interesting. What are we going to do? Send in our kids to force those people out, risking our kids' getting hurt, knowing full well that the settlers will just go back the next day? That's kind of silly, no? So Avraham Poraz, the minister of the interior, says, fine. Leave them there. We'll just pull the army back and let them fend for themselves. They're not willing to recognize the rule of law? Let them deal with the Palestinians on their own, without the army to protect them. The outcry, as one could have expected, was immediate.

But people here can still surprise you. A couple of days later, I sat with a friend in Café Hillel (rebuilt since the bombing, and thriving), and we got to talking about that. He's to the left of where I am, and I expected him to say Poraz was right. After all, he's got a kid in the army. And he's in favor of pulling out. So why would he want his kid to risk getting hurt evacuating people who will just go back, again and again?

"I don't know," he said. "Rationally, I see his point. But I just couldn't do it. Leave them there? They'll get massacred. I don't think we can do it. We just can't."

"So," I asked him, playing devil's advocate, "you're willing for your kid to go in there, to get into a scuffle (assuming, in the best-case scenario, that the settlers won't actually use weapons), possibly get knocked off a roof, or tossed off a porch, or thrown down the stairs, just to get them out, when you know they'll go back the very next day and we can't really stop them?"

He thought for a moment and said, "I don't know. I really don't know." He paused and then continued, "The way I see it, we've been due for a civil war for a long time. I guess we ought to just have it now and get it out of the way."

It could come to that, couldn't it? A negative consumer price index in 2003, the first in the country's history, has just been announced. We're giving land in exchange for nothing. And there's a feeling that we've let terror win. It wouldn't take much more to unleash the forces of fury.

Maybe we ought to have the whole country read Isaiah Berlin. About Great Goods. And choices. And losses. So that instead of arguing about civil war, we could begin to speak about what really matters— about whether enough people here are willing to lose enough of what they love and believe to save something of this place, to make sure that something remains.

Are they? Time will tell.

Coming Home

Adi Avitan, Benny Avraham, and Omar Souad came home today.

I remember the day they died. And I remember the day they died again. They were killed, we now know, 1,210 days ago, at the very start of the war, in the attack in which they, or their bodies, were captured. The number 1,208 was mentioned today by Hayim Avraham, Benny's father, as the number of days that the families survived without knowing. Now, he's getting his son back. Not alive, but back. And for the first time in 1,208 days, he and his family will go to sleep knowing with certainty that Benny is dead, that he's not in the hands of the same sorts of "people" who blew up a bus full of children and civilians in the heart of Jerusalem today, or who for more than three interminable years kept the most basic humanitarian information—that the boys were dead—from their suffering families. Those families will go to sleep now knowing that their boys are not suffering. That they didn't suffer, at least for long.

The prisoner exchange, in which we returned more than four hundred prisoners for three dead bodies and a suspected criminal named Elhanan Tennenbaum, has been the subject of intense, and now impassioned, debate in Israel. There are those who think we've made a grave mistake. And those who aren't sure. And those who believe that you simply have to "bring the boys home," no matter what the cost.

That's been the refrain of everyone today, those who agree, and those who don't. Israel "brings the boys home." No matter what. It may make strategic sense, it may not. It may get us information about Ron Arad, the Israeli navigator who was shot eighteen years ago, five days after our daughter, Talia, was born. It may not. It may have been worth it. It may not have. But it has made one point clear. We bring the boys home.

Israeli national television has been broadcasting nothing else (except for periodic interruptions for coverage of the aftermath of today's bus bombing—the bomber, by the way, was a Palestinian policeman from Bethlehem) all day. At one point, Avi had a friend over, and they joined me watching TV. Here they were, two fourteen-year-olds, headed out to the same army, and perhaps even the same fronts, in just a few years. I watched their eyes as they followed the rebroadcasts of video segments of these parents who've been interviewed incessantly over the past three years and four months, when they didn't know whether to mourn or to hope. I watched the kids as they saw the more recent pictures of parents who now know that the hope is over but that relief is ironically just beginning. And I saw the kids processing. Wondering. What will be? What could be? What would be? Who would do what? At what expense?

And for that moment, to me at least, the prisoner exchange seemed worth it. Without question. For these kids, kids watching TV now but kids who will soon be doing what Adi, Benny, and Omar were doing, need to know that we bring boys home.

Adi Avitan, Benny Avraham, and Omar Souad came home today. But they came home to a country very different from the one from which they were kidnapped. A country that's been at war for three years. A country that, when they were killed, was just weeks post Camp David, when we thought that virtually anything and everything was possible. To a country that no longer yearns for a peace, but that still hopes for the sort of quiet we enjoyed for a while. Until this morning's bus bombing.

They were kidnapped on October 7, 2000, just weeks after everything began, when we were foolish enough to imagine that things were bad. When we had no idea how bad they could get. Or would get. They've come home to a country that has stared evil in the eye and persevered. And that brought them home, against all odds.

Adi Avitan, Benny Avraham, and Omar Souad came home today. They came home to a country that is not afraid to cry. Israeli television tonight alternated between coverage of Beirut and of the air force base at Ben Gurion Airport. Beirut, with the fireworks lighting the sky, the back-slapping among the prisoners we returned, the sickening, endless speech by Hezbollah's Hassan Nassrallah in which he intimated the possibility of more kidnappings and hinted at the possible release of information (just information, though) on Ron Arad in exchange for all the remaining hundreds of prisoners we still have, evoking laughs, jeers, and clapping from the throngs of people listening.

And then the TV cut to the air force base, at which a quiet ceremony took place. A ceremony in which no one laughed. Where people cried. Where you could have heard a pin drop, and where you watched fathers and mothers, sisters and brothers, and a few grandparents, stifle their cries and wipe their tears away.

They came home to a country in which the carnage of burning buses in our cities, in parts of the country far from anything contested (unless, of course, the whole country is contested, which is clearly the case) has grown so intolerable that we're building a wall, a wall that keeps them out but also pens us in. But it's also a country in which many of us see, sadly, no alternative to that fence, as problematic as it undeniably is. They've come home to a country that will soon be "brought to trial" at The Hague for the "crime" of that wall, a country that's now referred to in some quarters as an apartheid state because of that fence.

I thought about that apartheid accusation a few times tonight, especially when the coffin of Omar Souad, a Bedouin, a career soldier who decided that defending the Jewish state was how he wanted to spend his life, was carried from the plane to the jeep. Six soldiers, three on each side of the coffin, arrayed to carry him one step closer to his final home. Four who looked Jewish. One who looked Bedouin, though it was hard to tell. And one, an Ethiopian. All by the side of Omar Souad, and then, all saluting him. And then the chief of staff, and the bearded IDF chief rabbi, standing at the side of his coffin, saluting him and standing at attention. Quite an apartheid state.

And then during the ceremony, the two Jewish fathers standing together and reciting Kaddish. And after the Kaddish, an imam, by the side of Omar's father, chanting an Arabic memorial prayer, as his mother sobbed and the honor guard stood at attention, along with the prime minister, the president, the chief of staff and others. So much for the apartheid state.

Adi Avitan, Benny Avraham, and Omar Souad came home today. To a country that's not been weakened by the past three years, but that's been hardened by it. I drove Talia's car pool for the first time in years yesterday morning. She's got a five-minute walk to school, so we never drive car pool, but this wasn't school. She and some friends had to be at the Jerusalem Convention Center at 7:00 A.M. to be bused someplace else for part of their draft process, so I drove them. Three kids, not really kids anymore, whom I remember just years ago as chatty adolescents, now talking quietly as I drove through the still awakening city and its mostly empty streets, talking about what forms they'd filled out, what they'd have to do during the day. And when I got home from work at about 9:30 that night, she still wasn't home. She got home closer to 10, grabbed a bite, and went to sleep. No fanfare. No complaints. In the past three years those girls have learned a lot. They've learned that the battle to stay here isn't over. That we have real enemies, and that if we're going to be able to stay here, they, too, are going to have to do their share.

Watching the ceremony tonight, witnessing the agony of families who should have been told three years ago that their sons were dead, I saw Tali watching them. With eyes of steel. Because she, like her friends, knows that the enemy isn't a concept. They bomb the cafés she eats in. They blow up the buses she rides. And they kept these parents awake for 1,208 nights, not knowing whether their sons were alive or dead, suffering or in peace. Our kids get it. They know what sorts of neighbors we have. And they're not running. They grow up too fast, I think, but they know who they are and what they stand for. Few of us would want it otherwise.

These kids get it long before they get drafted. A father of one of Israel's POWs (not one of the three returned tonight) came to Avi's class last year. He talked about how his son was captured and what they're doing (and have been doing for more than twenty years) to try to get him back. But kids will be kids. They're not afraid to ask what they want to know. At the end, one of the kids asked him if he's worried that they're torturing his son. No, he said, he didn't think about that. "But when I get into bed each night," he continued, "I worry that maybe he's cold."

Avi talked about that for days. And on the rare occasion that he still lets me tuck him into bed at night, I think about that, too. You know, at moments like that, that we just have to bring the boys home. No matter what.

The country to which the boys came home tonight is one in which kids who shouldn't have to be hardened, unfortunately, are. When we heard the news of the attack on the bus this morning, I text-messaged the kids to make sure that they were OK. They were supposed to be in school, but who knew where they really were? So I text-messaged them on their phones: "There was an attack in Jm this morning. Let me know you're OK." Talia wrote back to say she was fine. Avi wrote back a short while later, in classic cell-phone prose fashion: "Im fine and all my friends are fine. It was my friends bus tho so if he would have been late 2day he would have been killed."

That was the whole message. When Adi, Avi, and Benny were captured, it would have been unthinkable to us that a fourteen-year-old could talk about such things so matter-of-factly. Or that he could come home and tell us that the mother of one of the kids in his school is still unaccounted for, but half an hour later, still want to discuss the relative merits of the iPod versus the new Dell MP3 player. But that's what things have come to. And perhaps because of that ability to compartmentalize and to stare evil in the face, we're still here. And no one's thinking of budging.

I remember the second time that Adi, Benny, and Omar died. For a year, every Shabbat, our shul had been mentioning them and the other six (Tennenbaum among them) just after the Torah reading, in a prayer for Israel's captured soldiers. First a prayer for the state. Then for the army and its soldiers. Then for those in captivity. There were only nine names on that list, so after hearing it week after week, you know the list. You know it almost by heart, and you certainly notice if someone changes it. Then, about a year after they were captured, the army declared them dead based on new intelligence. Some of the families sat shiva but didn't really believe it. And in our shul, that next Shabbat, the person reading the "mi she-beirach," the prayer in which their names had been mentioned, started reading, and then stopped. It was as if he couldn't bear to read the list without their names. As if even though he didn't know them, he couldn't give up on the hope that they might still be alive. So he didn't mention any of the names and, instead, said something like "all those held in captivity." It was a moment that few of us who were there will ever forget. I was struck then by how personal this was. How despite everything that is wrong here, and that's quite a bit, there is so much that is right. And how the more they push us, the more we are bonded, even to people we never knew.

It is, I think, one of those immeasurable things that makes living here so compelling, despite everything. It's one of those things that remind us what a real home is.

As does the evening news. Throughout the entire broadcast tonight, there were two Hebrew words at the bottom right-hand side of the screen—*"Ve-shavu vanim"*—"And the sons will return." It's a quote from Jeremiah 31:16. The entire verse reads, "And there is hope for your future, declares the Lord, your children shall return to their country." And that's exactly what happened.

Adi Avitan, Benny Avraham, and Omar Souad came home today. Tomorrow we'll bury them, along with the victims of today's bus bombing.

Yehi zikhram barukh. May their memories be a blessing.

A Plane, a Bus, and a Trial

A group of us at the office have begun working with a guy who's a colonel in the air force. A few months after we meet, our friend (we'll call him David here, even though that's not his real name) asks some of us if we'd like to come to his base, to see some training, watch some takeoffs and landings, and learn a bit about the air force. A few of us are interested, and we pick a Sunday, a month hence, when everyone can do it.

When the day arrives, we meet at the Mandel Foundation's building and board the bus for the hour or so ride to the base. The bus heads up Hebron Road, past the intersection with Emek Refa'im, and past the Inbal Hotel. From here it should be a pretty straight shot out of the city.

The bus's radio is playing in the background, softly enough that the driver can listen and we can still talk to each other. But a few minutes into the ride, the bus driver turns the radio much louder, and the bus grows silent. We can tell by the tone of the announcer that something's happened.

A bus has just been bombed, on Emek Refa'im Street, across from the gas station near the Inbal Hotel. First indications are that it was a suicide bomber. The line was the 14A. No reports on casualties yet, though with the bus virtually incinerated, it's got to be bad. Police say that it's fortunate that the gas station didn't get hit. Had it blown up, things would have been much worse. The announcer cuts to eyewitnesses, but the bus driver turns off the radio. We've all heard this before, and we know we're not going to learn anything for a while.

It's quiet in the bus, except for a few people on their cell phones, trying to call friends and family to make sure that no one they know was on the 14A at that hour. It's the hour when people are going to work, when children are heading for school. That's why it's the preferred hour for the murderers who do this.

No one says what was on everyone's mind, which is that we were just there, four minutes ago. That if we'd gotten a somewhat later start, we'd have been there. But it stays quiet on the bus, and all of a sudden, a grown-up's field trip to an air force base doesn't feel like very much fun.

But we go ahead with the plan and, an hour later, enter the base. David takes us into a briefing room, where novice pilots are being instructed about the maneuver they're going to practice that day. They're paired up, two per F-15, and the officer describes how one plane will be the Israeli and one will be the enemy. Using his two hands, he describes the positions the two planes will assume, the minimum distance between the two that they must maintain, and what will constitute a "kill." When there's a kill, he says, you just fly back to the base.

The kids nod their understanding. And they're kids, nothing more. Half of them literally don't shave yet. Their boyish faces seem out of keeping with their pilots' jumpsuits, with the sort of exercise on which they're about to embark. A few ask some questions, and a few minutes later, they're dismissed to make their way to their planes.

David hangs behind for a moment, explains to us what they're going to do, and tells us that our bus will drive us to the other edge of the base so we can watch him take off. With that, he, too, goes to get suited up.

We board the bus and ten minutes later are in a hangar. So is David, with his F-15, and a young trainee with him. It's stunning how small these planes are. Tiny, rickety-looking, compared to the jets most of us fly in all the time.

They climb the ladder into the cockpit, and go over a seemingly endless list of checks and rechecks. David nods to a technician outside the plane, and the transparent cover to the cockpit begins to close. Before it does, David yells to us, telling us that the noise will be very loud, and that we should plug our ears with our fingers. With that, the cockpit shuts, and seconds later, the F-15 begins its creep out of the hangar.

Around the plane, other technicians are still checking and rechecking the plane. They're looking under the wings, inspecting the tires. One by one, as the engines get increasingly deafening, even with our ears plugged, the technicians peel away from the plane. The plane begins to move, and there's only one kid left just behind it. Just before the plane is out of reach, he reaches out. He touches the wing, closes his eyes, and then slowly brings his fingers to his lips. And kisses them.

Everyone else is watching the plane. After all, it's kind of cool to see your friend piloting an F-15. But I'm not following the plane. I'm looking at the kid, wondering what it must be like to be eighteen or nineteen, to know that two people you care about are about to hurl themselves high into the sky, and that their coming back home depends on whether you just did your job right. The kid, too, follows the plane with his gaze as it makes its way out of the hangar and to the runway, and then he turns and walks away. There's another plane to get ready. No time to loiter. No time, it seems to me, to be a kid, either.

I thought of myself when I was that kid's age. Away at college in New York. Where my biggest worry was midterms, or whether I'd get to go see my girlfriend (now my wife) that weekend near Boston, where she was in college. Nobody's life depended on me. To be more precise, it occurs to me as David's plane turns the corner and disappears from sight, nothing at all depended on me. For the life of me, I can't imagine what it must be like to be these kids.

We get back on the bus and get driven to the control tower, from which we'll have a better view. (David, it's clear, has a lot of pull on this base.) The room at the top of the tower is a beehive of activity. And it's full of kids. Kids in khaki. Kids in air force gray. Some of them on phones. Some of them punching away at computer terminals. Some with binoculars, watching each plane coming down to make sure that its landing gear is fully descended, they tell us.

And the planes are coming, and coming, and coming. Every ten seconds or so a plane approaches the runway and lands. Almost. Its back wheels touch the ground, and as soon as it's clear that this would have been a successful landing, the engines spit fire, and the plane climbs into the sky again and disappears. And throughout, the traffic on the runway and in the skies is managed by this troupe of overgrown teenagers, doing their job as if there weren't much to it. They're used to this, apparently.

David and the trainees have returned to earth. Drenched with sweat, their jumpsuits soaked through, they file into the debriefing room. Little videocassettes, taken from the cameras in their planes, are shoved into players, and they analyze their moves. For a few seconds, the clouds are on the top of the screens. Then the clouds are on the bottom. Now, it's clear, they're flying upside down, still maneuvering. And they're pointing and talking, taking notes and asking questions, as if it's driver's ed, as though they're just working on perfecting their parallel parking. Actually, I realize, they're only two years older than I was when I took driver's ed.

When David invited us to the base, I thought I'd get a kick out of watching all the hardware. Instead, I can't seem to do anything but think about the kids who use it.

We make our way back to Jerusalem, and suddenly, the bus bombing that we'd more or less forgotten about surfaces once again. The news is reporting very little else. Eight are dead, including a few high school students. Sixty wounded. It's the second bus bombing in the city in just over three weeks and the 110th Palestinian suicide bombing in the past three and a half years.

Our bus will take the same route back to the Foundation that it had taken on the way out of the city, so we'll pass the site of the attack. I can tell that some of us want to get a look, to see what happened. Half an hour later, we get to the site of the bombing. But to my surprise, traffic is flowing. No bus. No nothing, in fact. It's all cleaned up. There's no sign that anything had happened there.

Part of me feels relieved, but part of me is sickened. What, they can blow a bus to smithereens, killing eight people and wounding many dozens, and we're so used to it that we clean it up just like a fender bender? Is that what we're getting used to here?

The driver turns on the news again. More updates on the status of the wounded, a few of whom may not make it. And there's an interview with a police commander, who reports with pride that the street was opened to traffic just two hours after the attack.

Then, the news cuts to the next story. Tomorrow, at the International Court of Justice at The Hague, hearings will begin on Israel's controversial security fence. Lots of people don't like the fence. The Palestinians claim (quite rightly) that the fence is an enormous hardship for them. Israeli leftists don't want the fence. The world calls it the apartheid fence.

I look back at the street with its traffic flowing smoothly as if nothing had happened. It's a capital city that's gotten used to being attacked. And I think of the kids on that air force base, doing the extraordinary as if it were nothing, because they know that without them, we can't stay alive here. And I listen to some commentator droning on about the ICJ hearings tomorrow.

I wonder if the International Court of Justice will hear anything about how our kids live. About what they do all day long, at the age when the children of those ICJ judges sitting in judgment of us at The Hague are probably gallivanting around some European university campus. Or about what happens to other kids here, kids who simply get on a bus in the morning to go to school. And end up in pieces on the sidewalk. I wonder if they'll hear about that, or think about that.

And I know the answer. The truth is, they probably won't hear anything about that. And if they did, I suspect, they really wouldn't give a damn.

The Morning After

It's one of those quiet mornings at home. The paper, as expected, has the faces of many of the dead splayed across the front page. We don't know any of them.

The phone rings, and one of the kids answers it. "God," I hear them say. And moments later, "Yallah, bye," a combination of Arabic and English that in this strange country is considered Hebrew.

"You're not going to believe this," we're told. "You know that memorial near our old apartment, to that girl, Iris, who was stabbed outside her house? Well, one of the boys killed on the bus yesterday, a boy named Lior, was her nephew, her brother's son."

Micha's at the table, trying to figure out the relationships here. Finally, he gets it. "You mean that family first had their daughter killed, and now their grandson got killed?" he asks.

"That's right," we tell him, still trying to make sense of this.

"Wow," he says. "They must be really sad."

There's not much to say to that, so no one says very much. The kids take their lunches, zip their backpacks shut, and file out the door on the way to school.

I watch them head out, just another morning, and hope today's a better morning for Jerusalem's kids on their way to school. And try to remember what it was like when they went to school in Los Angeles. Nothing like this, that's for sure.

And I wonder how, when the International Court of Justice begins to discuss our oppressive fence later today, they'll mask the hypocrisy of the whole thing.

They won't try to mask it, I realize. Because they don't have to. Because this trial isn't really about us, or our fence. It's about them. It's about a Europe that did nothing to protect us in the 1940s, and now relishes any opportunity to show how evil we are, in some unspoken hope that our alleged wrongdoings now can finally take the spotlight off of what they didn't do. And did do.

I'm glad that Micha doesn't know about that. I bet he'd think that was pretty sad, too.

Unacceptable. Unjust.

A couple of years ago, our office started using a new driver. The previous one, it turns out, couldn't make a living after the tourists abandoned the country and left for the States.

Heading for a meeting, I got in the cab, sat in the back, introduced myself to Shlomo (who appeared to be in his midfifties), and told him where I was going. As we made our way across the city, I noticed a photograph on the dashboard. A young woman, probably in her twenties. An informal photo, in a Plexiglas frame glued to the dashboard. You don't often see things glued to the dashboards of luxury Mercedes cars, so I was curious. I leaned forward a little and read the words at the bottom of the frame. "Limor, HYD"—"Limor, May God Avenge Her Blood."

Now I was even more curious. This was clearly going to be a sensitive subject, but this is Israel, and subtlety has never been a strong suit of this society. So I just asked.

"Is that your daughter?"

"Limor. She was twenty-seven. And beautiful."

"I'm sorry."

"She was killed at Moment Café."

I had no idea what to say. So for a moment, I said nothing, and then he continued. "You know, they keep telling me that it will get easier with time. I'm still waiting."

He turned up the volume on the classical music station a bit, maybe to drown out the rest of the world. I don't know. He stared out the windshield, and I stared out the window, certain that anything I said would be absurdly trite. And, of course, I'd only met him a few minutes earlier. Even had I had anything to say, this probably wasn't the time.

We still work with the same driver. Sometimes it's Shlomo who picks me up, but usually it's Nir, his son, probably in his midtwenties, too. Between the two of them, they keep the cab running almost twenty-four hours a day, or so it seems. Because most of my trips to and from the airport are at night, it's Nir I usually see.

Each time we wind our way back into Jerusalem from the airport, Nir takes the same route to my house. A left at the Wolfson towers, up into the middle of Rechavia, following the narrow roads until the car is alongside Moment Café, now rebuilt, opened, better guarded, and full. There are sometimes faster ways to get to Bakk'a, days when the traffic in Rechavia is ridiculous. But he never varies his route. We always go by Moment. He never says anything, and I don't ask. Limor's picture is there, looking out at both of us, almost as if to remind us that we're really not in a hurry. So what if the traffic is a little thicker in Rechavia? The five-minute difference isn't that significant, compared with everything he lives with and thinks about each time he looks at his dashboard.

It was Nir whom I thought of when I first woke up on Monday morning. The radio had gone off at 6:15, and the news was prattling on. Helicopter. Missile. Killed. Sounded like a regular morning newscast. Until I was awake enough to get the name. Sheikh Ahmed Yassin, the founder of Hamas. Strange, but I thought of Nir. Before anyone else. And I wondered if he'd heard yet. I wondered how he'd feel knowing that we got the guy who killed his sister just about two years earlier, in March 2002. I wondered if this would provide any comfort whatsoever. I doubted it.

Certain things we don't have to wonder about. Like whether Yassin, the most outspoken and powerful Palestinian to advocate the use of suicide bombers and the complete annihilation of Israel, deserved to die.

Not everyone agrees, I guess. British foreign secretary Jack Straw called the killing "unacceptable" and "unjustified." But "unacceptable," I think, is a mild way of describing Yassin's résumé. Yassin was crystal clear: This conflict is not about the territories captured in 1967. It's about the whole Jewish state. There can be no "Zionist" entity in the Middle East, which is a Muslim part of the world. There can be no compromise, no negotiation. The Jews must go.

You've got to give him credit for clarity.

And for persistence. Under Yassin, Hamas was responsible, in the last few years, for 425 bombings, resulting in 377 deaths and 2,076 injured. "Unjustified"? The Sbarro Pizza parlor. The Dolphinarium, packed with teenagers. The Moment Café. The #37 bus. Café Hillel. The #19 bus. Many, many others. And most recently, the bombing at the Ashdod Port, a strategic target that ultimately resulted in the cabinet's decision to get rid of him and to let Hamas know that we've had enough. And that we have no intention of leaving.

Very few Israelis whom I know are terribly worried about the "justice" of the decision to kill him. If he didn't deserve to die, no one does. And some people do deserve to die. No one I know shed any tears that he's gone. But no one I know went out into the street to fire assault rifles into the air in celebration. Or gave candy to children to mark the joy of the event. That, most of us agree, would be "unacceptable."

Was killing Yassin smart? That's the only question. The morality of the killing is, to my mind, not an issue. And as for the wisdom, who knows? Whether it ultimately weakens Hamas and makes it possible for the Palestinian Authority to take over when we pull out, as Sharon says he plans to do, remains to be seen. What we've got in the meantime is a stalemate of dread.

Sharon, by the way, is apparently trying to get out of the stalemate. It was only weeks earlier that he shocked the world, and infuriated many members of his own Likud party, when he revealed his intention to withdraw from virtually all Israeli settlements in the Gaza Strip, with or without signing a final peace agreement with the Palestinians. Insisting that the isolated settlements there make no military sense and are incompatible with a peace settlement, Sharon told the Israeli newspaper *Ha-Aretz* that there would be "no Jews in Gaza" after his plan was carried out.

Israel begins to discuss unilateral withdrawal, and Hamas, unimpressed, continues to kill us. And to insist that we've got to vacate the entire Middle East, because leaving Gaza isn't enough. And tries to blow up the Ashdod Port, to make the point. So we got Yassin. Long overdue, to my mind.

On their side, the Hamas leadership has gone underground. Abdel Aziz Rantisi, Yassin's successor in the Gaza Strip, is threatening unprecedented reprisals and ultimate "liberation of the homeland." The IDF, undoubtedly, is now aiming for him. One assumes that Rantisi knows there's not much point in his buying green bananas.

But Rantisi's threats have not gone unheeded in Israel's cities. People here believe him when he speaks of reprisals. There are security checkpoints virtually everywhere, and now they're really checking. I had breakfast yesterday at Café Hillel, another reminder of Yassin. My secretary actually asked me to change the location. "Don't eat there this week," she pleaded. "It's just not a good idea."

But the point is that we're not leaving. That's exactly why Yassin had to go. So I didn't change the venue and went to Café Hillel.

The café, like Moment, is completely rebuilt and is usually packed. It can be hard to find a table at breakfast. Not yesterday. There were six of us in the whole restaurant, plus the waitress and the very alert guard outside the door. On the way to breakfast, walking to the café, I looked into the buses making their way down Emek Refa'im. Almost empty. Five or ten people on a bus, in rush hour.

When I finally got to the office, a colleague told me that on the way home on Wednesday, he was driving past one of the open-air markets of Jerusalem when an elderly woman knocked on the window of his car. She had sacks of food from the market, she showed him, and she lived a few blocks away, too far for her to walk. But she was afraid to get on the bus. Would he drive her home?

A couple of days ago, the editorial page of *Ha-Aretz* carried its daily political cartoon, this one of a Domino's pizza guy (yup, Domino's and Office Depot have made it here) on a motorcycle, delivering a pizza to a family. Nothing unusual about that. Except for the fact that the family is pictured behind sandbags, barely willing to stretch out an arm to take the pizza. That pretty much summed it up.

But the cartoon missed one thing—why we're in this mess. Yes, for the moment, things are a bit edgy, but we've been here before. What Israelis need to remember, and what the rest of the world needs to understand, is why Yassin hated us. He hated us simply because we're here. And that was why we had to get rid of him. Because he had pledged to keep killing us until we left.

But we're not leaving. Where would we possibly go? Does Europe want us back? It didn't work out very well last time we were there. Nor does it seem that the French have learned very much since 1943.

Last Sunday night, Elisheva and I went to a lecture by Aharon Appelfeld, one of Israel's preeminent novelists. Tali and Avi were out, so we left Micha by himself. He was lying on the living room couch, reading the latest Harry Potter tome, determined to finish it, fairly oblivious to our imminent departure. We told him that we had our cell phones if he needed us and that he should go to bed by 8:30. He barely looked up but muttered, "OK." We knew he wouldn't go to bed on time, but we couldn't exactly complain that a fifth-grader wanted to stay up late because he was busy reading a novel.

Appelfeld told his story. Of an idyllic eight years in a completely assimilated, wealthy, Jewish European home. Of his mother being shot by the Germans. Of him and his father being taken to a slave labor camp. And of his decision to flee the camp, because he knew he wouldn't survive it. And so, at the age of eight and a half, he found himself alone, in the forests of Europe, masquerading as a Christian, struggling to survive. He worked in the home of a prostitute, buying her groceries and cleaning her house, until one of her drunken clients called him a Jew. He fled. He worked for horse thieves, who would drop him through stable skylights so he could then open the stable doors, enabling them to steal the horses. He told of the nights he slept alone on the forest floor, of the days when he ate the moss off of trees to stay alive. At the age of ten.

And I thought about Micha, exactly that age now. I wondered. If he were alone in the forest tomorrow, would he know to do that? Would he have the presence of mind to work for a prostitute or for horse thieves? Would he figure out that he could eat moss off of trees if he was starving? I doubted it.

In the days since Yassin's death, since the palpable sense of dread has pervaded every nook and cranny of life here, I've thought of Appelfeld at ten. Of Micha at ten. And then I thought of Abdallah Quran, also ten. He's the boy from the Balata refugee camp who was given, apparently unbeknownst to him, a bomb to carry across a checkpoint. A ten-year-old who tries to make a living for his family after school by transporting packages across the checkpoint, he had no idea who put the bag on his cart.

The explosive had a remote control apparatus. Whoever put the bag on his cart was going to use a cell phone to set it off. And presumably blow Abdallah to high heaven, too.

That incident didn't make it to much of the international press. But when Hussam Abdo, the sixteen-year-old who tried to walk an explosive belt through a checkpoint two days ago, got caught by soldiers, there happened to be a camera crew on hand, and the whole thing was filmed. Turns out, Hussam was given one hundred shekels (about twenty-two dollars) to carry the explosive and blow it up. He was also promised seventy virgins in heaven, he said.

The good news, I first thought, was that the Palestinian community was outraged. Tamam Abdo, his mother, said to the press, "It is forbidden to send him to fight. He is young, he is small, he should be in school. Someone pressured him." Finally.

But then, I read the rest of the interview. "If he was over 18, I wouldn't feel so angry . . . then it is his decision," she said. Ah, another beautiful humanist sentiment. Or her neighbor, Sadia Abdel Rahman: "We have to carry out serious attacks. This is not a children's game. This is an embarrassment."

I guess we all get embarrassed by different things. When Israel sent an F-16 in July 2002 to drop a one-ton bomb on the home of Salah Shehadeh, then the military chief of Hamas in Gaza, we got him. Israelis were pleased about that. But a one-ton bomb is a formidable weapon, and in killing Shehadeh, we killed fourteen other people, including nine children. Israelis were outraged and mortified. Shehadeh, like Yassin, deserved to die. But Israeli society was in an uproar. Not like that, people said, both on the left and on the right. We can't begin to be like them. That's the whole idea of living here, of having a country to call our own. If we're not going to be different, even better, what's the point?

Eventually, the government apologized. And the IDF changed its policy. So last September 6, when the IDF decided to get Yassin, we sent an F-16 again, but this time with a quarter-ton bomb. The bomb worked perfectly, and the pilot hit his target. But the building was only damaged, and Yassin was scarcely wounded. And what was the reaction of the typical Israeli? Satisfaction. We'd learned something. We missed, true, but at least we were different.

I'm struck by the fact that very little coverage of the killing of Yassin has made any mention of the unsuccessful attempt on his life in September. It's because, I think, the reason that we missed reveals a dimension of this conflict that most of the world doesn't want to see. It upends the moral equivalence that the international press broadcasts. It suggests that some people in this conflict still think about what's "acceptable" and "just."

We're just days away from Passover. Already the stores are filling with Passover products. Israelis are cleaning. Buying. Inviting. And remembering. Remembering Pesach two years ago and the bloodbath called the Park Hotel. And remembering that Hamas, and Yassin, was responsible for that one, too.

Will this Pesach be quieter? It's hard to know. One hopes so. Prays, in fact. But no matter what happens, there will be a certain satisfaction, even if a sad one, in knowing that people who blow up our Seders can't do so with impunity. That's the difference between life now and life when Aharon Appelfeld foraged for his food in the forest. Appelfeld grew up in a world in which people could shoot his mother and send him to die, and there was no one to defend him.

That's what's changed. That's the bottom line. I can't imagine a decent human being feeling joy at the death of another. Joy, no. But satisfaction? Yes. Because there has to be a price to pay for the wholesale murder of Jews. There simply must be. Anything else, Mr. Straw needs to understand, is what's truly "unacceptable."

Tell Shlomo

Just a day or two after I post these thoughts about the cab drivers Shlomo and Nir on the Web, I get an e-mail from someone I don't know. But the name sounds vaguely familiar, and curious, I open it up:

From: Stephen Flatow
To: Daniel Gordis
Subject: Shlomo
Date: Fri, 26 March 2004 3:41 PM

Dear Rabbi Gordis—

I just read your account of driving with Shlomo and his son. Tell Shlomo that time does make it easier. When my daughter was killed by Islamic Jihad in 1995 I was told by a friend a few weeks after the attack that "the first year is the hardest." Of course, I thought "what did she know?"

But she was right. After the first yahrzeit (actually noted twice because of the differences between the secular and Hebrew calendars) the mid-afternoon stares into space began to diminish.

Nine years later, I don't cry as often, although you don't know what will trigger an outburst, and you don't forget. In fact, you can never forget the Limors or the Alisas of this world. From a father sitting in the United States this erev Shabbat, please tell Shlomo and his son Nir that we're also thinking of Limor, and her family, too.

Shabbat shalom.

Stephen M. Flatow

Of course I remember. I can barely move, and I stare at the screen, reading the note, over and over. Alisa Flatow, the Brandeis University student, aged twenty, here for a semester of her junior year, murdered when an Islamic Jihad suicidal terrorist drove a van loaded with explosives into the bus on which she was traveling. She suffered a serious head injury from shrapnel and never regained consciousness.

I remember her because Elisheva had also gone to Brandeis, though long before Alisa, and somehow the connection had stuck. And because Alisa's parents had had the moral courage to donate her organs, in a time and in a country in which that act of generosity and compassion was uncommon and, in some religious circles, even frowned upon.

Now, almost nine years later, with Stephen Flatow's e-mail on my screen, I'm struck by the awful, agonizing fraternity to which I'm witness. Growing up where I did, in suburban Baltimore, I knew Jews who felt connected to each other by virtue of the European town from which they'd come, or because of some suspected distant family link.

This is different. And unspeakably sad. But also remarkably compassionate, and moving.

I print out Stephen's e-mail and put it in my briefcase. It won't be long before I see Shlomo again, and I'll show him.

A few days later, he picks me up. I tell him about the letter and pass it to him. Later in our drive, when he has a moment, he reads it. He's quiet for a moment and then, almost in a whisper, says, "Tell him 'thank you.'" And then he says no more. For he can't speak.

Neither of us says anything, and except for the quiet classical music playing in the car, it's silent. What Shlomo is thinking about, I can scarcely imagine. As for me, I'm wondering about the powerful, unspeakable bond between two families who have never met, who are linked not by a common European town, or a distant family connection, but by having lost children simply because those young people, noncombatants in every sense of the word—were simply trying to live as Jews in the Land of Israel.

How many more families will join this fraternity, I can't help but ask myself. And then, because it's a question that I suppose most Israeli parents ask themselves: What if the next victim came from my family? Would it have been worth it?

I look at Shlomo, driving but staring at nothing in particular. And at the photo on his dashboard, almost staring back at him.

And now, for the first time that I can remember, I'm not sure. I really don't know.

An Ode to Ambivalence

I've taken more than my share of drives through the West Bank in the last three years, almost always in the company of friends (the West Bank is one area where I'm not terribly keen on getting lost on my own). And I'm stunned by how differently some of these people—all of whom are decent, moral, and Jewishly sensitive—see the places we drive through and the people we pass by.

I've got friends who drive through the West Bank and, gazing out upon a landscape virtually identical to how it must have appeared in biblical times, see *Eretz Yisrael*, the Land of Israel. For them, the idyllic images of the rocky, rolling hills, olive and acacia trees that dot the landscape, and even flocks of sheep grazing without any humans in sight, are a moving visage of what our ancestors probably saw when they were here. The pastoral beauty of the place and its obvious biblical resonance make it difficult for these people to imagine relinquishing this land to anyone, much less to those who for decades have dedicated themselves—and still dedicate themselves—to our destruction. For these friends of mine, who see and feel the land, its beauty, and our (I believe understandable) attachment to it, the trading of land for peace is so painful as to be either unthinkable or something that must come only after the Palestinians meet a series of expectations so demanding (no matter how legitimate they might be) as to render them virtually unattainable.

And if trading land for peace is hard, or impossible, then just giving it away in exchange for nothing strikes them as absurd, obscene. To them, it's incomprehensible, not the sort of thing that a sane country, or leader, does. Forget the security issues, they say. Just focus on the plain logic of it. Why would you take something you love, something that's part of your very soul, and simply give it to people who want to kill you, who will continue to want to kill you, in exchange for absolutely nothing? What's the logic in *that*, they ask.

As for the security issue, they add, why give in to terror? We left Lebanon and convinced the Palestinians that their continuous firing on us paid off. That's why, they say, five months after we left Lebanon, Camp David collapsed and we got the second Intifada. And if we leave now, they insist, we'll convince Palestinians yet again that terror works, and we'll be inviting more. "That makes sense?" they ask.

But other friends of mine, who drive with me along the very same roads, look out the same windows and see not the land, but the people who live there. They focus on the small villages and the larger towns that dot the landscape. They see small children, often living in fairly obvious poverty, and even adults who, if they are younger than thirty-seven, have never lived a day without our army's occupying them. And they see us, our soldiers, our kids, doing things in these places that we don't want our kids doing. They see a population of people without citizenship, not Jordanians and not Israelis, a population with no hope of having a passport as long as we're there, a people bound to hate us unless the situation changes.

Then, these Israelis simply decide that this reality is untenable. We must, they decide, simply end the occupation, for the occupation is (as even Ariel Sharon has now said) terrible for them and for us. Then these people, who see not *Eretz Yisrael* but an occupied, indigenous Palestinian population, lower the bar of expectations. They're willing to give it all back, often without making any demands on the Palestinians. All we have to do is set these people free, they say, and their democratic, humanistic nature will bubble to the surface.

As for giving in to terror, they respond, sometimes you have to admit that you've lost. Maybe we *are* moving more quickly because we're tired of being bombed and killed. Maybe that *is* what has pushed Sharon closer to the edge. But, they say, that's not a reason not to think. We might not like the idea that they've won this round, but even if we admit it, that doesn't mean that they have to win future rounds. We can still draw red lines, beyond which we wouldn't move. It's time to pull back, they insist, and even to acknowledge that the terror did pay off, for if we can't admit that the Palestinians may have won this round, then we won't make any accommodations to them, and then (since Palestinian fury is increasing, and the world's patience is decreasing), we're going to lose a lot more than just Gaza or the West Bank.

What strikes me on these drives, though, is that whoever I'm with sees with either one eye or the other. Either the land, or the people. Very few see both. Very few are willing to admit the truths on the other side of the Israeli divide. Very few can contemplate giving up on any of the convictions that animate them. They ought to pay more attention to the Israeli calendar.

We've just celebrated Yom Ha-Atzma'ut, Israel's Independence Day. When we first made *aliyah*, even though there was something incredibly exciting about celebrating Independence Day in a country where independence, even survival, is not taken for granted, there was also something peculiar, almost painful, about the whole thing for me. For Yom Ha-Atzma'ut comes immediately after Yom Ha-Zikaron (the memorial day for fallen soldiers).

Because these two days are scheduled one immediately after the other, what emerges is an annually agonizing transition. At the end of Yom Ha-Zikaron, a day on which cemeteries are filled with weeping families, a day during which the names of some 21,781 fallen soldiers are displayed one by one on television, a day on which the vast majority of Israeli families have someone to mourn, the whole country tries to make an impossible switch. We struggle valiantly to shed the grief, to try to embrace the euphoria, to move out of mourning into celebration. To leave behind the memorial candles and to light the fireworks. To walk out of the cemeteries and to pop open a beer as the party gets under way.

But it's really not possible. You can't really be in the first hours of Independence Day without the sting of Memorial Day still on your mind. Which is why the Knesset's decision to set things up this way was so brilliant. For what Israel has done with its calendar is to codify ambivalence. And in the face of ambivalence, important questions get asked. How should we most appropriately mark the miracle of our existence? With joy, at all that we've accomplished? Or with pain, because of a price so unbearably high? What is the best way to honor those who have fallen so that we might live here? By tenaciously holding on to what they helped us capture, or by thinking about giving it back, despite their sacrifice, so that the larger enterprise for which they gave their lives might survive?

Unlike the United States, which separates Memorial Day and Independence Day by more than a month (and which celebrates both with barbecues and sales, and little more), Israel reifies that angst, placing the holidays side by side, suggesting that those who believe that celebration is in order are right, but so, too, are those overcome by grief. The placement of the holidays begs us to see the complicated nature of the question, urging us not to be complacent.

But it's not working, at least not in the polemics currently gripping this tiny state. We've got a debate in this country not so much about grief, but about love. And two kinds of love, each of which is not only legitimate but critical, are at stake: love of the land and love of the state. To drastically oversimplify: The settlers love the land more than anything. Those who want to withdraw love the state more than they love the land.

Who could argue with love of the land? Despite what much of the left says, one needn't be a fanatic to love this land, to believe that for a Jew with a Jewish soul, giving it away is like giving up a child. Much of the books of Joshua, Judges, Samuel, and others takes place in precisely the land we may now have to give up. The liturgy that Jews have recited for thousands of years, and still do recite, is filled with petitions that we be permitted to return to the land, and much of the Torah is a tale of the Jewish people marching their way from slavery to their Promised Land. Even Jewish ritual makes that point. Even if we are in Pennsylvania and the bread we've just eaten came from Iowa, the Grace After Meals still offers thanks for the Land of Israel. Consider all that, these people say, and you could just give it up? Hand it over, for nothing in return? How?

There's nothing fanatical about that. At least not necessarily. But love of the land becomes fanatical when it completely ignores the love of the state.

This is a different sort of love. This is a love born not of belief, but of history. The state was created largely by Jews who had lost faith but gained a sense of history and its discontents. They saw what Europe had become, and they decided that the course of history had to be changed, that the Jews needed a place in which to determine their own fate. The UN Partition Plan in 1947, they will tell you, passed the vote in the General Assembly not because the UN cared about the sanctity of the land to Jewish souls; it was simply aware that without a country, there would be no Jewish survival. And for a brief moment, it actually cared about that.

If we're going to make it here, it seems to me, every one of us is going to have to give up part of what we love. Those who love the land will probably have to recognize that either we give up part of it, or we'll have none of it.

But those who love the people they see as they drive through those hills, who dream of a Middle East at peace, need to give up a dream. For the Palestinians will not be our friends. And for as far as the eye can see, they will hate us. Simply for being here. For existing.

Those who love the state, the disciplined army that we call the "Israel *Defense* Forces," will have to give up on the notion that we don't use the army against ourselves. For we will. It's becoming clearer that there will be no way to follow through on Sharon's plan, assuming that it progresses, without using the army in a way that we've never imagined before (except for a small foretaste when we evacuated Yamit in order to give back the Sinai). Our image of the army is going to have to change, too.

None of us will be able to have all of what we want, all of what we love. Survival in this part of the world can't be about "all or nothing." It is about "some or nothing." Most of us would have some, rather than nothing. We've had nothing in the past, and we know what that led to.

But accepting "some" rather than "all" requires compromise and ambivalence. Which is exactly what the Knesset tried to build into the calendar here.

I spent Yom Ha-Atzma'ut asking myself: Can we restore that ambivalence? Can we revive the sense of personal agony at the decisions this country is going to have to make? Can we create a discourse in Israel that recognizes that loving the land is not necessarily fanaticism, but that loving the state more and accepting the compromises that love will demand is not a sign of weakness or of moral murkiness?

I'm not sure. Dismantling settlements and uprooting settlers could lead to civil war. Or to a misplaced triumphalism of the left. Or to a hatred so deep that we never get beyond it.

Or, perhaps, it just might lead to the embracing of agony, and with that, a sign that some of the profundity of Judaism has returned to the Jewish state. Then we'd know that the state named for the One Who Wrestled with God (which is what the word *Israel* actually means) has finally earned its name.

Three Girls, Three Graves, One Torah

A Torah came home this week.

In about 1990, a group of pre-twelfth-grade girls from Pelech, Tali's high school, went on the school's annual trip to Poland. One day while in Krakow, they noticed a young man selling dolls. They were "Jew dolls," made to look like traditional Jews. A bit weird in Poland, perhaps, but not particularly noteworthy, until some of the girls noticed that the "books" that these dolls were holding looked remarkably authentic. The more closely the girls looked at these books, the more convinced they became that these books had been cut from a real Torah scroll.

They asked the doll-maker where he'd gotten the calligraphed parchment, and he told them that his uncle had a big scroll of it in the nearby town of Limanova. Asked where the uncle had gotten the scroll, he told them that during the war, it had been in the house of a Jew, and his uncle had taken it after the Jew disappeared. "Could they see it?" they wanted to know. He agreed to bring it back the next day.

True to his word, he showed up the next day and showed them what he had left. What remained was basically Genesis, Exodus, and Leviticus. The two other books, apparently, had been carved up for the dolls. The girls instinctively knew what they had to do. They pooled their relatively limited pocket money and bought the Torah from the man for whatever they managed to scrounge together.

They carried the partially destroyed and unusable Torah with them for the remainder of their trip. As the time to depart Poland grew closer, however, they were faced with a dilemma. All Jewish property from before the war now belonged to the state. The doll-maker had had no right to sell it, they had no right to buy it, and they certainly had no right to take it out of the country. If Israeli kids were caught smuggling Polish government property, matters would be most unpleasant, to put things mildly.

They talked it over, and after a while, the teacher from that summer reported, "*ha-lev gavar al ha-sechel*"—"the heart trumped reason." They decided to smuggle the Torah out of Poland and bring it home to Jerusalem.

At the airport, however, each girl was required to put her bags onto the X-ray machine. When the first girl in line was told to put her bags on the belt, she passed the Torah to the next girl in line. When that girl was told to do the same thing, she surreptitiously passed it to the girl behind her. And so forth. For the next few minutes, the Torah silently made its way back through the line, until it seemed that they were not going to get it out.

And then the belt broke. The machine just quit. The Polish authorities, too preoccupied with fixing the belt to inspect all the bags being brought through, just ushered the remaining girls by, the Torah included. They brought the Torah to a place in Jerusalem where such scrolls are repaired, but because this work is exceedingly expensive, there was no money to fix the scroll. With time, the girls graduated. They went on to the army or National Service, to university. To marriage, to kids, and to careers. The Torah remained unrepaired.

Fourteen years later, yet another senior class went to Poland. Talia was part of this group. The girls had an extraordinarily powerful experience and, during their trip, heard the story of the Torah that their predecessors, now in their thirties, had smuggled out of Europe. This class resolved to raise the money to get the Torah repaired, and upon their return, a few of them took the lead and got to work. A considerable amount of money was raised, the Torah was repaired over many months, and this past Sunday evening, it was danced into its new home in the auditorium/synagogue where, instead of being carved up for dolls, it will be used regularly and read by young women who actually understand it and who live by what it says.

The ceremony itself was a religious ceremony, so it was women only.

Elisheva and Talia went at the beginning, and I joined during the "speeches" segment, which was open to men, too. It was, despite the heat and the overly cramped space where people were sitting in the aisles and on the floor, standing on the sides and outside the door, incredibly moving. And as I listened to the teachers, the students, the rabbi, some graduates, and others tell the story of this Torah and of the two classes that had rescued it, a few mentioned that these girls are *dor shelishi la-shoah*, the third generation since the Holocaust. True enough.

And as I thought about that, I asked myself what inspired these girls to do this. How did the sense of urgency, the sense that this Torah couldn't be allowed to languish in Limanova and be cut up until there was nothing left, piece by piece and scattered to the winds, come to be so powerful for these girls? How did they know that this Torah simply had to come home? How, in a world in which last year's news is ancient history, did they know that the story of the Jews of Limanova is their story, too?

I watched Talia watching the speakers. I couldn't get a seat anywhere near her, but I could see her. Listening intently, her eyes, at certain moments, brimming with tears. Later, in the hallway of the school, just outside the auditorium, Elisheva and I talked about what the past six years have done to our kids. How grounded they are. How they know what they stand for. How despite everything they've been through, there's very little (on the surface, at least) that seems to frighten them. And a night like that, we said to each other, the opportunity for her to be part of something like this, reminded us why we came, and why there's nowhere else we'd rather raise our kids.

Musing on that, I was reminded of a conversation I'd had with Talia just a couple of weeks earlier, at the end of Yom Ha-Zikaron, the memorial day for fallen IDF soldiers. Yom Ha-Zikaron is a quiet day in Israel. A very quiet day. Stores are closed, restaurants are shuttered. The music on the radio communicates the sense that this is not a day like all others. Channel Three television does nothing but list the names of the soldiers who have died.

At the end of the afternoon, just hours before Yom Ha-Atzma'ut (Independence Day) celebrations were about to begin, Tali and I were sitting outside on the terrace, chatting. I asked her about her class's ceremony at Mount Herzl that morning.

"It was nice, actually. Shira [her principal] told us to spread out across the cemetery and to find a grave at which we wanted to recite Psalms. I decided to go to the section from 1948."

"Why there?"

"Well, I figured those were among the oldest graves, and they were the least likely to have family come and visit them later in the day.

"I went with two other friends. I went to a grave from the War of Independence, and read some *tehillim* [Psalms]. Then one of my friends who'd been at a grave not far away told me that the gravestone she'd stood by noted that it was someone who was killed in a battle for Jenin. And you know, Abba," she said, "it's pretty amazing, isn't it, that here we are, all these years later, still fighting in the same places, and we haven't given up?

"And then, my other friend came back, sobbing. She'd found a grave of someone who'd been killed in a battle for one of the places slated to go back [in Sharon's disengagement plan], and she was crying and saying, 'It's such a waste. These people died to get us those places, and now we're just going to give it back, with nothing in return? It's too much to bear.'"

Talia was quiet for a minute. I waited and didn't say anything. Then after a pause, she said, "I hope I don't have to go back there next year."

"Where?"

"The cemetery."

"Why?"

"Because, Abba, I'm a senior. There won't be a school trip next year. All my friends are going into the army now. If I go back there next year, it'll be for a funeral. For someone I know."

She's right, of course. She's at that age when all her friends are getting drafted, just as she is. And she's right that she could end up back there, as we were reminded eleven times this week (with six soldiers killed by a Gaza mine, and five more killed by a similar mine just days later). And she's right that if she did end up going there, the pain would be unbearable, more than any eighteen-year-old should have to know.

So what keeps these girls on track? How, and why, do they know that that Torah simply must come home? Why do they still weep at graves for people they never knew? Why are the stories on that mountain as real to them as the stories of the people in their own families?

That, when you boil it all down, is the magic of this place. It's the magic of living in a home where the kids and their parents breathe in history and a sense of belonging with every breath that they take. The implicit debate among those three girls, about what's a price worth paying, what should make us proud, what should devastate us, how we should understand the events playing out all around us, are what this country is about.

I was struck, listening to Talia's story, about how whole these young women are. For there was an era in which significant streams of early Zionism were a wholesale rejection of the biblical tradition. Poems like Alterman's "The Silver Platter," among many, many others, were an almost explicit claim that the biblical tradition had failed us. Bialik said the same thing. The Jews of Europe, he insisted, had ended up emaciated, defenseless, pathetic (his view, not mine). We didn't need just a new state we needed a new kind of Jew. Israel would be a place not only of Jewish sovereignty, but a place where the sick and defenseless European Jew would be brought home and then repaired and reborn.

And these girls are the new Jew. They're headed off to the army, confident enough to smuggle a Torah out of Europe in spite of the possible consequences of getting caught.

It's because of moments like that, in a packed auditorium, that the highly divisive society called Israel doesn't depress me. And it's why the histrionic headlines emblazoned across each morning's newspaper do not exasperate me. Because the divisiveness and the infighting, as exhausting as they can be, are often about a wounded but recovering people still trying to figure out what it wants to be when, one day, it recovers from its wounds. It would be unrealistic to imagine that the healing could come any faster. And it would be hard for me to imagine something more important to argue about.

When my daughter comes home from the military cemetery on Mount Herzl and tells me about the implicit argument with her two friends after their visits to those graves, I sense that, despite its myriad problems, this country is working. For what they're debating is how you make a home. When seventeen-year-old girls know that a Torah can't be left in Poland, or that it can't be left in a warehouse unrepaired, this place is working. Because repair and homecoming are what this place is all about.

. . .

Homecoming was the issue again this week. For how else are we to explain the fact that suddenly, this week, experts in *halakhah* (Jewish law) were sought for one radio talk show after another? The issue—"Is it permissible to send soldiers into Zeitoun, and then Philadelphi, in house-to-house and roof-to-roof searches, in order for them to look for fragments of the bodies of their comrades who'd been blown to smithereens the day before?" How does one balance the command not to risk life for anything except to save life, with the command to do whatever we possibly can to make sure that every Jew gets a Jewish burial? Can we put soldiers—kids, really—at a modicum of risk, so that the parents of their friends will have something, at least something, to put in the ground and have a funeral? Can we put soldiers in harm's way so that these very soldiers and all their friends will know that if, Heaven forbid, something like this happens to them, we'll get them home?

The rabbinate allowed the searches, but the country agonized. Many of us knew that the answer that had been given wasn't the only defensible one. The rabbinate basically said that depending on the likelihood of finding parts of the body, and the assessment of the risk, that, yes, "some" risk would be acceptable in order to bring those kids, or whatever we could find of them, home.

But what is "some" risk? What if more kids had been killed, by snipers or by a roadside bomb, in that operation? What would we have said then? Why, one could have asked, accept any risk whatsoever? Why, in the end, did the rabbinate rule this way? And why would any soldier risk his life to go look for a tiny piece of flesh on a Gaza rooftop? For what possible purpose?

Because, I think, there's something inexpressible about the commitment to ingathering at the core of this society. The Torah had to be brought home. The three dead soldiers we traded for a few months ago had to come home. And these eleven kids, or whatever we can find of them, have to come home. Which is why dozens upon dozens upon dozens of kids risked life and limb to crawl on their hands and knees, in enemy territory, to find whatever they could.

People argued about it. My taxi driver told me, "No way. It's just not worth it." Elisheva thought it was. I wasn't entirely certain. "If, God forbid, it had been our kid who had died there," I asked her, "would you want one of his friends [and I mentioned the names of a couple of kids who now hang around in our house, doing homework and playing their music way too loud, but who in relatively short order will also be drafted] to risk his life to go find what was left?" She looked at me, said nothing, and turned around and walked away. Rightly, of course, because the choice is unbearable. There's nothing to say.

It wasn't the issue of burial that was at the core of the debate this week, I think. It was a matter of bringing whatever we could find home. Just as those girls had to bring whatever was left of that Torah back home with them.

At the end of the ceremony at Tali's school, a few of us who hadn't been present at the religious service wanted to see the inside of the ark. It was beautiful, and on the *parochet* (the cloth covering at the front), there were some verses embroidered. The crowd was so thick that for a minute or two, I couldn't get a glimpse of what was written. But as people looked and moved away, I finally got to see. In beautiful lettering, embroidered with a love that was palpable, were the famous verses from Jeremiah 31:15–16 that had been chosen to welcome the Torah home:

> *Ki yesh sachar li-fe'ulateikh,*
> *Ve-yesh tikvah la-acharitekh*
> *Ve-shavu vanim li-gvulam*

> There is reward for your labor
> And there is hope for your future
> Your children shall return to their country.

Indeed.

WOUNDED, AND
HEALING

June 2004~January 2005

Born Again

On Monday afternoon an observation point was named for Limor, the slain daughter of Shlomo, the taxi driver from my work. In Gilo, the neighborhood in which she grew up and in which her family still lives, the neighborhood from which we heard all the shooting at the beginning of the war, we gathered to dedicate the memorial and to remember.

It was one of those glorious Jerusalem days. Clear blue skies, not too hot. And a totally normal Jerusalem afternoon. Buses making their way up and down the streets. People in cars on their way home from work. School kids hanging around. Mothers pushing strollers in the park just below us. Boys riding their bikes around the park, watching the proceedings. And a full crowd for the ceremony.

The emcee for the event trotted out the numbers. Since September 2000, Jerusalem had been attacked 591 times. Gilo, the neighborhood we were sitting in, had been attacked 180 times. And 209 Jerusalem residents had been killed. One of Limor's friends spoke about how the days go on, and life goes on, but she, and Limor's family, are not the people they used to be.

Despite the obvious sadness, the overall feeling was different. There was security at the event, but mostly because the mayor had been expected to arrive. (He didn't show—he was with some Chinese businessmen, itself good news if the business community is returning.) And the cops were chatting more than watching. Amazingly, even with her picture in the front, and the pain of her parents still so palpable that it was sometimes hard to breathe, one of Limor's family members spoke about the search for peace, the hope for the day in which we will put away our weapons.

Even in the face of the pain, and all the numbers, people are beginning to stir again, to dream of something different. Which is appropriate, because with the quiet that we're now having, something different seems to be emerging.

Micha called me at work last week to say he needed some money for his B'nai Akiva youth group meeting. Why, I wanted to know. Because they were going to the Israel Museum, to the annual Hebrew Book Week Festival. A bunch of fifth-graders, perfectly happy to have an activity at a book fair. And he insisted that he go with money—it wouldn't be fun if he couldn't buy a book. And then he hesitated. "Ema's out of town, Abba." I know, I told him. (I usually know when my wife is out of town.) "So, can I take a bus to the museum?"

I paused for a second, and then knew there was only one possible answer. Either you believe in this place, or you don't. We let our kids take the buses even when things were terrible, so now, there was really no reason to say no.

"Sure, take the bus," I told him.

He was relieved. He didn't want to have to tell his friends that his parents wouldn't let him ride the bus. These kids, when they think about their home, don't think about buses exploding. They think of book fairs at the museum.

I heard Avi chattering away on his cell phone the other day, in Hebrew, and asked him nonchalantly who he was talking to.

"Hannah," he said.

"Hannah?" I was surprised, I'll admit, that this immigrant kid from Los Angeles, and a girl who came here from Atlanta, both of whom grew up speaking English, were laughing and talking at the speed of sound in Hebrew. In a language that a hundred years ago virtually no one spoke.

"What's so surprising about my talking to Hannah?" he wanted to know.

"Nothing. Just that you were speaking in Hebrew, that's all."

He looked at me, incredulous. "We live in Israel, don't we?"

I don't know if he's aware of the rebirth that the naturalness of his speaking Hebrew signifies. But one day, I hope, he will be. For Israel, to those of us who've decided to make a go of it here, is about rebirth. About a new life. About a language restored. About healing a wounded people. About the future.

I was at Ma'aleh Ha-Chamishah, a kibbutz about twenty minutes outside Jerusalem, a few nights ago. On my way into the hotel for the meeting, I noticed that there was no guard. For the first time in years, I just walked into an Israeli hotel without being frisked. A couple hours later, on my way back to the car, I passed a lounge in the hotel where a group of elderly people were sitting playing cards. They were speaking Hebrew, but the bluish purplish numbers tattooed onto their left forearms were a clear giveaway that these weren't native Israelis. No, they'd come from a place very different.

And twenty yards away, a huge throng of American college kids on a Birthright trip, checking into the hotel and making a huge racket. The people sitting and playing cards didn't seem to mind the sudden invasion. I guess that when you come from where they've come from, a whole bunch of Jewish kids, even loud ones, and even a busload of kids who desperately need showers, is pretty good news. It's actually why you're here.

The buses we think about are the ones our kids ride to the museum, or the ones these dirty Birthright kids just got off of.

Which is why last week's Israel Day Parade in a major East Coast American city was so distressing to me. At the end of the parade route, the organizers decided to display the burned-out carcass of one of the buses on which people were incinerated in some Israeli city. There are, indeed, places for those buses, for the story of terror must be told. The Hague. The next UN conference on Human Rights.

But not an Israel Day Parade. What is a bus like that doing at a parade? Is that image of Israel the one we want thousands of young American Jewish kids to remember? Twisted skeletons of buses? Blackened metal? Is a freak show what we want kids to think the Jewish state is all about?

When a friend of ours wrote to Elisheva and to me separately last week, asking us whether to go to the parade with her kids, we each wrote back to her individually, and only later found that we'd said the same thing. Go to the parade. March. Have fun and be counted. But when you get close to the end, duck out. Don't take your kids (who haven't been to Israel yet) anywhere near that bus. It is the last thing they should see at a parade like that.

Because that bus isn't what will get her kids to fall in love with Israel. As effective as terror has been as a mobilizing tool, it's not what we're here for. Those of us who love this place love it for the same reason that we love people. Because with them, we're more whole than we can ever be without them. And what Israel has done for the Jews is to make us whole. Bruised, to be sure, but whole. When there are posters plastered all over the city announcing that the twenty-sixth volume of the Talmudic Encyclopedia is now available for purchase, I marvel. I never saw posters announcing the appearance of a book, plastered all over the city, in Los Angeles. New movies, yes. A book? Never. Not even Harry Potter. To me those posters are about rebirth.

When your kids don't want to go to the Annual Hebrew Book Week Festival without money, the Jewish people are more whole. When your son can't understand why it's a big deal that he's chatting with a girl in Hebrew, there's Jewish renewal.

Which brings us back to the memorial for Limor, and the gorgeous blue sky that stretched across the horizon. As we turned around and gazed at the view, we could see a vast panorama in the Judean hills. Sandy, rolling hills that look exactly as they must have looked centuries ago. Except for the fact that in the middle of the vista, a city rises out of those hills. An ancient city, but a modern city. A wounded city, but a healing city. A city that once hunkered down behind barricades and guards, but where the kids are once again riding their bikes and the strollers are once again being pushed in the parks. A city where we send our kids to school and don't really doubt anymore that we'll see them again at the end of the day.

Those are the same hills that the prophets must have seen, no? Could they, quite possibly, have been the very same hills that Zephaniah saw, when he exclaimed (3:14–15):

> Shout for joy, Fair Zion . . .
>
> Rejoice and be glad with all your heart
>
> The Lord . . . has swept away your foes . . .
>
> You need fear misfortune no more

Could it be? Might it just be that this dream, too, is slowly coming true? Might it just be that almost four years after it started, we've won this war, and something new is about to be born?

And the Land Was Tranquil

I would have thought that people would be ecstatic about the quiet, the peace, the return to normalcy. But it's more complicated than that. To be sure, we're enjoying it. The cafés are full, buses are crammed with people. Guards have relaxed, and the skittishness that had taken over every dimension of life here has gone. Almost.

Almost, because people are nervous. Nervous that it might not last. Worried that this time, now that we know how bad it can get, the loss of the quiet will be even more painful than the first time around, when we didn't know that as bad as things were, they could—and would—still get worse. It happened so slowly, over so many months, that by the time we'd hit bottom, we were almost used to it. But if it ends again, this time we know how bad it will be.

No one's talking about peace. Rather, the term is *sheket*. Quiet, or tranquility. It started at the beginning of the war, actually. When we arrived in Israel in 1998, the evening news would always end with the anchor's saying *"Erev tov,"* "Good evening," or *"Laila tov,"* "Good night." But then, as thousands of us began to get used to going to sleep to the sound of gunfire and waking up to horrendous news, that stopped. Now, each night, the evening newscast would end with *"Erev shaket le-kulanu,"* "May this be a quiet evening."

That was all we wanted. Quiet. And now that we have it, that's what we call it. Quiet, not peace. And I'm struck that perhaps the word still means what it meant thousands of years ago, in the time of the book of Judges. For then, the land was tranquil, but always temporarily. I reread those chapters, just to make sure that I'm remembering correctly, and sure enough—quiet is a temporary condition.

It starts in chapter 3 of the Book of Judges. There's a judge named Othniel, who finally prevails over Israel's enemies, and we're told in verse 11, "and the land was tranquil for forty years."

The land may have been tranquil for forty years (or "a while," which is what "forty" often signifies in the Bible), but in Judges, two verses later, the Israelites are at war again. But things settle down under another judge, Ehud, and at the end of the same chapter, in verse 30, "the land was tranquil for eighty years."

And the same thing again in chapter 5. And again in chapter 8, the land is quiet for forty years under Gideon. Tranquility, it seems, is not the normal state of affairs. It has to be pointed out. It has a duration. And it has an end.

Struck by this strange story, and by how similar it is to ours, I think of showing Elisheva this ancient biblical use of *shaket*. Or of mentioning the fact that it's kind of cool that the streets just a block or two from our house are named Othniel, and Ehud, and Gideon. We're living inside the biblical story in more ways than one.

So over dinner that night, I make some mention of the quiet we're having.

"It's going to be hell when it ends," she says to me, without even a second's hesitation.

"What?"

And then she looks up at me, almost whispering so that the kids, who're talking among themselves, don't hear, and says, "What if it ends? I can't go back to what we had before. I don't think I could bear it."

Things have gotten better so gradually that I've forgotten what it was like. But I remember everyone's glances out the window whenever we heard a loud noise. We'd hear helicopters outside, and Elisheva—like most of our friends—would dash to turn on the TV. And I remember how at night—every night, for months on end—I'd wake up in the middle of the night, and she wasn't there.

I would awaken, at one, or two, or three o'clock in the morning, and notice that she was nowhere to be seen. So I'd go downstairs and find her, night after night, sitting at the computer, on the Internet, scanning the major Israeli news pages.

"Anything new?" I'd ask.

"No. Not for now."

"So come on up to sleep."

"I'll be there in a minute."

"If there's nothing new, you should get some sleep."

But to no avail. Eventually she would make her way upstairs, only to be exhausted in the morning, and to go through the same ritual the next night. And the next. And make her way through each day, biding time until the next bombing hit. Which it always did.

She's right, I know. If this ends, it's going to be horrendous. Maybe that's why nobody talks about the quiet we're having. Maybe that's why the news anchorman still says *"Erev shaket le-kulanu,"* even though it *is* quiet.

And that's why I'm not going to say anything to her about the Book of Judges.

The land of the Bible, it seems, is sometimes just not the place to talk about the Bible.

What Divides Us

Jerusalem occupies space in international headlines that is wholly incommensurate with its size. Big news, but a tiny city. We live on the southern side of the city, almost at the edge (Bethlehem would be a ten-minute drive if we could get there at all), but we can get to the northern edge of the city, if traffic isn't too bad, in just over fifteen minutes. As you head north to the Hebrew University campus, for example, you pass the Old City, then a relatively upscale Arab neighborhood called Sheik Jarakh, and then take a right and an immediate left to the university. If you were to take the right, but not the immediate left, you would end up, in just a couple of minutes, in Wadi Joz, and then Abu Dis. Not, shall we say, very Jewish neighborhoods. And not, shall we say, neighborhoods where many Jews willingly go anymore.

Fortunately, in all the trips I've made to the university, I've never missed that immediate left. During the past few years, such a mistake wouldn't have been pretty. Last Monday, though, a friend and I purposely missed the left and kept heading straight, first into Wadi Joz and then into Abu Dis. She's Palestinian, and for a long time she's been asking me to spend a day with her in Abu Dis, to see the "wall" up close. Seeing it, she was convinced, would make me a vociferous opponent of the entire project. I had no idea how I would react, but it seemed to me that if I lived only fifteen minutes away from parts of it, taking a good, hard look was the least I could do.

She agreed to pick me up in her car (if any of the neighborhood's residents stopped us, she told me, we'd be much better off if she did the talking) and told me to wear a baseball cap instead of my kippah. There's apparently a limit to the protection she could offer.

Being an obedient sort, I dressed accordingly, jeans and an American T-shirt, baseball cap and a camera, to look a little tourist-like. She picked me up as promised, and within fifteen minutes we were in Wadi Joz. She showed me Al Kuds University, which I'd often heard of but had never seen, and then, after a bit of winding around neighborhoods I'd never have found my way out of, Mukassed Hospital, the east Jerusalem hospital where Arab victims of the violence are typically taken by the Arab ambulances. It didn't look like much. She didn't need to point out that Hadassah Hospital (where the more seriously injured Arabs are taken) on Mount Scopus, a cutting-edge place by any standard, is about three minutes—and two centuries—away.

Her point having been made, we set out for her to show me the pièce-de-résistance, no pun intended. We took the main drag through Abu Dis, and there it was, looming right in front of us. You can't exactly miss it, the gray concrete masses towering above you, many meters in the air. She parked in front of a grocery store and told me not to speak Hebrew. English only. She went to talk to the grocer to ask him to watch her car, and off we walked to the wall.

The first thing you notice, once you're up close, is the graffiti. Much of it read "From Warsaw Ghetto to Abu Dis Ghetto," or "No to the Busharon Wall." The second was at least clever. The first, I thought, was a bit sick. The Warsaw Ghetto was part of a project very different from what's going on here, no matter how much one may be opposed to the wall. There were also a few spray-painted slogans like "*Kol Ha-Kavod le-Magav*"—"Thank You, Border Patrol," presumably not written by Palestinians. A few biblical verses about freedom, a Star of David made out of dollar signs, presumably not painted by a Jew. And a biblical verse, in Hebrew: "Have we not all one Father? Did not one God create us? Why do we break faith with one another, profaning the covenant of our fathers?" (It's from Malachi 2:10, though the wall didn't have a footnote.) That one, presumably, was written by neither the Palestinians nor the border patrol.

Some graffiti, I thought, was missing. Where was the slogan that said, "Stop the bombings, so they take this thing down"? Nowhere. Not a single indication that the wall was a reaction to something. It was as if the wall had just been someone's whim, a decoration, a project for someone with nothing better to do. Not an auspicious beginning to the tour.

My friend wanted to show me a school that she knew about that was on the other side of the wall, so we started climbing the long, dusty road at its foot. Several hundred meters up, we came across five young women, probably teenagers, though it was hard to tell, all in long dresses and full Muslim headdress, carrying schoolbooks. My friend asked them how to get to the school. It's on the other side of the wall, they told her in an Arabic that I could barely follow. How do we get across? They pointed to a place where the wall hadn't been completed and said you climb up there and jump down. How far down is the jump, my friend wanted to know. They said something and laughed, and I didn't follow it. I asked her what they'd said, and she, too, laughed. "They said it's a big jump, but if you get killed, you're considered a 'shahid' [martyr]." Somehow, I suspected that if I died making the jump, they probably wouldn't announce my new 'shahid' status in my synagogue at the end of services, so we bagged the visit to the school.

We got to the top of the hill, where some Israeli security guys were loading equipment into a building that had formerly been a hotel, but that now, because it stood at the top of the village, was being used as a lookout post. They eyed us suspiciously and then asked me a few questions, but didn't really bother us. We hiked around. While I took some pictures, she explained the layout of the village to me and then suggested that we go to her sister's house on the other side of the wall. No problem, since the wall (still not completed) ended there. So we walked a bit further, around the edge of the wall, cut through a field, and (after she'd called her sister on her cell phone to tell her we were on our way) went to visit her sister.

Her sister also speaks perfect Hebrew. She brought out soft drinks and water, and then sat down to tell us about life in the village, the hardships of the fence. How she used to drive her son five minutes to his school bus (he goes to school at the Arab-Jewish public school in West Jerusalem) but now has to go all the way around Ma'aleh Adumim, and how it takes forty minutes on a good day. It wasn't clear to me why they didn't just park on the other side of the fence as we had done, and hike to the car, but I didn't ask.

The story, to be sure, wasn't a pretty one. The wall is enormous, it's ugly, and at least here, it cuts through the middle of the village. Why it has to run right through the middle of the village was impossible to tell. The planning certainly looked callous, if not worse. And it makes life very inconvenient for a lot of people. No question. I asked them if the part of the wall we'd just seen had been the part that the Israeli Supreme Court recently said had to be moved. They didn't quite answer that one. They (sort of) said they didn't know, and I (sort of) knew that wasn't the entire truth. I sat and listened, drank enough soft drinks to be polite, but couldn't help thinking about one missing subject of conversation, in an afternoon devoted almost exclusively to the wall—why the wall had been built in the first place. That, neither my friend, nor her sister, nor, for that matter, anyone else we met during the rest of the day, seemed inclined to mention.

It was, as my friend expected and hoped, an unsettling day for me. But not for the reasons that she'd thought. No one can deny the massiveness of the wall. No one can deny that it's ugly as sin. Or that it poses real hardships. Or that it may not have been built in all the right places. But no one can deny, either, that the reason that we, like many other Israeli parents, worry much less about whether our children will make it home each day is because of that wall. And that the reason that Jerusalem, and the rest of the country, has been exceedingly quiet for almost five previously unimaginable months, is also because of the wall.

Before the wall, this was a different country. A country terrorized. By people who came from places like Abu Dis. People who, for the most part, can no longer sneak in, because we've built the fence.

It was their absolute unwillingness to mention Israel's need for the wall that, contrary to her expectations and her hopes, slowly but inexorably eradicated most of the misgivings I'd had about the fence, at least in principle (there are without question some spots that have to be moved). My friend and her sister are Israeli citizens, in addition to being Palestinian (a long story). They live on opposite sides of the fence. (Another long story.) But both speak Hebrew, both work in West Jerusalem, and both understand Israeli culture as well as anyone else. And neither, in an hour of talking about the fence and a day of touring the area, ever mentioned any reason why Israel might do such a thing. That silence, much more than the fence, is what I found disconcerting.

These are bright people, well educated and articulate. So why the silence? It's not possible that they haven't thought about it. I suspected, though I surely didn't say, that there's a kind of Faustian bargain being made here. What these people want, quite understandably, is their own state. That's their goal, and if I were in their shoes, that's what I'd want, too. But I suspect they close their eyes to the terrorism of the extreme Israel-hating fascists around them because they secretly hope that the violence will serve their needs. And thus, they can't put up any graffiti about stopping the bombings, for to even acknowledge the terror would be to admit their own passive complicity in it.

That duplicity is akin to the difference between the International Court of Justice (ICJ) and Israel's own Supreme Court. Everyone knows that the wall is a problem. Israel's Supreme Court said the same thing. Which is why our court ruled, just days before the ICJ issued its ruling (the ICJ hearings, in a telling coincidence, opened the morning after the bombing of the #14A bus that killed eight people and wounded sixty) that significant stretches of the fence had to be moved. "Eliminate the hardship," the Supreme Court effectively said, "as much as you can." While the ICJ essentially said, with admitted hyperbole on my part, "Eliminate Israel, as soon as you can." How else to explain a ruling that the fence must be taken down, and the Palestinians compensated for their losses, without any serious reference to Israel's security concerns?

Though Israel's right wing was outraged by our Supreme Court's ruling, many of us were proud. I certainly was. Not many countries can boast of a Supreme Court that has ruled in favor of those trying to destroy it, even in times of war. (In fact, though I'm certainly no expert, I'm hard-pressed to think of a single other example.) That's the ultimate difference between our court and the ICJ, of course. Our court said, "Survive, but do it with decency." Whereas the ICJ said, essentially, "We don't really care whether you survive or not."

There's no question we didn't build this fence the smart way. We built it too slowly. And we should have plotted the course of parts of it differently. And our soldiers guarding it are not sufficiently trained, which is why it was announced today that the patrolling of the fence will shortly be assigned to a private firm, presumably with better trained people. All of those problems are real.

But so were the problems that the fence was meant to address, and about that, no one seems to have anything to say. Not the ICJ, not the Palestinian *and* Israeli protesters who want it brought down, and not my friend who so desperately wanted me to see it.

In a way, though, I was also saddened by something else. By the fact that I wasn't more upset.

I'd begun the day a bit nervous at how upset seeing the wall was going to make me. I started out knowing that it wasn't going to be an easy day, suspecting that I would feel terrible for the people whose lives have been horribly disrupted by it. And throughout the day, I kept waiting to feel the revulsion I'd expected, the disgust at our infringement on their freedom of movement. But it didn't come.

Yet the infringement is real. The wall is ugly. The reality is horrid. So why didn't I feel worse? That question actually made me saddest. I left saddened not so much by the wall as by the fact that the simple but instinctive desire to stay alive has killed something else in us, something that no one should live without. Empathy. Simple human caring. I wished that I'd been more upset. I knew that the person I'd been when I came here six years ago would have been horrified. But I wasn't. Not anymore. Not after all we've been through. Something in us has hardened.

And I was saddened, almost beyond words, because I came and left, not really believing that anything better than this was possible in the future. Because I left convinced that though we may one day get to non-belligerence, we're not going to see peace. The hatred is too deep, the distrust too embedded. They see us as a massive military power, while we can't remember one instance when their leadership has said clearly (in Arabic, to their own people in their own language, which is all that matters) that we have a right to exist. They accuse us of not caring about their standard of living, and we see them as unwilling to acknowledge the violence we've endured for decades. Where they see a massive invasion and disruption of their village, we see protection for our kids. They read the ICJ ruling with approval, and we see Europe, unrepentant, repeating its wholesale willingness to sacrifice the Jews.

One wonders how, or whether, we'll ever get beyond that. One wonders how many people really want to. On either side.

When we made our way back to the grocery store to get my friend's car, we saw some kids huddled around the ice cream freezer just outside the store, chatting about what kind of ice cream cones they wanted to buy. I realized, suddenly, that they were speaking English, a perfect American English, without a trace of an accent.

I went over to them and asked them where they were from. San Francisco, they told me, delighted to meet another American. What were they doing there, I asked. Their whole family lives in Abu Dis, they told me, and they come for the entire summer, every summer. We chatted for a minute, and then they asked me what I was doing here.

"I live here," I told them.

"In Abu Dis?" they asked, with surprise.

"No, there," I said and pointed to West Jerusalem, clearly visible one hill over.

At which point, the eldest, probably about fourteen years old, looked alarmed. Her body language shifted. She shepherded her siblings and cousins away from the freezer, without buying any ice cream, and as politely as she could, ushered them away. Had we met at a Ben and Jerry's store in the Bay Area, it all would have been very pleasant. But because we met over an ice cream freezer in Abu Dis, thousands of miles away, I was suddenly the enemy. Because of the wall? Or because I exist?

My friend and I were quiet as she drove me back to West Jerusalem. "What did you think?" she asked. But she didn't want to know. What I thought was that though I genuinely like her very much and admire a lot about her, and though Elisheva and I enjoy having her and her husband over for dinner, the wall didn't create the gulf between our worlds. It just formalizes it.

What did I think? What I couldn't tell her was that I was thinking of Abram, and Lot, and the verse that says "the land could not support them staying together" (Genesis 13:6). And wondering if it was no less true today than it was thousands of years ago.

And wondering, if it's still true, where that leaves us. Nowhere good, that's for sure. Without much hope. With just a deep sadness, the kind that gnaws at you and won't go away. With the sense that, with apologies to Robert Frost, huge fences make tolerable neighbors.

And with the fear that this may, for the foreseeable future, be the best we can hope for.

To Hell in a Handbasket

A note from the post office saying that you've got registered mail waiting for you just can't be good news. So it was with some foreboding earlier this summer that I went to pick up my letter. I waited in line, signed for the letter, and was even more unhappy to see that the return address said "*Medinat Yisrael—Batei Mishpat.*" "State of Israel—Courts." Great. What now?

I left the post office and, walking back to the office, opened the envelope. It was a summons, requiring my appearance in a Kfar Sabba court (not far from Tel Aviv) at the end of September 2004, as a witness in a case against a defendant I'd never heard of. The good news was that I wasn't the defendant. The bad news, though, was that I was being called upon to testify in a case I knew nothing about.

Until I realized that Kfar Sabba isn't that far from Ariel, which is where I'd been a few years ago when I'd gone to help some Palestinians harvest their olive crop and to protect them (simply by standing among them) from some radical settlers (who, we hoped, would be less likely to harass or shoot at the Palestinians if they saw that there were some Jews in the group). When the day got a bit violent, I happened to photograph some settlers attacking these Palestinians, and ended up being visited in my office by some cops who took a few pages of testimony. This, I figured, was probably the aftermath of that long-forgotten day.

I wasn't very keen on the idea of testifying in court, for many reasons. I didn't have much to say about the day that I hadn't already said, I wasn't eager to waste a day in court, and most important, this country has become so hostile that the last thing I needed was yet another adversarial setting. But the summons was very clear about a whole host of penalties for not showing, so I cleared the calendar and saved the day.

Court, I tried to reassure myself, couldn't possibly be any more adversarial than what we're already living with. With Sharon proceeding with his plans for a disengagement from Gaza, and the disengagement scheduled to take place sometime around the summer, the political climate was heating up with each passing day. Leaders of the settlers were calling for soldiers to disobey the orders they will receive to remove them. In response, Yossi Lapid, the justice minister, accused them of "incitement to civil war." *Maariv*, one of Israel's major newspapers, quoted the head of a regional settlement council whose daughter was killed by terrorists and is buried in the northern West Bank, "If any one dares to come and touch my daughter's grave . . . whether a soldier or the chief of staff, I will shoot him."

In the meantime, the Shin Bet has increased security around Sharon, because of "specific and plausible" threats to his life from the right. Rabbi Yosef Dayan, of the West Bank town of Pesagot, publicly offered to perform a traditional kabbalistic *Pulsa DeNura* ceremony, to place a curse on Sharon. Before you laugh, consider this—he did the same to Yitzhak Rabin. Now I'm not suggesting any causality in the Rabin assassination (by a religious Jew) that followed, but it does give you a sense of the mood of the country. In the meantime, the attorney general has said that Dayan is "horrific," but that he will not prosecute him for incitement.

Then, Nadia Matar, co-chairwoman of Women in Green, a right-wing women's group, sent a letter to Yonatan Bassi, the head of the Disengagement Administration, referring to him as the head of the "Expulsion Administration," and called him the "modern version of the Judenrat [the Jewish Council that was forced into collaboration with the Nazis]—but actually far worse." So now we've got Jews—religious Jews at that—making obscene comparisons between Israel's government and the Nazi regime. It would almost be laughable if it weren't so appalling and shameful. In response, some members of the Knesset demanded that the attorney general investigate her, too.

Then, according to *Ha-Aretz*, the right-wing *Arutz Sheva* Web site published a letter from a Gaza Strip resident to his two brothers in the army in which he urged them to refuse orders to evacuate settlements. "Don't make me raise my hand against you," he wrote to his brothers, according to the newspaper. "What would I tell Mother if, God forbid, you were hurt?" The Hebrew term for civil war, you may be interested in learning, is *milkhemet akhim*, or "a war of brothers." Appropriate, no?

The left, though, refuses to be outdone by the right's lunacy. In today's *Ha-Aretz*, former education minister Yossi Sarid has an astounding op-ed piece. Referring to the Yom Kippur liturgy that begins by permitting us to pray with transgressors, he writes, "Despite the permission to pray with the transgressors, I would not want to pray with the settlers and their benefactors [this Yom Kippur]. . . . [Because] the God to whom we direct our prayers is, apparently, not the same God."

The right says that the Sharon government is worse than the Third Reich, and the left says that they have a different God from that of the settlers. Four years into the Intifada, we're finally putting an end to the terror (for the most part), and the country seems that much closer to going to war—with itself.

So I wasn't much in the mood for courts, or more adversarial tension, but a summons is a summons, and off I went. On the way out of the office and to the car, I took the elevator. There was another family in the elevator, an Arab man, his wife in full traditional Arab dress, and their daughter, about four years old, in a cute T-shirt, a little blue skirt, and the most adorable pink sandals I'd seen in a long time. She looked at me, and I looked at her. And then, in contravention of an unspoken but very clear rule of Jerusalem etiquette, I smiled at her and said "Hi." Not really done. Jews and Arabs don't speak in elevators here. You're supposed to stare at the floor, or at your cell phone, or pretend not to see each other. Anything but eye contact.

But the girl was cute, and what the hell, she looked at me first. So I said "Hi." And smiled at her. Her mother shot me a glance and gently pulled the daughter behind her. And then looked at the floor.

But the little girl kept looking at me from behind her mother's dress, and I kept smiling at her. Even as they got to their floor, and the mother pulled her daughter after her and out of the elevator, the little girl kept turning around and looking at me. She didn't quite smile. But she wasn't afraid, either. I guess she's too young to know that she's supposed to hate me. That we shouldn't talk in the elevator. That we shouldn't talk at all. Well, this country is a formidable pedagogue. She'll learn.

Elisheva decided to drive with me to Kfar Sabba. On the way, I told her that I was annoyed at wasting the day. That the prosecutor couldn't be terribly serious if he hadn't contacted me. That some friends had warned me that often these prosecutors have to press charges but do so as ineptly as possible to make sure that the defendants (whose political positions they agree with) get off. The whole expedition, I told her, was a farce.

No, she said, it's not. Either someone makes the effort to show that religious Jewish life and social decency (along with some regard for the rule of law) aren't antithetical, or the whole country is going to go to hell in a handbasket. Appreciative, but not entirely convinced, I tried to keep that in mind.

When we got to Kfar Sabba, I made my way to the courthouse and was met in the hall by the prosecutor, a friendly chap wearing a kippah. He seemed to want to do this right and suggested that we review the testimony that I'd given to the cop two years ago, to make sure that I still stood by it. Did I take these pictures? Were these the dogs I'd mentioned?

He reviewed the case against the defendant, which was essentially illegal use of a weapon, and then told me to wait until we were called in to the chamber. As we witnesses were cooling our heels in the hallway, seeing each other for the first time since the day of those events, the defendant showed up. No thinner than he'd been that day, and certainly not any cleaner, he was still wearing a kippah the size of the cover we'd had on our garbage cans outside our Los Angeles house. The rest of his getup was equally impressive: an originally white XXL crewneck T-shirt, now mostly brown, tzitzit (the four woven fringes of white string worn by religiously observant men) outside the shirt, some filthy cargo pants, and Teva sandals. Wisely, this time he seemed not to be toting a fully loaded M-16.

I don't know if he recognized us or simply deduced who we were by virtue of the fact that we were all waiting outside the same courtroom, but he figured out what we were doing there, and then it didn't seem as if he wanted to be our friend. He sat a few benches away, opened up a book of Psalms, and began to pray. Given that there was no defense attorney in sight, praying seemed like a pretty good idea. But he wasn't entirely engrossed in his prayer—periodically, he cast a look of sheer disgust in our direction. We had gone to the West Bank that day, after all, to help

Palestinians pick their (own) olives by running interference between them and the likes of him. You live here long enough, you learn to understand the looks he gave us: "Arab lovers—destroying the country."

It was the second time that day someone made it very clear that he didn't want to be anywhere near me. The first time was because I was a Jew. The second time was because I didn't hate Arabs. It's hard to win around here.

A short while later, the chief witness for the prosecution, the one who'd made the complaint to the police (one of the three settlers involved had stolen his bag) received a visitor. The visitor, a physicist from Tel Aviv who's rather widely known in olive-picking circles, started chatting with his friend and then noticed me. And then shut up completely.

He said to his friend, nodding in my direction, "Who's that?" he asked, looking me over quite intently.

"Oh, he's another witness."

"A witness?" A bit of discomfort in his voice.

"Yeah, he's a witness. Our case."

"Which side?" Ah, so that was the issue.

At which point, his friend the plaintiff laughed and said, "Don't worry. He's on our side."

The newly arrived visitor looked at me, somewhat apologetically, and said, "Oh, excuse me. I didn't realize."

"No problem," I said, and went back to reading my book.

"No, you see," he insisted on continuing, "you need to understand. Anyone wearing a kippah is a suspect in my book, you know, unless I know them, you know."

I did understand. And let him know, with a glance that would have made the defendant proud, what I thought of his assessment of Israeli social boundaries. Inexplicably, he got very defensive and tried to explain.

"You know, it's not a principle thing. It's just the situation. It's just the way things are." We were getting dangerously close to "some of my best friends are religious Jews," which I really didn't want to hear, especially from another Jew, so I told him it sure sounded like a "principle thing." He stuttered a thing or two, but then gave up, and found an excuse to walk down the hall.

Surprisingly, that was the first time I was upset the whole day. It was too bad that the little girl in the elevator got a clear message from her mother that she wasn't to look at me, but I'm used to that. And it wasn't exactly surprising that the defendant didn't want to take us out for a beer. But the disdain from the physicist was more than I could take. Here we are, in the only country on the planet the Jews have, and this guy—a Jew—looks at me with a vicious kind of suspicion because I'm—a Jew. Just not his type of Jew. And he decides, completely incorrectly, that he knows everything about me, because of what I'm wearing. And I'd naïvely thought, long ago, that living here was precisely about not being judged just because you're wearing a kippah.

Eventually, long after the time that had been printed on the summons, and long after the defense attorney showed up (the defendant must have trusted her abilities, for he stopped praying when she got there), we were called into the courtroom, whereupon Her Honor, the judge of the day, gave the prosecutor a tongue-lashing for having delayed the proceedings. He attempted an anemic explanation, but she made it clear that she wasn't in the mood, and he apologized.

Then, the wrangling between the prosecution and the defense began. Turns out our defendant was actually on trial for two different arrests, on two different days, but the same prosecutor and defense attorney were handling both. The defense was making some sort of claim about the need to separate the cases, at which point the judge ordered us all out of the courtroom. Out we went again. The defendant stayed in (he, presumably, was allowed to hear the arguments), and my physicist friend cowered somewhere at the other end of the hall.

When we were called back into the room, Her Honor explained that due to some legal technicalities, the case could not be heard today. We'd be called back at a later date to give our testimony. She clearly felt bad that we'd wasted our time, though, so she smiled at us magnanimously and said, quoting the traditional greetings for the period between Rosh Hashanah and Yom Kippur, "*Shannah tovah*," and "*G'mar chatimah tovah*." "A good year. And may you be inscribed in the Book of Life."

You, too, Your Honor, you too.

We left the courthouse. About half an hour into our drive home, Avi called my cell, wanting to know if we could drive him to his kickboxing class downtown. "We're not even in Jerusalem," we told him. "OK," he said, "I'll get there on my own. And oh, by the way, there was a bombing in Jerusalem a few minutes ago."

We hung up and turned on the radio. Only one dead, but you have to know how to listen to the news here. One, they said, was "grievously" injured. That means, in Israel-speak, that he'd be dead soon. Another report said that the woman terrorist was on her way to a bus when alert security forces stopped her, dramatically reducing casualties. Translation: the border patrol kids blocked her passage to the bus or the crowd and absorbed the blast with their own bodies.

We turned off the radio. That was yesterday. This morning, the radio went on again at 6:00 A.M. First, the Shema, as it's read every morning on that station, and then the news. The towns from which the two border patrol kids came. The locations of their funerals. And the times. And then interviews with the family. The sobbing in the background was more than I could take to start the day, so I turned off the radio.

Got to the office about two hours later, about 8:00, and checked the Web, and the radio. Three more soldiers killed, at 6:00 A.M. this morning, in a vicious shootout with two Palestinian gunmen who'd infiltrated an IDF outpost near Morag. More funerals. More interviews with families. Army officers speaking about a major lapse in security and an investigation sure to follow. Lotta good that'll do those families. Turned off the radio. Got off the Web. And got to work.

The news all day didn't get much better. When the day was over, I started home, and on the way out of the office, I passed by the receptionist. "*Shannah tovah*," she said, and "*G'mar chatimah tovah*."

I considered telling her what I thought the prospects for the year were, but figured it would take forever to first translate "to hell in a handbasket" into Hebrew and then explain the origins of the phrase.

So I just smiled at her and said, "*Shannah tovah*." And "*G'mar chatimah tovah*."

Even the Victors Ought
to Mourn

Many of us remember the images of Jews huddled around their radios across the globe, listening to the UN vote on November 29, 1947, as the General Assembly voted to create a Jewish state. October 27, 2004, wasn't quite as momentous, but it may prove to have been no less decisive. That was the night of the Knesset vote to proceed with Sharon's disengagement plan and to get out of Gaza.

The outcome was relatively assured even before the vote, but still, the sense of tension as the roll of the Knesset's 120 members was called was palpable. At home we were all crowded around the TV, watching and waiting. With the sense that maybe, just maybe, something good would come out of all the angst and hatred of the past years, months, weeks, and days. Even if it means concessions that many of us don't want to have to make. Even if it means concessions that break our hearts, for the land we love that we will have to leave, and for the people who have settled it with passion and with dignity, often in the most selfless of ways.

If you want to get a sense of what's really going on in this country, behind the vote and the Knesset, all you have to do is look at the billboards that have begun to spring up everywhere. Like windows on the soul, billboards in Israeli life offer a glimpse into the psyche of a country in turmoil. This week, in ways that those who distributed them probably did not intend, those posters evoked not just the cavernous rift in this society, but its agony as well.

"*Ha-mefaked, anakhnu yehudim, ve-et zeh ani lo mesugal,*" read one that has appeared all over. "Commander, we're all Jews, and this I cannot do." It is a call to soldiers, encouraging them to declare that even if ordered, they will not force Jews from their homes.

The phrasing was brilliant, I thought. Not "I won't do this," but "I can't do this." It evoked, in almost wordless fashion, the bewilderment of those in Gaza who will be moved. It suggested that the Knesset's decision is not simply wrong, but that it verges on a violation of nature. This simply cannot be done. It is an assault on too much of what we stand for, an assault on fairness, on decency.

Even those who favor the disengagement should, indeed must, understand this sense of betrayal. Because these Israeli citizens were encouraged by Labor governments no less than by Likkud governments to build homes in the Gaza Strip, and they did so with exemplary dedication. Because, all of Israel's protestations to the contrary notwithstanding, we are withdrawing under fire. Because Ariel Sharon effectively promised these people that this would not happen, and they supported him with that assurance in mind. Because homes will be destroyed, communities dismantled, playgrounds abandoned, synagogues emptied, *batei midrash* (houses of religious study) razed. Because those who left Yamit (in the Sinai, when it was returned to Egypt, and was then destroyed by Israeli bulldozers) could at least console themselves with the knowledge that it was land for peace, while this week we could not point to anything that we were getting in return for our evacuation.

Because there are cemeteries in the Gaza settlements, where these citizens have buried their parents, their spouses, and their children. And what should happen to those graves? Shall we disinter the children killed and buried there and force those people to relive once again the torment of those funerals? Or shall we leave the graves there, even as the Palestinians move in, as if we don't know what will happen to them, pretending that we don't recall the desecrations of Joseph's Tomb in 2000, or of the Mount of Olives before the Six-Day War?

Sadly, we hear little validation of the settlers' angst from those who favor the withdrawal. Where is the grieving on the left for a human tragedy of enormous proportions? Have we become so embittered that we feel nothing for those whom we may have to dislodge? Is that what statehood has wrought?

"*Yotz'im me-azah, matchilim le-daber*," proclaimed the other side. "Leave Gaza, and start speaking," shouts the left, as if there were anyone with whom to speak. What was intended to be a declaration of hope struck me as naïve, as a reflection of precisely what is wrong with those with whom I (hesitantly) agree that we need to leave, but who see our part of the world with an optimism I do not share. The arms-smuggling tunnels between Egypt and Gaza will continue, and Israeli papers warned this week that Palestinians may have smuggled in weapons capable of bringing down a plane. (The Ben Gurion Airport isn't that far from Gaza and is even closer to parts of the West Bank.) The firing of Kassam rockets will also continue.

Therefore, the residents will leave, but our forces will not be able to. Ironically, "*Yotz'im me-azah, matchilim le-daber*" confirms the sense of futility that has the Gaza settlers in its grip. We are leaving out of desperation, because too many of us are dying, not because we have a peace partner.

As the Israeli news was carrying live coverage of the Knesset debate and vote, it occasionally cut to Tel Aviv, where a memorial ceremony was being conducted as the country began to mark the anniversary of the assassination of Yitzhak Rabin. Cutting back and forth between the Knesset and Tel Aviv, the broadcast reminded us that these days, with their vitriol, histrionics, and character assassination, are harrowingly reminiscent of the period in which Rabin was murdered.

Another poster has appeared, in jarring red and black, with a large photograph of Social Welfare Minister Zevulun Orlev at the bottom. The poster reads "*Orlev shutaf li-devar akirah*"—"Orlev is party to uprooting," roughly translated. (Because Orlev, a member of the National Religious Party, though opposed to the disengagement, has not quit the coalition.) Again, we have the finger-pointing at an individual and the insidious invocation of halakhic-sounding language that was in vogue in the weeks before Rabin was murdered.

Which makes one wonder: Have we learned nothing? Has the sickness that produced Yigal Amir, Rabin's assassin, been completely forgotten?

This week was cause for mourning. Because of the physical conflict we are about to undertake. And because, as the anniversary of Yitzhak Rabin's murder reminds us, though we may have taken the first steps to save our bodies, we have a long way to go if we are to repair our souls.

But there is reason to be hopeful, as well. *Ha-Aretz*, Israel's leading daily, ran a cartoon on Wednesday morning, the morning after the vote, which showed Ariel Sharon sitting by Rabin's grave. As Sharon sits, almost Rodin "Thinker"-like, Rabin says to him, from the grave, "Shalom, haver," the words that Clinton said to Rabin at Rabin's funeral.

"Shalom, haver," of course, can mean either "Good-bye, friend," which was what Clinton meant, or "Hello, friend." And here, in the cartoon, "Hello, friend" is apparently what Rabin is saying to Sharon. The cartoon lends itself to a cynical, sad read, in which Rabin foreshadows to Sharon that he, too, will soon be killed, a prospect that has some sectors of this society very worried, particularly as the vitriol of the radical right escalates.

But the cartoon has a simpler meaning, though no less poignant. In this read, Rabin is saying to Sharon, "Welcome, friend," to the company of those who have tried to push unpopular concessions through the Knesset. To the company of those who understand that ultimately this country is not about real estate, but about what we do with, and in, the land that we keep. To the company of warriors, who, at the dusk of their careers, have come to understand that the sword (though we will always need it) will not end this conflict. To the fraternity of those who have come to understand that even in the volatile neighborhood in which we live, even without an "agreement," we will have to compromise. But because we want something different. For ourselves, for our children, for this state.

One can look at the political machinations consuming the Knesset, or the ongoing possibility that Sharon will be killed, or the myriad ways in which the process of leaving Gaza could still be derailed—and then one can despair. Or, one can take consolation in the cartoon in *Ha-Aretz* and realize that once again, a man who rose through the ranks of Israeli public life as a warrior has decided to pursue something different.

From warrior to statesman to seeker of peace. Or if not peace, then at least a parting. It happened with Rabin. And it's happening with Sharon.

Particularly in a week like this, the fact that this country, despite everything it has faced during the past decades and the past four years, continues to witness this metamorphosis in its leaders, is, to me, a tremendous source of pride. And with so much so unclear this week, it is a wellspring of hope, as well.

A Reprieve

I guess if you're the *New York Post*, nuance isn't high on your list of priorities. And a good thing it isn't. Sometimes it's nice to see someone call it like it is, because the rest of the world is so hopelessly confused.

Today's *Post* has a headline—the entire front page in *New York Post* style—that I'm saving. "Arafat Dead—And He Won't Be Missed."

Yes, Yassir Arafat is finally dead. But so is the world's judgment. French president Jacques Chirac went to visit him in the hospital, as if Arafat were some great statesman, not the father of modern terrorism. George W. Bush, who mostly gets it about Muslim terrorism, also couldn't help himself. "God bless his soul," Bush said upon hearing that Arafat was dead. Why, George? Why in the world should God bless his soul? After all the children he murdered? After the Massacre at Maalot? After the 1972 Munich Olympics? And many more, too many to begin counting. Why, why in the world should God bless his soul?

Jimmy Carter waxed a bit too eloquent, too. Upon learning of Arafat's death, Carter called him "a powerful human symbol," noting that "Palestinians united behind him in their pursuit of a homeland." OK, he was trying to give credence to Palestinian aspirations without saying too much about the man himself. But still, "a powerful human symbol"? Of what, exactly? To Carter's credit, at least he made it clear that he had no intention of going to the funeral.

Tony Blair, thankfully, seems to have kept silent, aside from an innocuous expression of sympathy to the Palestinian people, which in his position, there's no avoiding. One assumes that he didn't want to make the same gaffe that his wife, Cherie, made in June 2002, when she opined, in the presence of Queen Rania of Jordan, "As long as young people feel they have got no hope but to blow themselves up you are never going to make progress."

Which brings us to the real point, doesn't it? Cherie Blair was right about one thing. The Palestinian people would have more hope if they had a state. That much is true. But why don't they have one? One reason only, and he just died. The great irony of the Middle East is that under Ehud Barak, Israel did more to create a Palestinian state than Yassir Arafat ever did. Maybe Barak's deal wasn't good enough; it was certainly a position from which to bargain. But Arafat didn't want to bargain. He didn't want to be a real president or prime minister. He wanted to remain a murderer, so instead of bargaining, he unleashed the latest Intifada. And a murderer he stayed until the very end.

But the world, so infatuated with the oppressed, can't see right from wrong, cause from effect, solution from obstacle. Or statesman from terrorist.

There are two things this week that bear particular notice. Imagine that Ariel Sharon had died suddenly this week. What would have been the reaction of Palestinians and Arabs all across the world? Let's not pretend that we don't know, that we'd have had to wait and see. We do know. Assault rifles fired into the air. Israeli flags—and American flags, as well—burned by the dozen. Rallies and joy. Whooping it up in the streets.

And what was the reaction in Israel? Nothing. No rallies. No weapons fired in the air. No particular joy, and certainly not in public. If anything, a quiet, melancholy relief. A reprieve. A moment or two to wonder how things might have turned out differently if "God had blessed his soul" a few decades earlier. Might things here have looked very different, much sooner? And a sense that maybe, just maybe, things here might begin to change.

Which—and this is the second point—is why Ariel Sharon is in trouble this week. Imagine that—Yassir Arafat's death is a problem for Ariel Sharon. The same Ariel Sharon who pursued Arafat into Beirut in 1982 and probably would have loved to have killed him then must be disappointed that Arafat has now died. Because the whole premise of the unilateral disengagement has been that there's no one to talk to. And now? With Arafat dead, Mahmoud Abbas will take over, and he says that he's willing to talk. Sharon's claim has been that the disengagement has to be carried out because there is no one on the Palestinian side to talk to. Arafat couldn't be trusted, and no one else had any real authority. So, Sharon said, we'll do it ourselves. But now, with Arafat gone, maybe there *will* be someone to talk to. How will Sharon justify continuing?

Telling, isn't it? The inventor of modern Muslim terror dies. The world lavishes praise upon him. And the Israelis are stuck, trying to figure out how, in the face of the overdue death of the primary obstacle to Palestinian statehood, they—of all people—can keep trying to move peace forward.

A Talmudic Warning

In my more whimsical moments, as I ponder the extremism that characterizes today's discourse about settlements and settlers, I suspect I've found the solution. We need to get hard-liners on both sides to study the Talmud. For the Talmud is testimony to Judaism's celebration of multiple perspectives. In the Talmud's twenty-volume disputation, what emerges most clearly is that there is often wisdom on both sides of whatever the argument happens to be. The redactors of the Talmudic text chose to preserve not simply the legal position that prevailed, but both sides of the argument, eternally locked in a discordant embrace.

Thus, the Talmud is our tradition's sanctification of ambivalence. And ambivalence and nuance, sadly, are dimensions of intellectual life that seem to be rapidly disappearing from Jewish discourse, both in Israel and beyond.

Not long ago, toward the end of 2004, I was in a not-to-be-named Western European capital and, during my stay, had occasion to meet with the faculty of a well-known liberal academic institution of higher Jewish learning. The topic they wanted to discuss, they told me in advance, was how to foster in their students an ongoing commitment to Israel, even when many of them (both faculty and students) find many of Israel's actions reprehensible. Fair enough, I thought. I may not share their critical assessment of Israel's behavior, but they have every right to disagree, and the question of how to justify ongoing commitment even in the face of disagreement seemed worth talking about.

So I figured I'd meet them where they were. I began the session with a brief history of the last four years and reviewed my assessment of how Israel has conducted this war. And then I acknowledged a few of the mistakes that we've made, figuring that if I showed the group that I was willing to acknowledge those errors, perhaps we could have a more genuine, and less adversarial, conversation.

No such luck. I hadn't gotten very far into this topic before one of the members of the faculty interrupted me, very politely, and suggested, "Well, since having power inevitably means that Israel is going to abuse it, maybe the Jews would simply be better off without a state. Maybe Judaism would be a better tradition, a more moral tradition, without Israel."

At first, I wasn't sure whether he was serious. But he was. Dead serious. And to be truthful, I wasn't entirely sure where to cut into that argument. I thought of asking him where he was going to go when the rising Muslim fundamentalism in his own country makes Jewish life impossible in his community, but decided against it. Had I had more time to think, I might have asked him where he's seen a country that's a moral paradise while it's at war for its survival. But at the time, the best I could manage was something like, "Well, we tried the powerlessness approach on this continent about sixty years ago, and it didn't work very well, did it?"

But he was completely unconvinced. Having an army, he insisted, meant that we would make mistakes. And no one wants to make mistakes of that gravity. So let's not have an army. Which means, of course, let's not have a country. Let's just live in London, Paris, New York, Buenos Aires, and other assorted places and hope for the best.

Fortunately, most of the people in the group weren't quite as attracted to the idea that the Jews should just call it quits in the nationalism market, and a decent conversation ensued. But this guy's question kept ringing in my ears. I found myself grateful that Tali wasn't with us. I wondered how she would have reacted, as she is about to devote two years of her life to the army that he's ashamed of, to the country that he thinks we might as well just dissolve. While he continues to train the next generation of his own country's rabbis.

A couple of weeks later, I was across the Atlantic, in the States, and spent Shabbat with an Orthodox congregation in New Jersey. On Friday night there was an informal gathering in a home. About fifty people or so, and we're chatting about Israel, *aliyah*, Zionism.

One fellow can't resist. You can sort of tell by the look on his face that he knows he shouldn't ask this, but he can't help himself. "But do you really live in Israel?" he asks.

"Gee, I really thought I did," I wanted to say, but I waited.

"I mean, after all, you live in Bakk'a, which is a nice neighborhood, with a lot of Anglos. You work for an American foundation. Your kids go to schools of the sort that don't really exist in other parts of Israel. I don't know, it just doesn't seem like you really live in Israel."

I think I understand where the question is coming from. We've been talking about *aliyah*, and his is a committed Zionist community. But for whatever reason, he doesn't want to go. So, it seems to me, he'll feel better if he can convince himself that even the people he knows who've moved don't *really* live in Israel. They're really just like him.

Once again I'm not quite sure where to begin to respond. Should I tell him about what it was like to put my kids to bed when the shelling was so loud that the entire apartment shook? Or what it's like for those first few moments after you hear the bomb go off until you find your wife on her cell phone and confirm that your kids are OK? Or what it's like to send your kid to school with a gas mask? Not the sort of stuff they do in northern New Jersey, it seemed to me.

Or, I thought, maybe I'd just ask what his oldest kids are up to. Which Ivy League college did they choose to attend? There's nothing wrong with those colleges, of course. I went to one, and I wish that my kids could, too. But my daughter, who's old enough to be at one, isn't. In fact, in a few months, she's also going to move away from home. And dress in green. And spend two years in the army, where she won't get to choose a thing.

Maybe I should ask this guy if his daughter's in the U.S. army. Or the Peace Corps. Or doing "Teach for America." But what's the point? We all know the answer.

Now to be fair, I know that there are lots of American Jews who might like to live in Israel but who have no idea how they'd manage financially. It's not simple. And there are those who can't leave aging parents. Or who don't speak the language and are afraid that they might not be able to learn it. All of that's real.

But still, "Do you really live in Israel?" While we're sitting in a living room the size of my entire apartment? Is *that* the way to have a real conversation about painful decisions?

What was interesting about that Shabbat was that having flown from Western Europe to New Jersey, I suddenly found myself facing the opposite end of the political spectrum. Here, no one was asking whether the Jews would be better off without an army. No one here wondered whether it was time for the Jews to get out of the business of statehood. Precisely the opposite. Here, the problem wasn't the army, or morality. Here, the problem was Ariel Sharon.

During a Q&A session the next morning, the following emerged as a major issue for more than one or two people. "Let's say," one fellow asked on behalf of a group, "that Heaven forbid, Sharon proceeds with his plan to leave Gaza. And that he needs a lot of money to pay for all the relocation of settlers, moving roads, repositioning the army, reshaping the infrastructure, etc. And that therefore, Sharon goes to Washington, either personally or through an emissary, to lobby the president or Congress for loan guarantees to fund this project."

So far, I didn't see a real question, but I had a feeling that when I did, I wasn't going to like it. I was right.

"Do we, or do we not," the questioner then continued, "have a Jewish obligation to go to Capitol Hill and to lobby Congress not to give Sharon the guarantees? You know, to punish him, of course, for having gone ahead with the disengagement. To show him that we won't abide that."

Of course, it's not Sharon who would be punished, is it? Sharon, one can assume, will have all the protection he needs. The money will come from an already stretched budget. And it's kids—poor kids—who will go to school without the services they need. Sharon, quite rightly, will have the medical care he needs. It will be others (about a quarter of Israel's population lives at or below the poverty line) who will pay the price. Sharon has finished with school; it will be Israel's kids who will not have the basic educational resources that they need and deserve.

But does any of this come into play as these people—highly committed and very observant Jews—talk about whether they ought to lobby against Israel in Congress? Not in the least. Because they know what's right. And if Israel won't be the kind of country *they* want, why should it exist?

About this, the left and the right actually agree. The fellow from Europe says, "If Israel can't be the pacifist entity I wish it could be, let it not exist." And the right says, "If Sharon doesn't conduct his foreign policy the way that we think he should, let's punish Israel's poor."

What's one to do? Flee back to Israel, what else? After all, there, where the people actually have to live with the consequences of their utterances, one could expect the vitriol to be moderated. Right?

Wrong. Very wrong.

The morning paper on my first day back sported a photograph of Rabbi Moshe Hirsch, one of the leaders of the anti-Zionist Neturei Karta group leading a delegation of fringe ultra-Orthodox Jews to the Muqata'a (the walled compound first built by the British in the 1920s that the Palestinians took control of in 1994, a year after the Oslo peace accords, and transformed into the Ramallah governorate) outside Ramallah at the conclusion of the forty-day mourning period for Yassir Arafat. Religious Jews going to mourn the death of the murderer of Jewish women, children, and men? Absolutely. Why not? After all, if the Neturei Karta believe that Jews ought to have delayed creating the State of Israel until the Messiah came, then the State of Israel was created in sin. And it should therefore be destroyed, no? So what's so strange about Jews going to pay their respects to the person who basically invented Palestinian terrorism?

And then, as if that's not enough to make you wonder what's happening to the Jews, the announcement in the news of a poll showing that 52 percent of those living in Gaza (most people call them "settlers," but for a variety of reasons, I'll simply refer to them as "Israeli citizens living in Gaza") were committed to resisting the withdrawal with physical force. With their own bodies, or worse.

But then, since that didn't seem to dissuade Sharon from continuing with his disengagement plan, they decided to up the ante. They decided that they'd walk around wearing orange stars on their clothes, in a clear reference to the yellow stars that the Nazis forced Jews to wear under the Third Reich (until they sent those Jews into gas chambers and up chimneys).

To make the point that . . . what point, exactly? That Adolf Hitler and Ariel Sharon are in some way comparable? That Sharon, no matter what one may think of him, can be accused of wanting to eradicate the Jews? That there's anything that the Reichstag of the 1930s and the Knesset of 2004 share in common? That if you don't see the issue my way, then you're no better than, and no different from, the worst enemy the Jews have ever had? *That*'s what political discourse in this country has come to?

So there they went. Parading around in orange stars until the Ministry of Education said that kids could not come to school that way, and the broader public expressed outrage at the stars. What are they trying to say? That our kids—my kid, literally—who might well be ordered to carry out the withdrawal and who will obey those orders, are akin to storm troopers?

That's the kind of accusation, in a society such as this, that could easily start the whole thing unraveling. So the Gazan Israelis backed off and dropped the stars. And said, "Oh, and we're sorry if we offended any survivors. That was the farthest thing from our minds." But forget the offense for one moment. The really troubling thing is what they thought. Just like the academic from Western Europe, the hard-liners from New Jersey, and the kooky anti-Zionist Neturei Karta hassidim praying at Arafat's grave. What do they all have in common?

It is, I think, an inability to deal with internal conflict, with personal discord. If an Israel at war can't be a moral paradise, who needs Israel? If talking about *aliyah* makes me uncomfortable, let's point to the non-Israeliness of those who *have* gone. If Sharon goes ahead with the disengagement, the question isn't "How do I continue to love Israel even when I think that a grave mistake has been made?" but rather, "How do I punish Sharon?" Even if the punishment I choose to exact further endangers Israel.

Sixty years after Jews stood perched on the edge of extinction, and this is what we've come to.

One person who gets it is IDF chief of staff Moshe (Boogy) Ya'alon. He recently met with the leaders of those Israeli citizens of Gaza and the West Bank and requested that they tone down the rhetoric. Don't put the soldiers in an impossible situation, he said, and stop asking them to refuse orders when the order to withdraw comes.

They refused. "We can't," they said, "it's too late." A direct quote. Ya'alon spoke to the press afterward and expressed his worry about the very future of the state. And he used the word *churban*, which means "destruction," but which is a heavily laden Hebrew word. It's synonymous in our world for the destruction of the Temples, the end of sovereign Jewish life. Say *churban*, and literate Jews see Jerusalem going up in flames. Say *churban*, and Jews think of the Temples in ruins, a calamity that the rabbis attribute to senseless hatred between Jew and Jew.

Funny how history repeats itself, no? Actually, not funny at all.

Tonight, it's still heating up. The news is reporting that earlier today, in the evacuation of an illegal settlement in Yizhar, shots were fired for the first time. The IDF is trying hard to downplay the incident, saying that a soldier simply fired in the air. Maybe. Maybe not.

And in the face of all this, Sharon is insisting that the disengagement will go forward. If anything, he asserts, he plans to move up the timetable. And send the army in to pull those people out if he has to.

Reasonable minds can differ, obviously, as to whether the withdrawal is a good idea. Both sides have strong arguments to make, and all arguments have their weaknesses. That's precisely why this is so agonizing.

But it's one thing to have an opinion, and another to decide that if things won't go the way I want, I'd rather have the whole enterprise topple. That's the one thing that left-wingers in Europe, right-wingers on the East Coast of the United States, the anti-Zionist Rabbi Moshe Hirsch, and the Gaza-dwelling star wearers all have in common. They agree that if it doesn't happen their way, it shouldn't happen at all.

What they all lack is a sense that though they'd rather things were otherwise, they'll stick with the enterprise no matter what. What they all lack is the sense that though they have strong opinions, they recognize that there might be some legitimacy to other viewpoints. What they are all missing is the Talmudic insight that discourse is genuinely religious—and wholly Jewish—when conflicting opinions coexist on the same page, locked in respectful combat for generations to follow. What we, and they, are missing, is the sort of nuanced thinking that once made Judaism profound.

Jerusalem didn't fall, our tradition insists, primarily because of the Romans. It fell due to infighting among the Jews. That's the Talmud's way of warning us.

So far, we've lost our ability to listen to each other. But if we're not careful, we're going to lose much more than that.

This Is Why We're Here

There's a new bookstore on Emek Refa'im Street. Tamir Books, part of a larger chain. Nothing worthy of notice by Barnes and Noble standards, but in Israeli terms, it's a nice place. Well stocked, well lit, and clean, with a knowledgeable and helpful staff.

The only downside is that I pass it on my way home from one of our offices, which means I walk by it often. And I'm not very good at walking by it without going in. Or at going in without buying something. So this new little bookstore is getting to be a bit of a financial liability.

But it's a liability that I'm more than happy to have to contend with. Because I think this bookstore is a miracle.

A miracle? A bookstore? Actually, yes. But we'll come back to that.

In the past few months we've had more than a few Americans over to the house while they're here on missions to Israel. So we talk to them about what they've gone to see. Yad Vashem, the national memorial to the victims of the Holocaust. The security fence, the national attempt to stay alive. An archaeological site, often Masada. Briefings with this government official or that one. An Ethiopian resettlement project. Stuff like that, all well and good. And invariably, a visit to an Israeli army base.

It's hard for me to put my finger on why there's something distressing about that visit to an army base. But it troubles me. So I ask people, "If you were going to France for two weeks, would it ever occur to you that one of the must-sees was a French army base?" The answer, obviously, is no.

Or bring things closer to home. "If some Israelis were going to come to the States for a couple of weeks, and you wanted to show them the country as best you could, would you take them to an army base?" Obviously not. So why here? What's really going on here?

And then a good friend from the States comes over. He's on a mission, but not just any old mission. He's on a men's mission. And sure enough, Yad Vashem. Masada. A meeting with a representative of the foreign ministry. And a visit to an army base.

But not just any visit to an army base. No, their bus takes them to a base where they're given a VIP welcome and some better-than-average army chow, and where after a few minutes of instruction, they're given a chance to fire M-16's at a firing range. "Totally awesome," he tells me with that "toys for boys" look of glee on his face.

And now, I'm more than bothered. I'm pretty sick. Part of me wants to ask him who's paying for those bullets. We are, obviously. But that's kind of petty and misses the point. The real point, of course, is that what our kids have to do during the day and during the night, in the cold and in the heat, in the mud and in the dust, these guys are doing as a bit of sport. Because it's cool.

But it's really not cool. And what's worse, it communicates entirely the wrong idea about what Israel is. Firing M-16's is really not why we have a country. We don't have a country so we can have an army. We have an army so we can have a country. That's why you don't take people to Fort Bragg if they're coming to the States for a tourist visit. Because Fort Bragg, as important as it may be, is not what the States is *about*. The United States is about the Smithsonian. The White House. Capitol Hill. The National Archives. Disneyland (maybe). Fort Bragg exists so the United States can exist. Not the other way around.

One day, shortly after learning about this firing spree, I mention to another visiting group that this whole phenomenon troubles me. Most are uninterested. A few look sheepishly at the ground, suddenly fascinated by the shoelaces on their Nikes. And one or two ask, "Fair enough. So where do you suggest that we go instead? What would you suggest we see?"

That, too, is a fair question. So I suggest the bilingual school in Jerusalem, which is actually a euphemism for binational, where Jewish and Arab kids study together (otherwise, basically unheard of in Israel), in both Hebrew and Arabic. Or Alyn Hospital, an orthopedic hospital for kids that does unbelievable rehabilitation. Or a park in our little neighborhood on a Shabbat afternoon, I say. And just look at the people. Young and old, religious and secular, immigrants and natives, all walks of professional and economic life, hanging out together, playing with their kids, carefree, rebuilding a Jewish society in a part of the world where you'd have thought that by now, life would have come to a grinding halt. And hasn't. Not by a long shot.

Or go, I tell them, to Yad Vashem and see the trauma with which this country still wrestles. But from there, go to the emergency room at Shaarey Zedek Hospital, a Jewish religious hospital, and see the Arabs lining up for care, and the devotion and respect with which they are treated. And ask yourself, how does a country like this, formed out of the ashes of twentieth-century Europe, somehow manage to transcend the horrors of Nazi Europe and to reach out that way? Not perfectly, and not all the time. But much more than anyone would have expected.

Or go to Tel Aviv, and we'll seek out the most cutting-edge, Jewishly informed art and music scenes. Maybe Achinoam Nini, the singer. And others. And witness a people come alive, after the precipice. And from there, we'd head to the area of the old bus station in Tel Aviv and look around. Homeless people, and prostitutes. Foreign workers not given their due. And we'd ask, how is it that one country can produce both Achinoam Nini and the bus station's neighborhood, with its poverty and neglect? The answer? This is about nation building. A long, slow, difficult, messy—and in our case, miraculous—project.

Maybe, if we get lucky, we could have you meet Aharon Barak, the Chief Justice of the Supreme Court. The court that has ruled that the route of the fence must be changed. That has limited the use of torture by the Israeli security forces, arguing that in order to preserve the Jewish sensibility and soul that underlie this country, it is even worth risking Jewish life. How many countries have a court that rules that way about their enemy? In times of war?

And then, it occurs to me. "Go to the Tamir Bookstore on Emek Refa'im," I tell them. They look at me, incredulous.

"Seriously," I insist. Go to the bookstore. And there, not on the army base, you'll find the real miracle that this place is. A store full of books in a language restored and brought back to life, like the nation that reads that language. A store with hundreds upon hundreds of new titles, written exclusively for a country with a population less than that of the Los Angeles metropolitan area. Pulitzer Prize–quality literature, and the Hebrew equivalent of Harlequin romances. Guidebooks, cookbooks, and children's books. Mysteries and memoirs. History, philosophy, art. Some international best sellers translated into Hebrew. A tiny store by B&N standards, but an enormous miracle nonetheless.

And it reminds me that a few weeks earlier, I'd passed by Tamir and, in the window, saw dozens of copies of a new book I hadn't seen before. A bright red band across the bottom of the cover caught my attention, so I took a look. *The Poems*, by Hayyim Nahman Bialik, Israel's unofficial poet laureate, the antitraditional but deeply learned national muse, who died in 1934.

Intrigued, I decided to go into the store to check it out. Bialik has been dead for three quarters of a century. So what could be new about a book of his poetry? A new edition, it turns out. A new light commentary, an introduction to each poem, a brief biography.

In the throes of everything it's been through in the past four years, this country is still reading, discussing, and publishing poetry. It's a country alive. A people revived. Which, when you get right down to it, is why we live here.

So I take a copy off the shelf, fully cognizant that as we already have a copy of Bialik's collected works, there's really no justification for this. (And thus, it will raise some spousal eyebrows, at best.) But I want it. I take it to the cashier and, still feeling a little bit guilty, say to her, "Gift wrap, please." My friend Pini will like this. I'll give it to him.

She's working on the wrapping, and I'm already missing the book I haven't yet given to Pini. So I go back to the shelf and take another one. "Wrap that one, too?" she wants to know. "No," I tell her. "This one I'm keeping." This one is why I'm here.

On the way out of the store, I notice another new item on one of the display tables. A box, also with a wide red band across the bottom. Doesn't look like a book, doesn't look like a CD. I've got no idea what it is. So, my two newly acquired copies of Bialik in hand, I walk over to the table to read more carefully. "Yossi Banai reads Psalms."

Yossi Banai is a pretty popular singer and, more recently, a newly religious folk artist. I look a little closer. It's a CD of Banai reading nineteen different Psalms, put to music by another artist. "Is this any good?" I ask one of the salespeople, who's just walking by.

"We can't keep it in stock," she says.

I look at the price tag. Not terrible, but with the volumes of Bialik in hand, Yossi Banai might be pushing my luck a bit. So I hold off. Maybe the next time I walk by, I tell myself.

A week or two later, a colleague of mine hands me a Tamir bag after we finish a meeting. "What's this?" I ask her.

"I saw it at Tamir, and I thought you'd like it."

"What's the occasion?"

"None. Enjoy," she says, and bids the office adieu.

When I get home, I open the wrapping, and it is, of course, Yossi Banai and his CD of Psalms. I call her up to thank her. Forget it, she says. "It's just hard not to buy that stuff when it comes out, no?"

That's what we're about, I tell myself after we hang up. Displays with books and CDs. Poetry and music. Modern verse and ancient verse. The antireligious Bialik alongside the newly religious Banai. A people in the only place in the world where the rich tapestry called Jewish life can come to life in this way.

It's really not about the square kilometers. Or the precise lines of the borders, as important as they are. It's about the content, not the contours. It's about the substance of what gets built here, what gets revived. It's about what gets healed, renewed, and bequeathed to another generation.

"Don't you see?" I wish I could say to my friends before they go to those army bases. This place isn't about guns. Precisely the opposite is the case. It's about life.

A WAGER, AND
A PRAYER

February 2005~October 2005

Lucky, Don't You Think?

Micha and I were doing some of his Talmud homework together last night, when he needed a break. So I suggested that we watch the news. We flipped on CNN, which Micha thought was pretty boring. Almost immediately, though, CNN got to a story about Israel preparing to let the Palestinian Authority take over security in five Palestinian cities. Suddenly, he was all ears.

"What did she say Israel is going to do?" he wanted to know. I explained. "Why would we do that?" he asked.

"So we can have peace," I told him, suddenly struck by how ridiculous that must sound to an eleven-year-old kid who probably can't remember not being at war, who actually doesn't know what it means to be at peace.

"What, we give them the land and then we just trust them not to start attacking us again?" Well, yeah, basically, I told him. I knew that that sounded pretty Pollyannaish on our part, and I was struggling to figure out something more encouraging to say when I realized that I didn't quite know how to do that. Come to think about it, given the past few years, it *does* sound kind of naïve. I was suddenly really sorry that we'd taken a break from Talmud.

"Well, if we give them the land and then they start firing rockets again or sending suicide bombers, do we get our land back?"

"Our" land, I noticed that he'd said. That was interesting. He can't remember not being at war, and he can't remember the days when we didn't have that land. He's never known a different map.

Do we just get our land back? I didn't know whether to laugh or cry. To laugh, because the idea that we'd just magically get the land returned to us was so cute, or to cry, because he's right. What does, in fact, happen, if this whole thing is a wager that doesn't work out? Not a bad point, kiddo. No, I told him, we don't get our land back.

"Well, Abba, right that the whole world thinks Israel should give back the land?" Terrible English, translated, I realized, from the Hebrew. Yeah, right. "And right that every time Israel does something to them after they attack us, the world thinks Israel was wrong?" Yup.

"Well, do you think that after we give back the land, if we have to attack them again because they keep firing on us, the world will understand this time?" I don't know, I told him, appalled by how convincing an eleven-year-old could be. "Well, Abba, they won't remember. We won't have our land, and the world will still hate us. I think we're just being dumb."

Out of the mouths of babes. Everyone knows that things here are changing, and changing rapidly. What we can't figure out is whether things are suddenly getting much, much better, or whether, unawares, we're careering toward another gross miscalculation, as we apparently did with Oslo.

Whichever it will be, what almost everyone seems to have in common is that they're unhappy. Those in favor of making these accommodations to the Palestinians are afraid that the relative peace we've got now won't last. They're afraid that Sharon will do something provocative to create an excuse for a military response, or that the terrorists will provide it. And those opposed, who are afraid we're being duped again and who say that if Oslo hadn't been derailed we'd have been in much more trouble than we are now, are worried that we might continue to make concessions until it's too late. For, as Micha pointed out, once the land's given away, that's it. There'll be no getting it back.

Still others are afraid of missing an opportunity that might not reappear so quickly. Abu Mazen (or Abbas, as he's typically called in the West) is proving not to be a doormat. The Kassam rockets raining down on the town of Sderot (inside Israel proper) and other places haven't completely stopped, but so far, the reduction has been dramatic. Jerusalem was on high alert yesterday because of fears that a bomber had gotten through security checkpoints and was now somewhere in Israel, and elsewhere we did snag a sixteen-year-old kid with an explosive belt yesterday as well; so far, though, we're catching them all in time. Six soldiers were wounded in combat yesterday, but no one died. All in all, it's been very quiet for a very long time.

So quiet, in fact, that people are getting nervous.

And they're getting nervous because of the prime minister's plan. Ariel Sharon is still trying to orchestrate his "disengagement," a withdrawal from (others would say "flight from") Gaza and some West Bank settlements. Preparations are being made, as Micha discovered last night, for Israel to hand over control of four or five Arab West Bank cities, including Ramallah and Jericho, to the Palestinian security forces. Israel's offering to release nine hundred Palestinian prisoners. Then Mubarak invites Abbas and Sharon to Sharm, again, for a summit. And Sharon accepts, right away.

One wonders how many people, on both sides, would still be living if Arafat had only done us—Israelis and Palestinians alike—the favor of dying a few years earlier.

Even the looming civil war that some are predicting if Sharon tries to pry the inhabitants of the Jewish settlements in Gaza out of their homes seems to be shocking people to their senses. Some, of course, are still convinced that civil war is really going to break out. I was meeting with a faculty member a couple of days ago about a conference she's planning at our institute in June, which will bring about sixty people to us from abroad. We talked about teaching, curriculum, faculty, the budget. And then she asked, "We should probably send them an e-mail, though, letting them know that there's a reasonable chance of a civil war in June, no?"

I just laughed. And said no. We're not going to send any such e-mail.

Because I just don't believe that at the end of the day we're going to be that stupid. Perhaps it's not coincidental that after months of a united front, cracks appeared in the settler bloc this week. This week— the week after Elie Weisel spoke at the General Assembly. The week after "Hatikvah" was played for the first time at the United Nations. The week that German president Horst Koehler addressed the Knesset and began his speech in Hebrew. The week that we were reminded, on the sixtieth anniversary of the liberation of what was left of the human beings in Auschwitz, that we can't afford to risk losing what we have.

This morning, the paper ran a front-page article about Rabbi Yaakov Meidan, a well-known rabbi from one of Israel's finest yeshivot, who encouraged the army and the settlers to negotiate before the disengagement how each side will behave, and suggested that both sides forswear the use of force. Interesting. I'm not sure how an army can commit itself to not using force, but at least someone seems to be thinking outside the box.

It's not easy, after so many years of this Intifada, after the seemingly interminable days, weeks, months, and years of bombing after bombing, the guards in front of every door, the faces of the dead on the front page of the newspaper, the dread of waking up in the morning and turning on the radio—to believe that something may really be changing. There's a danger in believing, of course. We've walked down the rosy path before and have been burned, badly.

Elisheva and I were watching the news the other night, trying to keep abreast of everything that's changing, when she turned to me and asked, "Do you think it's for real?"

"I don't know," I said. "Kind of hard to believe it, no? What do you think?"

"I think I can't do it again," she said to me, in a virtual whisper. "I just can't go back to that again, not after this." And she reached for my hand, a signal that she didn't want to talk, that there was too much at stake for words to capture.

And I remembered Avi telling me at the very beginning of the war, "I can't do this anymore." He did stick it out, but that was a long time ago. Things got a lot worse after that, and now, Elisheva's right. We can't delude ourselves; we know how bad it will be if this falls apart. It will be literally unbearable.

But there's a chance that all of that may be changing. And that mere possibility is going to force major change for lots of people. Those Jews—both inside Israel and out—who have fashioned their entire Zionist orientation on the notion of Israel at war with an implacable Arab or Palestinian enemy are going to have to do the readjusting. There are lots of Diaspora Jews, and Israeli Jews, whose Zionist passion is expressed mostly in terms of hating our enemies. This position has its more sophisticated versions and its less sophisticated (more racist) formulations. But what they all share is that their conception of what it means to be an Israeli or a Zionist is to be at war. To be united against an intractable enemy. To know that we are at war for our lives, for our very survival, and that all other issues are secondary.

What happens if suddenly we're not at war anymore? Then what? What will they be passionate about then?

And once the religious right loses its territorial aspirations, its considerable—and admirable—ideological passion will likely get focused elsewhere. They'll probably start devoting themselves to what's happening inside what's left of this country. What kind of a society this is. How Jewish it is, and how it is Jewish. How this place is different from some sort of Sweden in the middle of the Middle East. What if those people who now live in Gaza, and the many thousands who support them, can actually get beyond the focus on borders that now lies at the heart of their Zionist passions and ask penetrating questions about the rapidly disappearing Jewish core of this society, and take *that* on as their new challenge? What would happen then? For better or for worse, secular Israeli society may also be in for a rude awakening.

Rude awakenings seem to be the order of things these days. A couple of weeks ago, Talia came home from her yeshiva for a home-cooked dinner and said, quite matter-of-factly, "Oh, I'm getting drafted on Tuesday."

That's nice, honey. Would you pass the salad, please?

Micha perked up. "You're going into the *army*? Now?" He looked at her with apparent disbelief. Or was it something else?

She's not actually going into the army now; that happens this summer. But still, it was a big day for her. She came home the next day to drop off her newly acquired duffle bag with all her gear. (It may have been newly acquired, but it was far from new; it had the names of half a dozen previous "owners" scrawled all over it.) We chatted a bit about what the day had been like. Long, she said. What did they do? A lecture about this, instructions about that. They'd also given the eight hundred women being inducted that day flu shots, dog tags, ID cards, etc., and taken blood. "What did they take blood for?" I wanted to know. "DNA, in case they need to identify us later," she said.

Lovely. What do you say to that?

I thought, before she went, that that day was going to be a momentous one for me. That it would probably have made our being here feel permanent, because you can sell a house or change jobs, but you can't get your kid out of the army. Or even out of the country, actually, once she's in the army.

Sending a child into the army punches our ticket here in a way that buying a house or getting a job doesn't. I remember the day that our moving van, filled with all our earthly possessions, showed up at the home we'd bought. Before it arrived, I'd expected that we'd be thrilled. It had been a year and a half since we'd had our own furniture, our own dishes, the pictures from our walls.

Somehow, though, for both Elisheva and for me, that day was much more traumatic than we'd expected. We were excited to be settling down, but when the enormous truck parked in front of the house, and a crane started lifting everything in, our move suddenly felt permanent. This wasn't an adventure anymore. It was real. We'd emigrated. We lived here. Suddenly, going "back" wasn't nearly as simple as buying some tickets and grabbing a cab to the airport.

But if that step years ago felt permanent, this is the real deal. She's not ours anymore. No more writing a note to get her out of something if she doesn't feel well. No more deciding what's too dangerous for her. No more helping her figure out what the best use of her time is. She belongs to them, not to us. They, not we, will set her agenda, her schedule, her assignments. They, not we, will decide what risks she should take. Because now she's part of something much bigger than a family. This, more than anything else we or she has ever done, makes our being here "official."

So, I would have figured that the day would have evoked some sort of patriotic rush. But it didn't, not really. We were proud of her, obviously, but there was something nagging at me that I couldn't put my finger on.

Two days later, completely coincidentally, I was in New York and had a meeting with one of our faculty members who's in New York this year. We decided to meet on Columbia's campus, the campus on which I lived and studied when I was exactly Talia's age. It was winter break, so the campus was pretty deserted. And it was cold, so there weren't too many people hanging around outside. But there were a few. Kids, exactly my daughter's age, hanging out, walking in and out of the library, lounging around the bookstore. Doing exactly what I'd done there almost thirty years earlier. Doing what I suddenly realized I wished my kid was doing.

Which was when it dawned on me why I wasn't terribly thrilled when I saw Talia walk through the door with a duffle bag bigger than she is. What I really would have liked would have been for her to have come home not with a duffle bag and a new monochromatic wardrobe, but with Plato's *Republic*, Augustine's *Confessions*, and maybe some Hannah Arendt. *Eichmann in Jerusalem: A Report on the Banality of Evil*, perhaps. She could probably relate to that after the last few years.

What I would have liked is for her to live in a world very different from the one she inhabits. One in which she could live here but not be at war; one in which she could live here and instead of spending two years doing things that she won't even be able to tell us about (in that way, the army's perfect for a teenager—it actually becomes illegal to talk to your parents about your life), one in which we might actually talk about what she's read or what she's thinking about. What I wish is that she was starting two years in which she could think about what a different world might look like, rather than spending two years hunting down the bad guys.

What if eighteen-year-olds just got to go to college here one day? Now, *that* would be a change, no?

In the meantime, though, they don't. And their siblings know it. We were walking to the home of some friends last Shabbat, and as we have on hundreds of occasions, we passed the memorial at the side of the street to Iris, the nineteen-year-old soldier who lived in the house across the street from her memorial. Micha's seen it more times than he can count, and he doesn't even notice it anymore. But this time he stopped and looked. And read.

We were a couple of minutes late, so I urged him on. But he hung back for a minute and then said, "Abba, what's this mean?"

"What does what mean?"

"What it says here."

I looked at the stone. Nothing terribly complicated about it. The stone had the insignia of the IDF on the upper row, and below it, in simple Hebrew:

In memory of the soldier
Iris Azoulai, *hy'd*
Here her blood was spilled
by a murderer
whilst in the performance of her mission
2 Heshvan 5751 21.10.90
Nineteen years old when she fell
May her soul be bound up in the bonds of life

I looked at Micha staring at the stone and then again at the words. What was there not to understand?

"What do you want to know?" I asked him.

"I don't get it," he said.

"Get what?"

He looked toward Tali, who'd walked ahead with Elisheva and Avi, and then up at me and said, "I thought girls don't get hurt in the army."

I took a deep breath and then held his hand. "They don't, not usually," I told him as we started walking.

"But this girl did," he said.

"She did," I admitted. And I knew that I should tell him that Tali would be OK, that that was what he really worried about, but I couldn't say it. There was something about even verbalizing the unthinkable that I just couldn't do.

"Things are getting better here," I told him. "Those sorts of terrible things are going to stop."

I don't know if I thought I was telling him the truth. But it might just happen, that's the amazing thing. Not tomorrow, and not next year. But maybe in time for Tali's kids, who, if we're lucky, might not come home with a green duffle. It's that knowledge, that awareness, that has many of us so hopeful that we're afraid to admit even to ourselves how great it could all be if it worked. Even the people I'd least expect to be hopeful can't help but be carried along by it all.

Last Friday night, I was in shul sitting near a friend who is politically way to the right of me, who's been banging the drums of warning for four years now. Every Shabbat. Week in and week out, he's got some warning about how we've got to get tough with them or, more recently, how we'd better not give away the store. He sat down next to me and then made some comment about the blossoming of "Oslo II," which I assumed was a prelude to how this was all going to backfire.

"So what do you make of it?" I asked him.

"You know," he said. "I'm not sure anymore. Abu Mazen might really make a difference." I was just grateful that we hadn't been at a point in the service where we'd have been standing. I would have fallen over.

The service continued, and the singing picked up. Within minutes, the whole room was reverberating with the sounds of people who, pretty serious political divisions and lots of other differences notwithstanding, get together every week to usher in Shabbat, which is itself, on a certain level, about imagining a different kind of reality. And in the midst of it all, with the singing so powerful that we could barely hear each other speak, my friend leaned over to me and whispered into my ear, "You know, who knows what will be here? But I'll tell you . . . we're so damn lucky to be living here, don't you think?"

I looked at him and looked at the crowd. I looked at my kids, speaking bad English as they translate from Hebrew, going to the army instead of to college. Kids, though, who would never dream of not going to the army. And kids who, when they look at the map, see "our" land and know exactly where they belong. Kids who, if the adults don't screw this up, might just enter adulthood in a very different kind of reality. Maybe.

Not bad, not bad at all. And I thought again about what he'd said. "We're so damned lucky to be living here, don't you think?"

I do. I do, indeed.

Yeah, Right.

Boarding my flight at Newark for the trip home, I'm exhausted. In line at the door of the plane, there's nothing I want except to get into my seat and fall asleep. A flight attendant at the door offers me a paper, but I thank her and decline. I've seen the news. Abbas and Sharon, Mubarak and Bush, all at Sharm al-Sheikh. Another summit. But summits have come and summits have gone, and I don't want a newspaper. I just want to sleep.

But as I'm walking past the newspaper cart, the *Yedioth Ahronoth* catches my eye. At the top of the page, on the left, a little emblem printed on the page. "*Gilayon Meyuhad*," it says. "Special Edition—The Sharm Summit."

Special edition? OK, I'll take one.

She hands me the paper. A smiling Abbas, standing next to a smiling Sharon, with a green and perfectly manicured Sharm (which, of course, was Israel's from 1967 until we returned it under Begin in 1982 after the Camp David Accords). And in huge print across the page, in white letters with a blue border, two simple Hebrew words: "*Ha-Intifada Histaymah*"—"The Intifada Is Over."

That's cool, I think. A paper to keep. I'll bring it home to show the kids, since we get the stodgy *Ha-Aretz*, which never has graphics like this.

I flip through the pages. The expected stories. Sharon and Abbas declared an end to the violence. Sharon pledged to end military operations against Palestinians, and President Abbas said that the Palestinians would end "all acts of violence against Israelis . . . wherever they are." Sharon said that the agreement is part of the goal of "quiet, dignified and peaceful lives for all the nations in the Middle East." Abbas said, "the calm that is currently prevailing in our territories signals the start of a new era, the start of a hopeful peace."

It may last, and it may not. But either way, it's a newspaper I want the kids to see. I fold it up, and put it in my carry-on so the stewardess doesn't pick it up if I fall asleep.

A short while later, the guy next to me gets up from his seat. I glance at his paper. It's *Ma'ariv*, the other tabloidesque Israeli daily. A similar picture of Abbas and Sharon, but a different headline. "*Ulai Ha-Pa'am?*" it says. "Maybe this time?"

Also worth keeping.

When he returns, he takes the paper and puts it on the floor. "Do you want your paper?" I ask him. "No," he says, "take it." I do.

The next morning, the kids are hanging around the dining room table. As I'm unpacking, I pull out the *Yedioth*. "Take a look at this," I say to them.

Avi looks at the headline, and says, "Yeah. Right."

And Talia, home for some reason, asks, bewildered, "You actually *believe* that?"

I thought I did. And I look at them, so dismissive without even having to think about it that suddenly, I'm not sure.

The Bird's Nest in Shul

A week ago Friday night, shul was packed as usual. We were sitting in our regular seats along the right-hand side wall, facing most everyone else. As we were making our way through the service, I noticed a few of the fathers getting their sons' attention, pointing to something on the wall, to our right, and apparently above us. From where we were seated, the only thing that I could see that they might have been pointing to was the large white stone plaque, not far from us, in memory of the two young men from the shul who died in the Yom Kippur War. But that plaque has been there for a long time, certainly ever since we joined the shul, so I knew that it couldn't have been that.

But what was it? When we got to a point in the service where everyone stands, I was able to move a bit, and I craned my neck to see what they might have been pointing out to their kids. There's an arched window there, almost carved into the thick walls of the old Arab building that's now a synagogue, a building that was a shoe factory until the Arab owners and residents of the neighborhood "fled" (a loaded term if ever there was one) in 1948. The smaller semicircular window at the very top of the arch was open a few inches, and wedged between the frame of the window and the glass pane, a bird had built a nest.

The nest rested there precariously, mostly outside the shul but partly inside, the occasional twig already having fallen in and come to rest on the sill way below. But precarious or not, there it was. The weather has gotten warmer, winter is receding, and the birds, apparently, are getting ready to usher in a new round of life. Once I saw it, I, too, like the kids and many of their parents, was mesmerized by the nest. There was something uncanny about the array of twigs that some bird apparently wanted to call home. Perched where it wouldn't seem to have a chance, it was built against all odds and was hanging in there—for the time being.

Its fragility, the knowledge that even an accidental nudge of the window would send it falling to the ground outside the synagogue, made it all the more arresting. The nest, it struck me, was precisely in the position that we are—signs of new life all around, a thaw of sorts, but a pervasive precariousness all at the same time. One breeze that's just a bit too strong or a slight push on the window, and the nest will be gone.

And us? Life seems to be beginning anew here, too. As painful as the thought of the disengagement that lies ahead is, and as violent as the reaction that some fear will accompany it may be, there are signs of renewed life here. Of a country that wants to get beyond the endless conflict. A country the majority of which wants—despite the pain of the decision—to get out of a place that tens of thousands of our soldiers—our kids—have to patrol, against impossible odds. There are more than a million Palestinians in Gaza, and six thousand Israelis in Jewish settlements. The force that it takes to keep that small group safe, most Israelis have decided, simply doesn't make sense. Especially when it's clear that we're going to leave: either now, or when the world forces us out.

Those who live in Gaza obviously disagree. They think we're being duped (possible), that they're being shafted (no question), and that Sharon has cleverly manipulated a democratic process to adopt a position precisely the opposite of what they thought he would do when they elected him (true).

All that's true. But in the rest of the country, there are murmurings of people ready to move on, anxious to begin to work on other parts of this enterprise. There are signs of a country that wants to address the economy, the poverty, the health care crisis, and the crumbling education system. And there are signs that the prime minister, after a lifelong career of defending and capturing land, now understands that Israel will not survive with those lands and that population under our control, and therefore is waging what is to my mind a courageous and seemingly Sisyphian campaign to get the plan through, before it's too late.

So how do people deal with precariousness? I can't say that this is true of the whole country, but in our little pocket of Israeli life, we deal by holding our breath and by not thinking about it. No one's talking about what's happening, or what could happen. We haven't had a political conversation at the Shabbat table in months. No one brings it up. When someone accidentally says something about the world of geopolitics, it gets treated as if they made an unfortunate social gaffe, as if the only polite thing to do is to pretend that no one heard it and to move on to something else. Even our kids don't talk about it anymore. They're a bit split on the disengagement, but they read the paper, draw their own and independent conclusions, and never, ever mention it. Everyone's just holding their breath, waiting to see if it will happen, and if it does, waiting to see if all hell is going to break loose.

At work, faculty and staff still gather over coffee and the morning papers as the day gets started, but no one says much about what is—or is not—happening. As if the papers were about some country far away. As if whatever unfolds here isn't going to alter forever the fate of the place we call home.

At a recent faculty meeting someone actually asked if that was healthy. Is it fair or responsible, he wanted to know, to be training a significant slice of the social and educational leadership elite of the country, and not to talk about the simmering internal conflict that is shaking the very foundations of this society? Can we not address the very real possibility of civil war in just over three months?

Everyone nodded. An important set of issues, indeed. So what should we do? What kind of conversation should we engender? How do you have the discussion without its deteriorating into useless prattle? We chatted about it for a few minutes, and then before you knew it, the subject had changed. And I haven't heard anyone raise it again since.

Because we're all in that proverbial nest. A breath too loud, a move at the wrong time, and the whole thing could come crashing down.

Those opposed are praying that somehow, Sharon will lose the budget vote this week, sending the country into elections and into a paralysis that will prevent the disengagement, a disengagement they're convinced would be a terrible blow to Israel's strategic and diplomatic position.

Those who are in favor are holding their breath, hoping that he stays in power—and stays alive—long enough to get this done so the country can start planning a future. The far right, though, is not holding its breath. It's already burning tires on major highways, in a foreshadowing of the civil unrest they plan to unleash. They want us to see how disruptive they'll be able to be even without touching a trigger (an option some of them have not forsworn).

And though the disengagement is, on the surface, simply about Israel's borders, it actually threatens to undo a fragile social and religious truce that holds all of Israeli society together. When those opposed to the disengagement tried again last week to get approval for a referendum on the disengagement (a referendum that they are convinced they'll win, putting an end to the disengagement, which is why Sharon is refusing to have such a vote), they were warned by the left that if a referendum does take place, the left will engineer things so that there's also a referendum on civil marriage (which does not exist in Israel, which the left very much wants, and to which the right is opposed, since it wants to protect the hegemony of the Orthodox chief rabbinate over such matters). Another item for a referendum, the right was reminded, could be the exemption that the ultra-Orthodox currently have from military and national service. (The left would end it, while the right wants to protect it.) Or they could call for a referendum on the fragile social agreement that religious and secular Jews have constructed regarding Shabbat policy. (The left would like public buses to run, for example, while the right has thus far prevented that in most of the country.) Suddenly, the pro-referendum enthusiasm of some of the far right, which cares much more about domestic religious issues than it does about foreign policy issues, seemed to wane.

So, what do we have? Those threatened with removal from their homes in Gaza are threatening violence, some even promising that they will shoot soldiers who come to dislodge them. The left threatens to undo the fragile social contract that allows a simmering religious war to be held in check, and the prime minister's security is so nervous about his being killed by another Jew that they virtually crawl over him like ants. Either way, it's probably not exactly what Herzl had in mind when he spoke about the resolution of the Jewish Problem, is it? Or is it?

But what's amazing about this place is how optimistic the people with whom we work and socialize still feel. There's no reason to suppose that a nest can be built on a marginally open window, but apparently, it has managed to survive all the forces that could bring it toppling down. And so have we, despite it all. For more important than anything else, the war has subsided, and a fragile peace is in the air.

The hotels are starting to fill up again, and the tourist sites aren't the abandoned wastelands they were until a few months ago. The sidewalks are packed, and though there are still guards at all the stores and all the restaurants, they're fairly relaxed. A quick peek here, a pat down the back there, but none of the nervousness and methodical "wanding" that you used to see. Not too deep down, people here really think—or at least very much want to hope—that the worst may be behind us.

Even the kids sense that the terror simply seems to have passed. Two weeks ago, the week before the bird's nest appeared, I had guard duty outside shul on a Shabbat morning. It was freezing and threatening to pour (it didn't). Avi used to hate when I had to stand out there. He'd tell me when he was younger that he was worried that something would happen to me, that if a terrorist showed up, I'd get hurt. (I never bothered to tell him I probably wouldn't feel a thing if I got blown up.) But now he's older, more cynical, and less worried. We were walking home later that morning, when he told me he thought that guarding the shul was a dumb idea.

"You know," he said, "I really don't see the point of your standing out there and freezing to death [not his precise wording, to say the least]. Nothing's happening anymore."

"I agree," I told him.

"Well, they should either stop the rotation, or you should get off the list."

"We'll see."

"It's useless, anyway, you know."

"What's useless?"

"To have you guys guarding the shul."

"Why's that?"

"Why's that? Because, Abba, one Arab guy, even unarmed, could take the whole lot of you," he said, laughing. "What we need in this shul is some Sephardim. Sephardi guys are serious. What are you Ashkenazim going to do if a bomber comes by? Offer to write him a check?" And with that, enormously proud of his sense of humor, he burst out laughing.

It was, in fact, pretty funny, and we both found ourselves laughing the rest of the way home. He was undoubtedly amused by the idea of his father or any of his father's friends actually doing any good in guarding the shul if we had to. And me? I was amused by his highly adolescent, self-impressed sense of humor, and relieved that we were now joking about needing some Sephardim in the shul, rather than having Avi tell me that he's worried that I'm going to get blown up when I get a shift. If the beginnings of some sort of peace have my kid laughing at me, I'll take it. Any day.

For the first time in years, we had a real Purim. Costumes everywhere, parties inside and out. Some security, to be sure, but infinitely less than in recent years. Cities across the country had parades and carnivals for the first time in years, because this year, unlike the situation in the last few years, the security costs didn't eat up the whole budget. They actually had some money left over for the fun. That's an improvement.

Even Israeli soccer is cause for optimism. Last night I started watching the Israel-Ireland game, when Ireland scored a goal from a seemingly impossible angle just four minutes into the game. Convinced that we were going to get massacred, I turned off the TV in disgust. But this morning, I went to get the paper, and lo and behold, on the front page, a story about the game, tied at 1–1. In the very last minute of the game, Israel tied. With a goal by . . . Abbas Suan, an Israeli Arab from Bnei Sakhnin.

The pictures in the paper of Suan's (Jewish) teammates hugging him doesn't prove anything, but it sure was a nice way to wake up. Certainly better than the story in February when Suan was booed by Israeli fans when he was introduced, and then again every time he touched the ball during the game. Have the fans learned something? Probably not. The game was moved out of Jerusalem, where the fans are the most sickening and racist. But still, today's pictures were better.

And then, a couple of hours after I looked through the paper, I was cooking for today's Purim Seudah, a big afternoon feast. Stuck in the kitchen for what seemed like an eternity, I turned on the radio for some distraction. A couple of minutes later, the host on Galei Tzahal, Israeli Army Radio, announced that the next song, "In My Heart," a new song written by Jewish and Arab artists together, would be played simultaneously by Galei Tzahal and Voice of Palestine radio. It will be, he announced, the first time that Palestinian radio has ever played a Hebrew song. He cut over to an interview (in English) with Voice of Palestine's director, Bassem Abu Sumaya, who spoke about the song and the symbolism of the simultaneous broadcast.

"Does that mean you're stopping the incitement on your station?" Razi Barka'i (the Israeli) asked.

"We don't engage in incitement."

"Now, or are you saying you never did?"

"We're not in the business of incitement. We report. When the facts on the ground are the facts of war, we talk about what is. Now that there is a chance for peace, we talk about that."

Abu Sumaya avoided the real issue, obviously, but Barka'i let him off the hook. They spoke about the song a bit more, wished each other well, and cut to the music, entitled *"B'libi"* in Hebrew, in which both peoples express their love for the land.

Well, I thought. Here we are, three weeks after I was outside my shul freezing, and now I'm standing in the kitchen, wearing shorts and a T-shirt with the windows wide open. The paper and its article about Abbas Suan, with the photo of him being hugged, is on the counter, and on the radio, Army Radio and the Voice of Palestine are doing a simultaneous broadcast of a new song about peace. Makes you wonder what might be. If nothing goes terribly wrong.

A very big if, indeed.

Which brought me right back to that bird's nest. Yesterday, when we were in shul, I suddenly remembered the nest. I was, for a moment, hesitant to check. Because last year, there had been a nest in that same window, and then one day, it was simply gone. I remembered that I'd been upset about the nest-no-longer all day. But this time, I did look up to see if this year's nest was still around.

It was, but there was something different. This time, there was a bird in the nest. It didn't move the entire morning. I know nothing about birds, but I assume that it was sitting on some eggs that it wouldn't abandon. It looked around periodically, shifted here and there, but didn't budge. As if it was unwilling to give up. On a new generation, new possibilities. A new start.

Like us, and this crazy, rickety, optimistic place that we call home. A place no less filled with promise than that nest, but a place no less vulnerable and no less likely to be sent falling, upended. Unless.

Unless we get lucky or smart. Unless everyone just holds their breath between now and July and does nothing foolish, so that at last, something better than what we've had for the last four years might really begin to fly.

A Rock and a Hard Place

It's the main issue consuming the country, but we're not talking about it much at home. Partly because we don't all agree, and the house ought to be one place where the tension can subside. And because when we first started talking about it, Micha had a horrible day at school.

It was probably a year ago when Sharon first made it clear that there would be no Jews left in Gaza when the disengagement was done. That was when people here began to realize that he was serious, damn serious, and started talking about it. Elisheva and I, with a few of our liberal sensibilities still intact from the days when we lived in the States, were just relieved that somebody was doing something, *anything*, to get us out of the stalemate, and we explained to the kids one day why we were in favor. Enough soldiers were getting killed there. It's bad for Jews to be dominating another people. Sharon can be trusted to watch out for our security interests. It will buy some much-needed goodwill with the international community. I'm not actually sure exactly what we said back then, but it was probably something along those lines.

Anyway, Micha got the point. His parents were in favor, so he decided that he was in favor, too. A few days later, though, he came home in tears, inconsolable. "What happened?" we had to ask several times.

His teacher at school, a (superb) religious public school in the Jewish Quarter of the Old City, had told the kids that they weren't going to discuss the disengagement, because she was not supposed to. Nothing, of course, could be more effective at getting the kids to talk about it, and a conversation ensued. Who's in favor, someone wanted to know. Of the twenty-three kids in the class, Micha and one or two others said that they were.

And then Micha got his first serious introduction to the divisiveness of Israeli society. A few of the girls in the class said that they couldn't believe that he would be in favor of throwing Jews out of their homes. How could he? And they started to cry. One or two stopped talking to him.

When he got home and checked his e-mail, it was filled with incredibly nasty notes from a few kids in the class. Some of it was so disgusting that I was tempted to save it and show the principal, or to call the parents, or both.

"Stay out of it," Elisheva warned me. "Don't get involved."

"Why? It's outrageous. His teacher's an idiot."

"It's not about his teacher. That's how life is here. He has to learn to weather it. He'll take care of himself. He'll be OK."

From the minute the kids were born, Elisheva has had a deep intelligence and an uncanny sixth sense about them, their needs, and what will help them that still amazes me. And I know she's right here, too, but I'm too upset with Micha's class to give in entirely. In a sort of compromise, I told Micha that he couldn't check his e-mail for a few days, so at least his waking hours at home wouldn't be consumed with the nastiness.

Elisheva, of course, was right. Micha managed to navigate matters at school. The formerly silent girls started talking to him, the incident passed, and Micha decided that he's opposed to the disengagement. And always will be.

And we haven't talked about it much since then. But now that the date is just months away, now that people are starting to "vote" in the public square by putting orange ribbons—signifying their opposition—on their cars, it's beginning to come up again.

"So what do you think?" the kids want to know. A good idea, or bad?

"I could make you a good argument for either side," I tell them.

"Go ahead."

So I lay out the reasons for being opposed. Israel has said that it would never retreat under fire, and with Kassam rockets still being fired from Gaza, it's clear that that's precisely what we're doing. When we gave back the Sinai to Egypt, we got a peace treaty out of the deal. With Jordan, we got a treaty without giving up any significant land. And here we're giving land back without any peace, something that we've said we'd never do.

And what's to stop Hamas from turning Gaza into a terrorist haven once we're out? They will, and the IDF will have to go back in to stop them. So all that will have happened will be that we'll have dislodged the seven thousand Israeli citizens who live there and destroyed their homes, but the army will still be there, for all intents and purposes. What's the gain in *that*?

And we're inviting the third Intifada. "Don't forget," I tell the kids, "the army's exit from Lebanon under Barak in the spring of 2000 and the outbreak of the Intifada in September of that year were separated by only five months." What if they were related? What if leaving Lebanon after years of being fired on convinced them that if you shoot at us long enough, and kill enough soldiers, we'll leave? And now, after four years of the second Intifada, when they've killed even more soldiers, and many civilians, we're leaving again. So why shouldn't they start again as soon as we're out of Gaza? The West Bank this time? Or Tel Aviv, or Haifa after that? Isn't it possible that getting out under fire is the worst possible thing Israel could do for its own security?

And what about the human side, and the settlers? Why should they be punished for the stalemate with the Palestinians? They're the ones who heeded the call of governments, both left and right, to move to those places. The settlements program was favored by Golda Meir and Yitzhak Rabin. And by people to the right. These settlers are the ones who left the comfort of other cities and towns and moved to these places when there was nothing, and over decades built model communities. *They* should have to pay this price? For what?

"So how could you possibly argue the opposite?" came the immediate question.

"Easily."

First of all, I tell them, we know that the world is eventually going to force us out of Gaza. Europe has made that clear, and even Bush has said it. And since we know that the world will force us out of Gaza eventually, why stay any longer than we have to? What will we say to the parents of the boys who will get killed there, when the army sent them there long after it became clear that Gaza would not remain ours? How would they go on?

What about the thirty thousand troops currently guarding the six thousand people who live there? Does that make *any* sense? That, in fact, is precisely Sharon's point. He says that current borders are simply not defensible. And doesn't someone like Sharon have to be taken seriously, at least about military issues?

And what about our souls? Is it good for us to have six thousand settlers there, living among a million and a half Palestinians? Many of them are the ones who in 1948 fled to these refugee camps from what is now inside the Green Line. Regardless of whose fault it is that they were turned into refugees, it's clearly not unrelated to our establishing the country. About that, there's no dispute. So we should now pursue them into that squalid refugee bog and build gorgeous settlements right in the middle of their squalor? To further antagonize them? To poison the waters here for yet another generation? That's good for *us*? That's the kind of Jews we want to be?

But even if someone didn't care about that, or said that God gave us this land so we have the right to stay there, how naïve can they be? Let's face it: if we can't get out of Gaza under Sharon, we probably can't get out of anywhere. Because Gaza's the easiest. It doesn't pose the security considerations that the Golan does, or the intermingled populations that the West Bank does, or the political and religious significance that Jerusalem does. So if we can't exit Gaza, we'll be in the territories forever, and the three million to four million Palestinians who live under our control will continue not to have a state.

And why should that matter to you? Because either we make those Palestinians citizens of *this* country, in which case it ceases almost overnight to be a Jewish state, or we deny them citizenship and admit that that's how it's going to stay for the long haul. And then the world will decide, perhaps correctly this time, that the Israeli situation is akin to apartheid, and it will do to us what it did to South Africa. It will impose economic sanctions—or worse—on Israel, until we begin to buckle under the weight of collapse. What, do you think F. W. de Klerk just woke up one day and decided to free Nelson Mandela? Or he just had a vision and decided to recognize the African National Congress? Hardly. His country was falling apart. And the world will be all too happy to do the same to Israel. Look at Europe and their resistance to playing against Israeli sports teams. Or their occasional refusal to invite Israeli academics to conferences. Or the boycotts of Israeli goods that have already started. It's begun already, and this while Israel is anxious for the Palestinians to make a deal. Close off the option by not getting out of Gaza, and the world will shut us down.

So it's simple. Get out of Gaza, or lose the country.

"Which do you want?" I ask them.

Not exactly a choice that teenagers should have to make, and they don't.

"So which of those arguments do you believe?" one of the kids asks.

"Both of them," I answer. "Both." This isn't a choice between a good option and a bad one, or the right thing to do and the wrong one. It's a choice between two miserable options.

It's a wager and a prayer. The disengagement is a wager that getting out is less bad for the country than staying in, but it's a guess, at best.

And it's a prayer. A prayer that we're not wrong again, as we were with Oslo. Because with Oslo, we got duped. And got a war from which we're just now beginning to emerge. So we're praying that this time it's not a goof.

Speaking of easy questions, all I need now is for them to ask me if I think prayer works. I hope it does. I pray it does.

Exodus(es), Redux

Pesach is one of those periods in Israeli life when it seems that everyone takes to the road and goes out to hike, bike, or picnic in some part of the country. Maybe the Seder, and the image of the Israelites and their Exodus into the desert, is what gets everyone out. Or maybe it's just the fact that people don't take the country for granted and still love the rocks, the hills, the desert, the coast.

This year we decided that with the disengagement coming up, probably sometime at the end of the summer, we should take the kids to Gush Katif in Gaza so that they could see what it is that we're actually leaving. I, at least, didn't want their impressions of these people and their communities to be based solely on the press, or rumors, or imagination. For or against (and the kids are actually split), I wanted them to see real people, real houses, gardens, synagogues, cemeteries. And the Palestinians who live around them. In other words, the whole complicated mess.

So we set out early Tuesday morning of Pesach to make our way to Gaza. Given the traffic jams that normally accompany every Pesach day trip, we left relatively early in the morning and decided to take the back way out of Jerusalem, which means going south, by Gilo and Beit Jala and the tunnel road to Gush Eztion. From there, we'd head southwest and wind our way over to Gaza, I figured.

We went past Gush Eztion, via the tunnel road that was the object of all the shooters from Beit Jala a few years ago and that is now shielded by massive concrete barriers on either side. As I looked at the map while driving, it seemed to me that a bit further south there was a road that offered a more direct cut, due west, and that might save us a bit of time.

Why not, I figured? So we kept heading south, when all of a sudden, any semblance of being in Israel disappeared. The signs were all in Arabic. There was very little traffic on the road, and what there was, was all Palestinian taxis and trucks (with different-colored license plates, of course, making our car stand out rather starkly). There were kids shepherding their flocks of sheep and goats on either side of the road, and older men in kaffiyehs, sitting by the side of the road or walking. More than anything else, though, people were staring at us with a look that more or less said, "What in the world are *you* doing *here*?"

I was hoping that the kids would stay in their earphone-induced trances in the back, and that Elisheva would continue to doze until I'd made the right turn and gotten us out of there, but no such luck. A few minutes later, the kids began to ask, "Abba, where, exactly, are we?"

"South of Gush Eztion," I said, as if that would be comforting.

The kids went back to their music, at which point Elisheva whispered to me, "I don't think this road was such a great idea. You notice we're the only Israelis near here? And there's not even any army in evidence?"

"You don't have to whisper," I pointed out. The kids were behind solid walls of MP3, and as for the danger outside, well, whispering wasn't going to help. I found myself trying to remember how long it had been since we'd switched the tires on the car, wondering how long, exactly, we might stay alive on this road if we had to stop to change one. I decided not to share that thought with her.

"How much longer till we hit the Green Line [and enter Israel proper again]?" I asked her, pointing to the map that she was holding.

She looked at the map. "A while."

"Meaning?"

"Meaning I don't know. The Green Line's not on the map."

Oh, yeah. That oft-forgotten little fact about Israeli maps. Hardly any of them show where the line used to be. As if, until recently, there was no reason to think that it would ever be important again.

"Well, how long till we're out of these Palestinian villages and back near something with a Hebrew name?"

"A while."

"Meaning?"

"Meaning, I don't know. A while." Still in a whisper, as if whispering would mean that they couldn't see us. I took the map and gave it a look. She was right. A while. What looks like nothing on an international map can actually take a long time when you'd like to be anywhere but there. I picked up our speed, to about 125 or 130 km/h, which usually prompts a gentle "You're driving a bit fast, no?" But this time, no objections from the copilot. An unspoken assent, basically, "Just get us out of here."

So we flew along in what will, after another Exodus one day, be Palestine, and eventually, hit an army roadblock. It was designed mostly to stop Palestinians from entering Israel proper from our direction. There was a line at the roadblock, as the soldiers made everyone in the cars in front of us (they were all Palestinians, in Israeli taxis) get out, searched their bags, the trunks, etc. When one of the soldiers saw us in the line, he flagged us over to the left side and into the lane for oncoming traffic. I lowered the window to answer his questions, but he didn't have any. He just gave us a look of complete bewilderment at seeing a car with people like us in a place like that, and waved us on.

"Where are we now?" wafted the question from the back.

"Safe," I wanted to say, but didn't.

"Was that Gush Katif?" Micha wanted to know.

"No, that was Gush Eztion before."

"What's the difference?" as if "Gush" was all that matters.

So, at the next gas station, we pulled over. Everyone out of the car. I took out two maps that together covered most of the country, laid them on the ground, and showed them Gush Eztion, Gush Katif, and our route.

"Where did we just go through?" one of the older kids wanted to know.

"Some Palestinian areas," I said nonchalantly and pointed to our route.

"That was pretty dumb, Abba," Avi said. To which Micha said, "Is the part we just went through going back, too?"

"Next time," one of the older kids said.

"What next time?" he wanted to know.

The sibling explanation continued: "Now we're giving up Gaza. But it won't be the last time we have to give back land. The part we just went through will be the next thing that gets put on the chopping block. They want all of this for their state."

I decided to let them talk it out, and said nothing. But their wheels were churning; that much was clear.

Forty-five minutes later, we drove though Sederot, where the Kassam rockets have been landing of late, and a few minutes after that, we crossed the Kissufim junction and made our way into Gaza, which suddenly, in relative terms, now seemed rather safe. It was also pretty empty. The enormous protest march wasn't scheduled until the next day, and we'd decided to come a day earlier to avoid the masses.

Now the kids had dispensed with their MP3 players and were looking out the windows, taking some pictures. Of the tanks on the side of the road. Of the horrendous and enormous Palestinian refugee camps, just a few hundred yards from the Jewish communities that were already visible directly ahead. Of the sign at the side of the road that said "Kfar Darom will not fall again," a play on the famous "Masada will not fall again" phrase. Or of the sign that said "Careful—tank crossing," or the one that read "We love you, Land of Israel." Not the roadside literature of the neighborhood my kids live in.

We drove around Gush Katif, the biggest block of Jewish communities in Gaza, for a while. We went first to Neve Dekalim, a large-ish community, with streets, and houses, and parks, and a little downtown with a shopping center. And a synagogue. And a cemetery just outside. It looked, as the kids quickly saw, not like a "settlement," but like a city. Which is exactly what it is.

"Which part of this is going back?" Micha wanted to know.

"Everything you can see," his sister told him.

"What, *all* of this?"

"Yup. All of it."

"And they get to keep all the buildings?"

"Yup."

"And they get to live in the houses?"

"Yup."

"What are they going to do with a shul?" Micha wanted to know.

"Loot it and deface it," one sibling replied.

"You don't know that," I interjected, trying to make this conversation a bit less wrist-slashingly depressing.

"Yes, we do," came the response. "Abba, you know what happened to the shul in Yamit after we gave it back to the Egyptians, don't you?" I do, so I figured I'd let that one slide.

It was now very quiet in the car. All of a sudden, the "disengagement" was more than a political hot potato. Or the reason for some signs, or an argument on the evening news. Now, it was about people, whom the kids could see on the sidewalks, walking with their families, pushing their strollers. Not wild-eyed maniacs walking around with M-16's, just people, real people, who look exactly like we do. Now the disengagement was about giving up well-tended gardens. Playgrounds. Homes. It's one thing, we were all seeing, to be "in favor." It's quite another to see the horrendous price a lot of people—many of them Israel's most passionate pioneers—are going to have to pay.

It's like visiting a community before the hurricane strikes, or before the flood rushes in. You know that what you're seeing looks permanent, but you also know that within hours—or in our case, weeks—it's all going to be erased.

"What do we get when we give all this back?" Micha wanted to know.

"Nothing," came the icy response.

"Well, do they have to pay for the houses?"

"No."

"Do they have to do anything?"

"They don't even have to make peace. They just get it."

"Then I don't get it."

I was tempted to explain Sharon's security reasons for getting out, or the high price, in life and in money, that the army pays to hold on to it, or the eventual apartheid with which we'll be faced if we don't stop ruling what will soon be an Arab majority between the Jordan River and the Mediterranean Sea, but I didn't say anything. None of that, after all, would address what he was really saying. That the cost seems enormous. That the pain feels overwhelming. That the risk is huge. And he's right.

I continued driving around, when Elisheva said, "Let's get out of here. I'm way beyond depressed." But Talia, who'd been there recently and who knew her way around better than we did, said we should go to another community, Shirat HaYam, which was just a few minutes away.

Five minutes later, having driven a short dirt road with refugee camps on one side, we came upon a giant fence with a soldier guarding it. "Is this Shirat HaYam?" I asked him. He nodded and opened the gate. We drove in and followed the solitary, single-lane road through the . . . the what? Not a city. Not even a community. About ten little caravans on the most beautiful Middle Eastern beach I've ever seen, and some abandoned Egyptian buildings that were now being renovated, even as we watched, presumably for the influx of people moving there before the disengagement. Through the car windows and through the aforementioned high fence, our kids watched the Palestinian kids walking by outside the settlement. One strip of sand, one fence, two utterly separated populations.

We spent some time there and then went on to other communities, but we left pretty quickly. Later in the day, after a few hours on the Ashkelon beach to try to recuperate, we decided to head back to Jerusalem.

"Traffic's going to be murder," Elisheva said.

"Well, we can take the same route we took to get here," I suggested, but her look said, "That's not even funny."

"How about 443?" I asked, referring to the Modi'in Road, which goes by Ramallah and enters Jerusalem from the north. That road had been impassable in the days of the Intifada (or at least made you a target for the daily shootings there), but it, too, is protected by concrete barriers now so sharpshooters can't aim as easily at the cars. And besides, we have peace now, right?

"Good idea. That'll probably be more open."

So we took Highway 6, Israel's new road, our equivalent of an interstate, E-ZPass and all, and got off the exit to the 443. After a little bit of driving Micha perked up again and said, "What's this road?"

We told him.

"This is ours, right?"

"Right."

"This we get to keep?"

Again the sibling chorus. "For now. This will go back when we give back the road we were on this morning."

"Abba, is that true?" he asked, incredulous that everywhere we went was destined to be given back.

"Basically."

"Well, what is going to be left?"

Not much to say to that. Luckily, he needed to change the batteries on his music player, and the conversation ended.

But his question lingered in my mind, long after the day was over. What do you say to the kid when he says, "There won't be much left, will there?" How do you explain that most people in the country are willing (with varying degrees of ambivalence) to give that all back, in the hopes that something better can emerge here? Or because we'd rather face uncertainty with the Palestinians than the certainty of apartheid. Or because we've all got kids in the army now, and the cost, many of us think, is just too high. For a twelve-year-old kid, who's lived most of the years he can actually remember in an Intifada, none of that would be terribly convincing, so I didn't even try.

Or could it have been because after a day of actually being there, seeing the people, their homes, their gardens—that the pain that these people will experience was so palpable that no words seemed adequate?

Two days later, we were on a different trip, a long and tricky hike in the desert at a place called Nahal Deragot, west of the Dead Sea. We went with a group of four families and joined the hundreds of others in the overcrowded dry riverbed, called a wadi, for the day-long hike that involves descending thirteen (dry) waterfalls with ropes. We were all having a fine old time, even though the wadi was overcrowded.

About midway into the hike, though, Elisheva slipped and took a pretty nasty spill. By the time I made my way to where I'd heard the big thump, she was lying on the ground, with a bad head gash, and who knew what else.

For the rest of the day, our kids and the other kids in the group got to see the answer to "What will be left?" As news of the "spill" spread, some former army medics hurried to the spot, from both directions. Army-issued bandages and other medical supplies started landing around us, until the area looked more like a military pharmacy than a desert wadi. There were two men, whom none of us knew, who were expert climbers and medics, who abandoned their groups, and stayed with her the rest of the day (after a physician, who himself had to climb *up* several of the waterfalls to get to her, had said that she could try to stand up) as she walked the remaining three and a half hours with her concussion.

When we were met by a volunteer medic crew that had been sent to check her out, the men said good-bye, and started back to their families and friends. When I tried to thank them, they brushed it off. When I insisted, they simply didn't understand what the big deal was.

When we finally finished our exodus from the wadi and got to the parking lot, in a pitch-black and almost moonless night, we decided to wait for a while for the rest of the families to get out (we'd gone ahead at each waterfall, because she needed to get to flat ground as quickly as possible). But when it appeared that no one else was getting out that night (and indeed, sixty people ended up spending the night in the wadi because the waterfalls are too dangerous to attempt after dark), there was only one car left in the lot.

I went to the people who had the car and asked where they were going. Hoshayah, was the answer (it's way up in the Galilee). What route are you taking, I wanted to know. The Jordan Valley, straight up north, they said.

"Do you think you could drive us to the gas station at the turnoff to Jerusalem and leave us off there?"

They took one look at Elisheva, with her head bandaged, and asked, "Where are you going?"

"Jerusalem, to the Terem clinic. The medic thinks she needs to get to a doctor."

"Get in. We'll take you."

"Just to the junction."

"We'll take you to the clinic. Get in."

"It's hours out of your way."

"Get in."

"Just to the gas station. We can grab a cab from there." I actually wasn't sure that we'd get one, but figured we'd deal with that then.

"Get in."

After some negotiation, which we lost, we got in, and they drove us all the way to Jerusalem, to the city entrance on the other side of town, where the emergency clinic was. After a farewell and a thank-you, where they tried to give us money since all our backpacks were still with our friends in the wadi, we waited in the clinic. I decided to buy some food, since we hadn't eaten all day.

"Anything here kosher for Pesach?" I asked the vendor, with all his piercings and spiked hair. "Everything is," he said and showed me the certificate on the wall. I bought a few things, at which point he said, "*Chag same'ach*," and "*Refu'ah sheleimah*." "Happy holiday. And a speedy recovery." We weren't at Kaiser Permanente anymore; that much was clear.

A short while later, a doctor of French origin decided that stitches were needed and saw to them, along with a tetanus shot. The next morning, as the checks continued in the Hadassah emergency room, it was first a neurologist of Spanish origin and then a Russian-speaking orthopedist. French, Spanish, Russians, Americans . . . The "ingathering of the exiles" is no mere phrase on days like that. Even that collection of immigrants, with all the different stories they could have told, added poignancy to what would have otherwise been an uneventful day at Hadassah.

The country is shrinking, true, but it wasn't for its size that any of us chose to be here. It was about what happens inside. At the bottom of a wadi. Or in a desert parking lot. Or in the waiting room at an emergency clinic.

Or in the hospital.

There was an Arab kid in the emergency room whose parents were coming to meet him but were still a while away. He apparently didn't speak much Hebrew, because the doctors and nurses were struggling to communicate with him until an Arabic-speaking nurse came by. When they'd calmed him down, our Avi, who'd overheard all that, went to take a peek at the Arab boy through the curtains around the treatment area.

Avi came back and said, "Abba, can I have some money?"

"For what?" I asked, as I gave it to him.

"The Arab boy. He doesn't have anything to eat, and his parents aren't here. I'm sure he's too shy to ask for anything. I'll go buy him some candy and a drink at the cafeteria." And off he went.

The next day, I went back to the bookstore and bought four more copies of that Bialik book I'd purchased a while back. One for the family who drove us to Hoshayah. And copies for the guys in the wadi. And for the medic who'd stuck with us.

A few called to say thanks a few days later, when the books had arrived in the mail, but were perplexed. "Why'd you do that?" they wanted to know. "We didn't really do anything." Six hours taking care of a woman they didn't know on a day they'd planned to spend with their friends and their families, and they don't think that they did anything extraordinary.

Which was the end of the answer to Micha's question. What will be left when we give it all back? You go through a Pesach like this one, and you know the answer. What will be left will be a country where "Exodus" isn't just a reference to the ancient past. And what will be left, undoubtedly, will be a smaller country.

What will be left is a country deeply wounded by the pain it is about to inflict on itself, by the price it is asking its most committed and passionate pioneers to pay for having heeded the call of previous governments to move to precisely where they now live.

But what will be left is also a people still in love with the land that it does have, and that hikes it and bikes it at every opportunity. That fills the roads to overflowing on vacations, and that fills the wadis. A place where the sense of shared enterprise is palpable, especially when you need it.

What will be left are people who, if someone gets hurt, respond so selflessly that it takes your breath away. And then don't understand why you're making such a big deal of thanking them.

What will be left will be a country in which, if you go to three different doctors in the space of a few hours, one will have made *aliyah* from France, one from Spain, and one from Russia. Where even the food cart in the waiting room reflects the fact that it's Pesach. It will be a country in which, despite all the years of conflict, kids still reach out to each other, across the chasms of cultures and of languages.

What will be left will be a country where, after this summer, people will have proven that despite the enormous and almost unspeakable pain involved, they have decided to have less land in the short run, rather than nothing in the long run. Because they will still love what they'll have. And because they can't imagine surviving without it.

What will be left, when the pain begins to subside, will be home.

Child's Play

When we lived in Los Angeles, on a tree-lined street with perfectly manicured houses and a private neighborhood patrol to guarantee that whatever happened in the rest of LA wouldn't happen near us, there was a little place called Circle Park, where the kids would play when they were young. And nearby, on the main road that approached the intersection where the park was, there were those ubiquitous yellow signs that said "Slow—Children at Play." In my mind, I can still see those signs—the ones with the picture of the seesaw, or the kid running after the ball.

We've been gone from LA for years now, but I thought of those signs again when Tali broke her nose. Actually, she didn't really break her nose—her brother did it for her. Quite self-impressed with his newfound pitching skills, Micha's been swinging his arm around, holding on to the ball, practicing his windup.

Which is fine, until the ball accidentally slips out of his hand one fine Shabbat afternoon and hits Tali squarely in the face. A visit to the emergency room that night and then a few more to the plastic surgeon in the coming days, and she's OK, all bandaged up, but her eyes are black and blue, and she looks more like a raccoon than anything. Mortified, she won't go out of the house, and truthfully, it's hard to blame her.

So her friends are coming by to visit her. By day and by night, there's a steady stream of teenagers parading through the house. Chatting, watching TV, sitting on the porch, hanging out. Mostly her high school friends, all dispersed now. Some are in yeshivot and on the way to the army, like she is, while some are already drafted. One night an old friend of hers from the neighborhood shows up. We've known him since he was thirteen, and the two of them have grown up together.

To us, he's still a kid from the 'hood. But a year older than Tali, he's already been drafted. He's done with basic training and is now in Gaza, doing what, we're not entirely certain. This kid and Tali head into the study, where the TV is, and a short while later we hear peals of laughter. Curious, I peer in. They're watching *Dave*, that absurd comedy about a presidential look-alike. I never thought the movie was terribly funny, but something about it has them in hysterics.

It's adorable, but sad, too. One more day at home, and then he'll be back in Gaza, which might as well be a different planet. There's something about this image, these two big kids sitting on the couch laughing at *Dave*, and the knowledge that the next day he'll be back in Gaza, an hour and a half away, in a world we can scarcely imagine.

The world doesn't see Israeli soldiers as kids who'd rather just be home, sitting on the couch, laughing at *Dave*. Neither, I'm sure, do the Palestinian kids who live near where he's doing whatever he's doing.

They laugh again, and Elisheva smiles at me. "Nice of him to come over," she says, "don't you think?" But I'm not really smiling. I'm thinking about that yellow sign and remembering the days when "Children at Play" meant seesaw and soccer. Not Gaza and God knows what else.

A couple of days later, I see that kid's father on the street. We say hello and chat for a minute, when I tell him how nice it was that his son came over to visit my daughter, when she was too mortified to go out of the house. "He's a good friend," I tell the dad.

Without missing a beat, the dad looks at me and says, deadpan, "Well, it's the least he can do, given that he spends the rest of the week assassinating people." I laugh, but he doesn't. There's a look on his face, not quite a smile. Something more distant. And I'm left wondering. Is that what his kid is *really* doing out there? What does it feel like, I want to ask him but don't, not to know what your kid is doing? And to suspect that it's something like that? And to know that if you'd stayed in the States (they came here a few years before we did) he'd probably be playing Ultimate Frisbee on a university campus somewhere, rather than doing . . . doing what?

. . .

On May 17, we know what other kids are doing. The "orange kids," at least, are out at the country's major intersections, raising Cain. A few are burning tires, and many more are obstructing traffic, in an ongoing attempt to disrupt life, to get the country to rethink the disengagement, to force Sharon to either call it off or to at least allow a referendum.

But Sharon won't think of it, and the country, frankly, is beginning to run out of patience. People really do feel for those about to lose their homes, their businesses, their lives, and many are wondering aloud whether a referendum wouldn't be such a bad idea. But this blocking the traffic, they think, simply has to stop. This is a pretty crowded country as it is, and with the blocking of major intersections throughout the country, life's becoming intolerable.

So the police clamp down and start arresting the masses of people performing these acts of civil disobedience. Among those arrested are kids, including some as young as twelve and thirteen.

The police want to book them and release them to their parents, but there's a problem. The kids won't identify themselves. Asked who they are, time and again, all they will say is "I am a Jew from the Land of Israel." *Ha-Aretz* runs an editorial that fumes at that phrase, claiming that they're emphasizing that they're from the *Land* of Israel, and not from the *State* of Israel. But the editorial misses the point, it seems to me. These kids are just repeating a phrase that Jews had used with the British decades earlier.

In the 1940s, when the British tried to limit Jewish immigration to Palestine, His Majesty's soldiers succeeded in stopping many of the boats headed to these shores. But some of the ships slipped through, and when they did, the boats were met by hundreds of Jews already living here legally, so that the British would not be able to tell who had a right to return to their home, and who, according to British policy, needed to be arrested and sent to camps, often on Cyprus. The British would arrest many of those found near the boat. But it was to no avail, because the illegal immigrants and those here legally had blended completely. And because when the British brought their quarry in for questioning, the only thing those who'd been arrested would say was "I am a Jew from the Land of Israel."

The point, of course, was "I have a right to be here." And that's the point that these kids are making. It's the point that their parents have taught them to make. Sharon is now the British. And the settlers are the refugees from Europe. And these kids are the ones who waded into the water to meet the new immigrants and to shield them from arrest.

"I am a Jew from the Land of Israel." That's all they'll say. And the cops, understandably, can't let the kids go if they can't reach their parents. And they can't reach their parents if the kids won't say their names. So for weeks, there are a few stalwarts, including a thirteen-year-old girl, who languish in prison, with no contact from their parents, because all they'll say, despite repeated interrogations, is "I am a Jew from the Land of Israel."

The police are at their wits' end and announce that eventually, of course, they'll figure out who these kids are. If the parents do not pick them up first, the police warn, the parents will be prosecuted. A lot of people are talking about what kind of parents would leave their thirteen-year-old kid in jail for days and then for weeks, and not contact them, all for the sake of some political cause.

But I'm wondering about something different: How different are we from them? Are we really different at all? Who are we to judge them, when we, too, took our kids away from Circle Park, the manicured lawns, and the little signs that said "Children at Play."

For some reason, I find myself thinking about the national military cemetery on Mount Herzl and its section for the kids killed during the siege on Jerusalem in 1948. These kids were used primarily as runners, to carry messages in or out. A lot of them made it, but some of them didn't. And now those who didn't make it through are memorialized near the soldiers who died in combat and, like the soldiers, have plaques commemorating the price they paid. The plaques list their names, their ages, and then the phrase *"Nafal be-milui tafkido"*—"He fell in the performance of his mission." A boy aged seventeen. And a girl aged fifteen. And a boy named Nisim Gini, born in Jerusalem and killed at the age of ten, "in the performance of his mission."

What does it mean to be ten years old and to fall in the performance of your mission? Or to be a nineteen-year-old soldier, like Iris Azoulai, stabbed just outside her home, two minutes away from our house?

How many more will join them, in jail or worse, before we figure a way out of this? What would it take for our kids not to have missions anymore? Or to be able to introduce themselves one day and say, perhaps with a tinge of memory, "I am a Jew from the Land of Israel," and mean just that?

Good, As Good As Can Be

I landed at Ben Gurion Airport, back from a quick trip to the States. Got my luggage, went through customs, and met Shlomo, our driver, at our usual spot. We've got this down to a routine. Same meeting place, and same casual hellos. He took my bags, and I asked him how he was. *Tov, kamah she-efshar.* "Good, as good as can be."

A fair response to a stupid question. How's he supposed to be? How does a guy in his fifties get beyond his daughter being murdered by a suicide bomber at the Moment Café? When he drives all day with her picture on the dashboard, how good could things possibly be?

So I tried a different tack. "What's new in the country?" I asked him. "Did you hear about the train disaster?"

"No," I said, beginning to dread what was to follow. It turns out that when a truck tried to cross a track as a train was approaching, the train collided with the truck, killing the truck driver and seven people on the train.

"Actually," he said, "the news should be on. You can hear for yourself." He turned up the volume, just as the hourly news began. First, an update on the train wreck. Then, the time of the funeral of a victim of a shooting attack by armed Palestinians two days earlier. An update on the Palestinian woman from Gaza arrested with a bomb belt on her way to Soroka hospital in Beer Sheva. She'd been treated there in the past, but this time, she said, she was out to "kill as many Jews as possible." Some more about the Trojan Horse episode, a corporate-spying-via-computer scandal that has captivated the country. And the traffic report. Delays on the road due to settlers burning tires on the road. And settlers passing out orange ribbons—the symbol of opposition to the disengagement—on the highway.

I looked out the window of the car, and sure enough, there were many more cars sporting orange ribbons tied to their antennas or roof racks than there had been when I'd left just days earlier. Half an hour later, we got to Jerusalem, and traffic slowed to a crawl. As the uphill road narrowed to two lanes (King David should have thought of this when he picked a city on a hilltop as his capital thousands of years ago), things got even worse as people in orange shirts tried to hand the drivers orange ribbons. Others simply stood on the side holding signs that said, "Jews Don't Evict Jews."

Some of the drivers were clearly annoyed that these kids, mostly teenagers, were causing such a backup of traffic. Maybe I was too tired from the flight, but it didn't faze me. True, the train wreck was horrible. The terror is picking up a bit. And the disengagement is a complete mess. But these kids are on the streets, opposing the government's stated official policy, and no one is rounding them up. The police drive by, and these kids have nothing to fear. They aren't hurting anyone. It's civil disobedience at its best. The painfully slow traffic notwithstanding, maybe Shlomo was right. Perhaps things really are "good, as good as can be."

A couple of days later, Micha had a piano recital. With all the nervousness thereunto appertaining, we walked to the conservatory on Emek Refa'im. As we got closer, I saw that the street was blocked off. Food carts and all sorts of merchandise were being set up on the side, as people got ready for a street fair scheduled to start a short while later.

There were police stanchions with guards at the sides, armed with wands to check us as we walked into the area. We walked closer, and I got ready to open my bag for them to check. But they weren't interested. They just watched us walk by and kept chatting to themselves. As if to say, "Those days are gone." For now, at least. For now, the old Jerusalem is back.

At the recital, the teacher (who happens to be a religious Jewish woman) made all the usual thanks, to the parents, to the kids, and then to the people who had helped Rasha get to class. I didn't pay it much attention. I just figured that Rasha (an Arab name) lived far away and needed help getting to her lessons. But when it was Rasha's turn to play, I found out what the big deal was. She seemed to be in her late teens, maybe early twenties. And she's blind. And autistic. And played with a passion that had the entire audience spellbound. When she was done, the awe in the room was palpable. She couldn't see us, but she heard the applause, and she knew what she'd done. As she was helped back to her seat by one of her "chauffeurs," her smile said it all. Hers is, quite simply, a life saved. Not bad. Not bad at all.

Then, the next student (and her teacher) played a version of the Brahms Sonata in F minor for four hands. It's a long piece, and it gave me a few minutes to wonder. What would have happened if the roles had been reversed? If a Jewish blind kid, also autistic, was growing up in an Arab country, what would happen? Would people have lined up to drive her to her piano lessons? Would the other parents, of a different religion and nationality, have been so thrilled for her accomplishments? Would the teacher have clearly loved her so?

I realized pretty quickly that it would be hard for a teacher to love a Jewish child like that in one of those countries. After all, those nations unceremoniously threw out all their Jews decades ago. It puts all the garbage here into a bit of perspective, I thought.

Eventually the recital ended, and we headed back to Emek Refa'im. By now the street was packed with thousands of people, bands playing, restaurants plying their wares. Used books for sale on every block. And people having the time of their lives. We walked to one end of the festival, checking out what we wanted to eat. "Pretty amazing, no?" I asked Elisheva.

"Yup," she said, "and basically right in front of Café Hillel."

I hadn't thought of that. But there it was, long since rebuilt, right in the midst of the festivities. A block down is Caffit, where a bomber walked in at the height of the Intifada, but was overpowered by vigilant patrons before he could press his button. Caffit, too, was now surrounded by the festive crowds, with the security outside basically asleep. And at the other end of the street, that small stone memorial to the victims of the #14A bus bombing. There, too, crowds, music. Laughter. And very little security.

On the same street as Café Hillel, Caffit, and the Bus #14A memorial, a street fair. Music, food, laughter. And no obvious security. We've won. We've definitely won. Shlomo was right. Things are, they really are, as good as they could be.

A few nights later, we had Micha's "graduation" from elementary school. Getting there, I knew, was going to be wretched, for the settlers had planned to shut down the country's roads. "Stop for a minute, and think," was their motto for the evening's operation. But it actually meant, "Stop for an hour while we slow the roads." The police were out in force, helicopters chopping up above, water cannons positioned at critical junctions (and used, later in the evening). There were orange T-shirts everywhere and, on a few street corners, a relatively new phenomenon—a few kids timidly handling out blue ribbons, too, representing those in favor of the disengagement. (Blue, obviously, is the color of our flag, and, less obviously, is directly opposite orange on the color wheel.) Cars were honking, people were shouting.

The vitriol on the radio was poisonous as we made our way to Gilo, where the graduation ceremony was held. Sharon was being vilified. The army was threatening to raid the hotel in Gaza where hard-liners were storing food and surrounding themselves with barbed wire. Hundreds of troops were said to be amassed, just awaiting the order. In short, a complete and colossal mess.

As representatives of both sides were interviewed on the radio, they agreed about one thing. Make the wrong move here, and we're finished. The right said that this disengagement is only going to lead to a renewed Intifada in the fall, for we'll have shown them that firing on us does pay. And the left says that if we don't pull out, the conflict will never end. The world will dismember us, and we will collapse under the weight of never-ending conflict. Complete disagreement, but both sides are talking about the end of the country.

Outside the graduation a good number of parents were milling about the lobby. With lots of orange ribbons tied to their briefcases and backpacks. And then, in the auditorium, the graduating sixth-graders put on a play based on Leon Uris's *Exodus*. It's a story about refugees with nowhere to go, trying to get into the land. About why the land is rightfully theirs. And how no one will keep them out. A pretty heavy-handed political statement, obviously. But I watched these kids, first during the play, and then at the end of the ceremony when they were given Bibles as gifts from City Hall, and I realized, they actually believe in something.

They believe in their right to have a home. They believe that there's one place on the planet where they genuinely belong.

It's elementary school belief, true, but it's also elementary. They just take their right to be here as a matter of fundamental faith. They believe that this is the place where they belong. Because of God, or history. What did I believe in when I was that age, growing up in suburban Baltimore? Anything? Anything at all? Shlomo again—lots of things here are, despite it all, as good as they could possibly be.

In the days that followed, ribbon fever heated up. The blues tried to keep pace with the oranges, and tied white ribbons to the blue ribbons they were distributing to make the obvious point. The distributors fanned out across the city, not just at major intersections, but, it seemed, everywhere. Everywhere you go, it's a ribbon fest. Orange ribbons. Blue and white ribbons. You can't stop at a traffic light without being offered one.

We were in the car on our way out of town a few days later, and we stopped at a red light. Both colors were being given out, with two teenagers giving out the opposite colors standing right next to each other. I opened a window.

"What, Abba, are you really going to take a ribbon?"

"Why not?"

"What color?"

"What color do you want?"

"Orange," came one reply. "Blue," said the other.

I took both. The orange one came unaccompanied. The blue one came tied to a white one. When we got where we were going, I tied all three to the cell phone antenna on the windshield corner. Elisheva was mortified. And then, when we got home, Tali saw the car.

"What's with the car?"

"What about it?"

"How can you have both colors on it?"

"We don't all agree. This way, the car represents everyone in the family."

"That's ridiculous. Our car looks like it was a float in the gay pride parade." (That parade, with its rainbow of colors, had taken place just a few days earlier.)

Talia's objections notwithstanding, I kept all the ribbons on the antenna. A bit bizarre, I'll grant, but what can I do? We own only one car, and we don't agree. And besides, though I've got my position, I'm not sure it's right. I see the other side's point, too. And with each passing day, as the Day of Judgment gets closer, I know that they, too, might be right. So I figure, I don't mind being the only (or at least one of the very few) car with all three colors. I'll live with the stares.

Today I had a lunch meeting at the Faculty Club at Hebrew University. Parking there is always a hassle. The person who invited you has to call in your license plate and other ID information to security, and then you have to reconfirm that you appear on the security list of approved cars. Then you go, drive up to the guard, and pray that it works. If it doesn't, it's always unpleasant. You're annoyed that after all that work, your name's still not there. The person who has now pulled up behind you, who can't move until your situation is resolved, often leans on the horn. Which only distracts the guard and makes everything move more slowly. So that by the time you get to your meeting, you're a jumble of nerves.

So I had my secretary check and double-check that I was on the list. "No problem," she tells me. "I spoke to them, and you're cleared." Great. So I head up to Mount Scopus and pull up to the guard, a young Ethiopian woman in her twenties. I lower the passenger window, and she asks my name. I give it to her, and she scans the list.

"You're not on the list."

"I'm on the list. We just checked. Look again."

Another scan, and, "You're not here."

"Great, so what do we do now?"

"Call the person who invited you, tell them to call security, and they'll call us."

"That's going to take forever."

"That's what you have to do."

None too pleased, I take out my Palm to look up my host's cell number, when the guard points to my ribbons.

"What's with all the colors?"

"Our family is split," I tell her, "and even those of us who do have an opinion, aren't entirely sure we're right. So we've got both. All three, I guess."

She laughed out loud. *"Ahavti, mamash ahavti,"* she grinned and said, meaning something like "I love it. I just love it." Then she looked at me and said, "You know, if everyone around here took that view, this country would actually work." And she tossed her head toward the now-rising gate and said, "Go park, and have a nice day."

I pulled forward, the ribbons rippling in the breeze, and drove toward an open space. And I thought, here we are. An immigrant from Ethiopia and an immigrant from Los Angeles. Chatting with each other in a language that is native to neither of them. On a campus that just decades ago, Israel lost to the Jordanians and had to recapture in 1967. And laughing about the craziness of the only country the Jews have and the only functioning democracy in this part of the world. Things could really be a lot worse.

Which brings us back to what Shlomo said. On the eve of one of the most painful and divisive actions the country has ever had to take (at least with regard to its own citizens), how are we doing?

A hard question to answer. Nervous. Worried. Hopeful.

In short: "Good. As good as can be."

Coming Attractions?

There was a moment, albeit a brief one, when I'd imagined we were done with parent-teacher conferences. At least for one kid. She was, after all, a senior in high school, and we'd already had the annual parents' meeting for her senior year. So we were done, I happily assumed.

But I was wrong. The high school meetings were, indeed, behind us, but what I hadn't counted on was the possibility that the army, too, could have meetings that parents are strongly encouraged to attend. But it does.

Talia, like a number of kids in her class, was being invited to try out for a competitive unit in . . . something. And to attract the girls, and to allay any fears that their parents might have, we were invited to an evening for parents and daughters on a military base in the center of the country.

So the three of us piled into the car and, after getting lost a couple of times, found the right exit for the base, parked, got through security, and found ourselves seated in the auditorium. We'd missed the opening film with all the pyrotechnics, but we did get there in time for the "intelligence briefing." The briefing was given by an officer, clearly bright, who told the girls what Israel was up against, in a tone that suggested that they were being exposed to the most intimate of state secrets, when in reality it wasn't much more than one could glean from a casual reading of most journals and daily newspapers. But he was cool, and more important, apparently extremely cute, so they listened carefully.

Half an hour later, though, the evening got to real business. It was time to convince the girls to try out for this unit. Because of the sensitive nature of the work and the fact that none of us had security clearances, we were given only the most minimal description of what they would be doing. And then the girls were asked to decide. Oh, well.

As part of the army's show and tell, they'd positioned three girls on stage, all of whom were in this unit and in their first year, and who apparently loved what they were doing. All three spoke in the most general way about their service (since everything they do is classified), but they did manage to communicate the sense of privilege they felt to be part of the unit.

While they were speaking, I noticed their uniforms. Even though they were all religious girls, they were each dressed very differently. One was wearing pants and a standard IDF olive-green short-sleeved shirt. One was wearing an IDF-issued skirt, down to her knees, and the same short-sleeved shirt. And the last one was wearing a different IDF-issued skirt, down to her ankles, with a long-sleeved uniform shirt, buttoned at the wrists and all the way up to the collar. Though I couldn't be sure, I assumed that this was planned. The army, we were being told, is a hospitable place for girls of all religious walks of life, and it will do its best to accommodate them. OK—we've got the point.

Later in the evening, after the unit's commander and the base rabbi had spoken, it was time for questions from the parents. Which, it turns out, was the real reason for the evening.

It quickly became clear that there were many families in the room who did not want their daughters in the army, who were worried about the impact that being drafted would have on their girls' religious commitments (and religious girls have the option of doing National Service rather than the army). The questions, asked mostly by fathers, were for the most part incredibly hostile. I would have liked to leave, but as Tali had to stay until the end to hand in some forms, there was nothing to do but wait it out.

So I more or less tuned out until one father stood up, obviously angry before he'd so much as uttered a word, and turned to the base commander and the base rabbi and asked (or, more accurately, hissed), "Do you make the girls work on Shabbat?"

The room was perfectly silent. Everyone knew the answer and assumed that a confrontation between the father and the base rabbi was inevitable. No one moved. Even the rabbi, who had to answer the question, said nothing. He stood at the podium, leaned into the mike, and, lost in thought, played with his beard. How, he was obviously wondering, could he answer the question honestly and still avoid a scene?

As he pondered the challenge, no one stirred. So it was with particular clarity and astonishment that we saw and then heard the girl on the right, the one with the buttons up to her chin and the sleeves to her wrists, with the skirt to her ankles, look the father right in the eye and, without being called on, say to him, "Of course we work on Shabbat." And then after a second's pause, "*Gam ha-oyev oved be-shabbat.*" "The enemy also works on Shabbat."

Checkmate. This isn't the scouts, she was telling that father. This is a serious business. We're not in this unit because we like the work. We're here because someone needs to do this. The future of the country depends on this. And in our heart of hearts, she implied, there's no contradiction at all between serving the state and serving God. They go hand in hand. Combined, they are the backbone of religious Zionism. She didn't say any of that, of course, but she didn't have to. The image of the hypermodestly dressed young woman openly telling the group, in front of her rabbi, that of course she worked on Shabbat—because the state needed her to—pretty much said it all.

It was quiet in the car on the way home. Partly because we were all tired. Partly, I assume, because Talia was processing how different this world was going to be from any that she'd known before, and how ill-equipped her immigrant parents were going to be at helping her navigate it. And because, at least for me, I couldn't help thinking about that girl on the stage and believing that despite it all, if this country was still producing kids like that, things here would all work out.

But that was a very long time ago. A year ago. Before the disengagement got serious. Before Israel started drowning in orange and blue. Before we had the cease-fire, and then last week's Netanya suicide bombing and Hamas's Kassam rocket reminders of how painful it's going to be when the lull and the quiet that we've so happily gotten used to inevitably come to an explosive end. It was before the march on Gaza by thirty thousand opponents of the disengagement, and the massing of somewhere between fifteen and twenty thousand troops to stop them from getting into what the army has declared a "closed military zone." It was before Israeli soldiers were declared heroes for refusing their orders.

Israeli society takes heroism seriously. Our kids are bombarded from kindergarten through the end of high school with visits from heroes from the front. The ones who survived Syrian captivity but gave away no secrets. The ones who volunteered for the most dangerous missions and came back to tell the story. The ones who lost limbs or came back paralyzed, yet still go on. The ones who lost their best friends and strive to live up to the challenge of honoring their memories. It can be a bit much to watch your kids hear this year in and year out, but you take a deep breath and try not to think about it too much, because you know exactly why the "system" does this. The country needs more heroes, and it needs more parents to raise their kids to want to be heroes.

Which brings us back to Monday of this week, and the march. The march called "The March to Our Brothers, the Heroes in Gaza." A clever moniker, indeed. For suddenly, the heroes are not the soldiers. The heroes are the people living in Gaza, who are about to be "exiled," or "transferred," both words that they use, and both words with powerful Jewish resonance. No, we were being told, now to be a hero means to insist that it doesn't matter what the government has decided. To be a hero means to resist the soldiers or to refuse orders. To be a hero this week means to scream at the soldiers, many of them eighteen- and nineteen-year-old kids who probably would much rather have been on summer vacation between their freshman and sophomore years. To yell, in front of the cameras, "What will you tell your children about what you did here?" "Aren't you ashamed?" "Soldier, it's not too late. You can refuse your orders!" "Jews don't exile Jews!"

And for seventy-two hours, in the sweltering heat of the Middle East summer, thirty thousand protesters and twenty thousand members of the security forces stood on opposite sides of a hastily erected fence. The protesters said they were going to march all the way to Gaza. And the police and soldiers said that they weren't, that Kfar Maimon was as far as they were going to go. And then the security forces formed a human ring, several people deep, around the group, and let no one move. The pictures on the news (not covered much in the international press, since Israelis weren't shooting anyone) said it all—a sea of orange, men, women, and children, on a massive pilgrimage for the sake of God. A Jewish crusade?

And across from them, thousands upon thousands of young men in uniform, looking confused, bewildered. By what they were seeing. By what they were hearing. And, perhaps, even, by what they were doing?

The future is now, I told myself as I watched the news (much more than I should have) throughout the week. There would come a time, we all knew, when the question of whether Israel would be democratic or Jewish would ultimately be put to the test. But that test, I'd thought, would come from Israel's Arabs. They're already 20 percent of the population now, and that number is climbing.

So now that mass immigration to Israel is over (there's only one numerically significant Jewish Diaspora community left, and it's not going to come in any meaningful numbers), what is going to prevent Israel's Arabs, who are justifiably not terribly committed Zionists, from becoming 25 percent and then 30 percent and then 35 percent of the population? And as that number grows, what will they do when they finally have powerful political sway?

And what should we Jews do as that clock ticks? Honor democracy and erode the Jewish content of the state? Or protect the Jewish character of Israel, and somehow curtail the democracy?

Though we've known that that choice was looming, we thought we had a few years before it became a crisis. But we were wrong, for the issue came to a head this week. Not because of the Arabs, but because of the Jews. This was the week when two of the most prominent rabbis in Israel ordered their students to refuse orders related to the disengagement. When soldiers were interviewed and responded that yes, they take their orders seriously, but what can they do when their rabbis tell them that Torah commands otherwise? When, in retaliation, Defense Minister Shaul Mofaz hinted that he would dismantle *hesder* yeshiva programs—sponsored jointly by the army and the religious communities—where the rabbis instructed their disciples to refuse orders.

This was the week, in short, when the secular government and its army (in which many religious Jews continue to serve) aligned against the almost monolithic religious bloc, each declaring that it would not back down, each declaring that the other was a threat to the State of Israel. It was the week of rabbis versus commanders, the week (or so it seemed to many secular observers) of those loyal to the state versus those loyal to God. It was, in short, the week when we got a glimpse of what this country could come to look like.

Because it's so frightening, many people around here are trying to comfort themselves, claiming that despite it all, democracy won. After three sweltering days, without enough bathrooms or sufficient water for fifty thousand people camped out in the desert in Kfar Maimon, the orange-wearing protesters gave up, didn't they? They went home, and lost. Didn't democracy win?

I'm not sure, though. Even if democracy won, it was bruised. The only question is how badly.

It shouldn't require twenty thousand troops and police to stop people from entering an area that the army has declared closed. In a functioning democracy, people might protest. March. Hold signs. Even block roads. But openly declare that they will enter areas the army says are forbidden? Siphon away forces that are critically needed in the war on terror? And encourage soldiers to violate their orders?

Now, it will be asked, how's that different from when left-wing pilots refused to carry out missions in the territories a few years ago, or when many more left-leaning soldiers refused to serve in the West Bank or Gaza? Fair enough. Maybe it's just the numbers that were different. Or the fact that this time, those who refused to follow orders were backed by an enormous edifice, in this case, the religious establishment.

But now, if only because of the scale, the threat to democracy looms larger. Israel amassed twenty thousand troops to prevent a protest from moving westward toward Gaza, and to me, the pictures look like Tiananmen Square in 1989. The reality is different, to be sure. But how long can it stay that different?

This time, democracy and the country got lucky, because the protesters gave up. But what if they hadn't? What if they had tried to push by the fence, and beyond the human chain? Dare we imagine what heat, exhaustion, dehydration, and passions can do in the desert with fifty thousand people in a tiny area?

And no, democracy didn't win so neatly, because the government was no better. By virtue of what authority did Ariel Sharon (or whoever it was) stop the buses that were bringing the protesters to congregate? What gave them the right to confiscate the drivers' licenses? Is it now illegal to hire a bus to take people to a protest? These buses weren't stopped near Gaza. They weren't stopped near a border. They were stopped all over the country, smack in the middle of internationally recognized sovereign Israel. Now it's illegal to drive the bus if the government doesn't like the purpose?

Of course, Sharon believed, perhaps correctly, that this had to be their last stand. That here, he would demonstrate that even though we've never imagined it possible, yes, the country *would* use force to stop the religious community. One can understand why he thought this necessary.

But there was a cost. It's hard to say precisely why, but it feels as if we've crossed an important line here. And what will happen next time? What line will we cross then? How much more has to shift before we no longer recognize the country we're all trying to save?

One Ribbon Has to Go

It's settler day. Some people from the States have asked me to show them around the "settlements," so that they can see for themselves what these places are like, and who lives there. So I team up with someone I know who lives in Shiloh, way over the Green Line, and who knows these communities infinitely better than I do. Together, he and I amass some reading materials for them. And then we arrange to take a few hours one day to show these people around.

The idea, at least in my mind, is to show them that the settlements—and the settlers—are a varied group, much too heterogeneous to be thought about as one cohesive unit. Maybe, if I'm lucky, I'll get them to understand why this disengagement is so problematic, so hard. Why I'm still so conflicted. Why we still have all three ribbons—orange, blue, and white—tied to the antenna on our car.

I ask Elisheva to drive me downtown to where I'm going to meet the group. We hop into the car, our three ribbons fluttering in the breeze, and in minutes, I'm there. "Have fun," she says. "Stay low and keep moving," a quip we started using back in the days when Jerusalem was a veritable shooting gallery.

After a quick visit to the Gush Eztion Museum, where they learn about the history of the Gush Eztion bloc, where they can get a sense of the deep historical roots Jews have to this region, our group heads off to our first meeting with a real "settler." She lives in Efrat, which though unquestionably over the Green Line, is really a bedroom community of Jerusalem. American by birth, she's very involved in Efrat politics and is extremely articulate, passionate, and fair. She leads us to one of the higher topographical points in Efrat and points out Bethlehem. Jerusalem. The roads that are occasionally blocked by the army. And she explains why. About where her children go to school. About where the attacks in her area have originated. About the attacks in Efrat itself.

And then she talks about the future. She looks our charges squarely in the eye and says, "I want them to have a state. And I'm even willing to give up land for them to have it. But they have to show us that they can rein in the terror. And before they do that, I wouldn't give them a thing. That's what's wrong with the disengagement—it's caving in to terror. But if they can establish a functioning government and start disarming the terrorists? I'd give them land for their state. They've got kids, too. And those kids deserve better than what they have now."

Already we can see our guests beginning to think and to rethink. Sure doesn't sound like the settler from CNN sound bites, does it? And suddenly, the disengagement seems rather strange. Why, in fact, would we reward terror?

The questions still ticking away, we and our armed guards board our bulletproof bus, heading north, past Jerusalem, past Ramallah, and still further north, to Shiloh.

It takes about an hour, perhaps a bit more, to get to Shiloh, the capital of Israel in the time of the biblical Judges, the site of the tabernacle under Joshua, the place where Hannah came to worship and to pray for a child. You can't get more biblical than this land. With rolling hills of olive trees, identical to how they must have looked thousands of years ago, the area looks largely uninhabited. And the map that my colleague has distributed—of the biblical area of the tribe of Benjamin—seems to confirm that. Jerusalem is on the map. As is Shiloh. And Beit El, Ofrah, Pesagot, and Talmon. And lots of smaller settlements, too.

Ramallah is on the map, as are a few other Arab villages, but not too many. The area of the tribe of Benjamin, as far as the map would indicate, is a pretty Jewish area.

When we get to Shiloh, we are given a tour of the town, with its large houses, paved, tree-lined streets, and schools. We're shown the spot where archaeologists believe that the Ark itself may have rested. And we meet with a rabbi who lives there, a Western, well-spoken, internationally respected teacher and thinker. He tells us that life in Israel is a matter of prophecy and politics, a balance of matters of the soul with issues more practical. And today, he says, he wants to focus on prophecy. He tries to give a sense of what it's like to raise one's children in the land of the Bible. Not in Jerusalem, with its tall buildings and metropolitan sensibilities, but in Shiloh, where they can play outside knowing full well that in this very field the Ark of the Covenant rested for generations. He speaks about the love of the land, of the sense of purpose that comes with reclaiming an ancient Israelite homeland for our own.

His passion is evident, but his presentation is so different from that of the woman we'd met in Efrat that I'm afraid our "students" for the day won't be able to compare her position to his. Not that I'm so clear as to what his position is. So I decide to try to get him to lay out *his* vision of the future. After all, in Efrat, the woman they'd met said that if the Palestinians reined in terror, she'd be willing to give up land. But the land that she'd give up would probably be *this* land. What would our host say about that?

When he was done, I thanked him and asked him if he might be willing to move away from prophecy and to say something to the group about politics. "What do you see here in the long run?" I asked him. "How does your love of this land dovetail with a vision for how a semblance of peace eventually comes to this region?"

But he doesn't want to go there. "It's a fair question," he says, "but today I want to focus on prophecy. I don't want to think about politics today."

Not such a fair answer, it seems to me. For how are our American friends supposed to think seriously about what these communities mean for the future unless we hear from the people themselves what they have in mind? But he wasn't to be budged.

So we moved on from there to a very small settlement only a mile or two down the road. It's Giv'at Achiyah, a small collection of about a dozen caravans, and a visitors' center where they sell olive oil made from their trees and show a video about the area, their industry, and their hopes that when the Third Temple is built, the olive oil made here will be used on the Temple Mount. (The video does not mention, of course, that for the Third Temple to be built, the Dome of the Rock would have to be destroyed.)

The presentation is given by a young woman, probably in her midthirties, named Rachel. She works in high-tech in Jerusalem, we learn, but her passion for living out on these barren hills is obvious and impressive.

Here, though, sitting in the visitors center, one can see several small Arab villages not far at all from Giv'at Achiyah. And those villages don't seem to be on the map of the region that's been distributed. One of our guests catches on to this and asks Rachel, "How are your relations with the local Arab community?"

"They're fine," Rachel says.

"Do you work with them, or have any kind of relationship with them?" the questioner continues.

"No. But when we work our land, they just back off. It's fine."

"Fine relations," quite clearly, means something very different in this region than it does in the American communities from which these people come.

Someone else asks Rachel if this settlement is supported by the government. "No," she says, "we don't get a penny from the government."

At that moment, an army jeep drives by for the third time since our meeting with Rachel has begun. So I ask her, "What's the story with that jeep?"

"That's the army's patrol. They protect the settlement."

"Would you call that support from the government?" I ask.

"Well, yeah, we do get that. But our men help. We also patrol the perimeter at night." What that's supposed to prove I'm not entirely sure, but I drop it.

"I'm interested," I continue, "in hearing something about your vision for the future of this area. Obviously, you plan to stay. And seeing the beauty here, and knowing the Jewish history of the area, one can easily understand why. But as we can also see from these windows, there are quite a few Arab villages in the area. I'm curious about what you see as the long-term solution for these two populations."

She looks at me as if the question is absurd. "God gave us this land."

"OK, so therefore?"

"They can leave. We're going to stay here, so they can live under us, or they should leave."

It's quiet in the room. No one seems to want to breathe. Because suddenly we're getting to the point.

"Where would you suggest that they go?" I ask.

"Anywhere. Syria, Jordan. Anywhere. But this is our land."

I want to ask if she's thought about the fact that while we've had this land since 1967, many of the Arabs have families who've lived in those villages for hundreds of years. But I know she'll just tell me that we had that land in biblical times and that God gave it to us. That question won't move us very far. I'm tempted to ask her if she knows anything about Black September, and King Hussein's flagrant attack on the Palestinians in Jordan, or why she thinks that Jordan would be open to a mass immigration of Palestinians. But she'll say she doesn't know anything about Jordanian politics.

So I turn to my colleague, who lives in the area, and ask him, "How many Jews live today in the area of Binyamin?"

"Hard to say," he says.

"A rough estimate," I press him.

"In the Binyamin Regional Council Borders?"

"Fine."

"About 33,000 Jews, give or take."

"Great, and how many Arabs would you say live in the region?"

"Very hard to know."

"A guesstimate."

"About 300,000, more or less."

The group looks at Rachel and at my colleague. And out the window at the idyllic, pastoral setting. The wheels are churning. Ten times as many Arabs as there are Jews, and we haven't seen an Arab all day. Ten times as many Arabs as there are Jews, and the map they've been given shows scarcely an Arab village. Ten times as many Arabs as there are Jews, and Rachel just says, "Let them leave."

I turn to my colleague again and ask him, "How many Jews live in the West Bank altogether?"

"Including greater Jerusalem?"

"No, without Jerusalem."

"About 245,000, give or take."

"And Arabs?"

"About 2.3 million, give or take a hundred thousand or so. Maybe 2.4 million."

Suddenly, they're all looking at Rachel. Saying nothing, but the echo of "They can leave" hangs in the air. Two and a half million people? Leave to where? And invisible, until they're gone. "Fine relations." Why? Because "when we work our fields, they back off."

We climb back onto the bus and begin the southward drive back to Jerusalem, through the same pristine hills, still beautiful, still dotted with green, still an echo of a biblical era long since vanished. But they seem different to me now, these hills. As if, despite their beauty and the love anyone with even a spark of Jewish loyalty would feel for them, they hide an ugly secret.

There's nothing we heard today that I didn't know before. Those numbers aren't secret, and the plight of the Arabs on the West Bank is regularly documented by *Ha-Aretz* writers like Amira Haas and Gideon Levy. But it's one thing to read it in the paper and another to hear someone, someone who looks and sounds completely balanced, just tell you that more than a million people can, and should, disappear. In my social circles, people don't believe that. But there's clearly another side of what we're becoming, and seeing it in the flesh has jolted me much more than I'd ever expected it would.

Is that what the past thirty-eight years have wrought? Since 1967 we've been sitting there, building there, without any serious thought as to what we were going to do in the long run. And to make that possible, we've become half-blind, it seems to me. That map shows the Jewish settlements, but not the Arab villages. We can spend the whole day touring the area, and not see 90 percent of the population. We hardly see an Arab vehicle on the roads. There are Jews, religious Jews, decent Jews, who can think about the future and say, without hesitation, "Let them leave." All two and a half million of them?!

Sitting at the front of the bus, staring out the enormous windshield at a vista that I can't imagine not loving, I know what I have to do. It's a small gesture, with no impact. It will make absolutely no difference. But when I get home, I'm going to take the orange ribbon off the car. Not because I'm sure that this Gaza move is smart. Not because I know how Sharon will handle the security problem of Kassam and Hamas in Gaza without the army there. And not because my heart doesn't break for the settlers and all they're going to lose, for it does.

But I'm going to take the ribbon off because at the end of the day, there are parts of the place called Israel that are becoming a country completely unlike the one I thought I was moving to. This wasn't why we brought our kids here. If staying in those territories is going to make us blind to the Arab population, then we have to withdraw. For when I was growing up, I intuited that the more we deepened our Jewish memory, the more we deepened our humanity.

But no longer. Memory, love of the land, even love of parts of the Bible, are coming at the expense of our humanity. What I've felt for a long time is no longer deniable. We have to pull out soon, before the poison runs too deep, before we're more calloused. We have to leave parts of the land we love, so that there's a Jewish soul left to cultivate the land we're left with.

What about Elisheva, I suddenly wonder. And I'm not sure what to do. There's no way she's going to want to take that ribbon off the car. I could just take it off, I assume, and tell her I don't know what happened, if she even asks. But that seems kind of cheap. No, I should talk to her about this. But then we're going to have a heated discussion, at best. And I'm wiped after today. Maybe I'll just take it off after all, and we can talk about it later.

Or maybe, I muse Solomonically, we'll just take off all the ribbons.

And have no opinion at all? What's the point of that?

The bus drops us off downtown, and I hop in a cab to get home. Five minutes later, we turn onto our street, and I decide. Hell, I'm just going to pull the damn ribbon off, and then I'll talk about it with Elisheva afterward. But after today, I just can't have it on the car.

I pay the cabbie, and decide that I'll take the ribbon off even before I go in the house. I see the car parked on the street, about half a block down. So I walk over, and then cross to the other side of the car, where the ribbons are hanging off of the cell phone antenna. Wondering how I'll ever get that knot undone, it takes me a minute to notice. There's no orange ribbon. The blue and the white are doing fine, still attached to the antenna, but the orange is gone. For a minute, I'm not sure that I'm seeing straight. But I check again, and sure enough, there's no orange.

Later, over dinner, I ask, as casually as I can, "Hey, what happened to the orange ribbon on the car?"

Without missing a beat, Elisheva says, "I took it off." And she looks at me, as if she's waiting for the barrage to begin.

"Why?"

She takes a deep breath. "I was on the treadmill today, watching one of the episodes of *Tekumah* [a TV show produced by Israel television on the fiftieth anniversary of the State, tracing the history of Israel from its beginnings to the present]. And I watched the episode about the first Intifada."

"And?"

"They showed these settlers just marching through the Arab village, just to piss them off, waving Israeli flags, as if either the Arabs weren't there, or it would be fun to spite them. And I decided that we're just becoming disgusting. So we should get the hell out."

She's quiet, assuming, I imagine, that I'm going to object to not having been consulted. Or argue the larger point with her.

"Guess what?" I tell her. "I was going to take the orange ribbon off when I got home today, and I was afraid you'd be mad."

She laughs. "You're kidding." Maybe she's thinking what I'm thinking, that this is some sort of Zionist version of "The Gift of the Magi." O. Henry would be proud. "Why?" she wants to know.

I tell her about my day. Efrat. Prophecy but no politics. Oil for the Third Temple. "Fine relations." "They can just leave."

And then it's quiet again. I'm not sure what she's thinking, but I know what's going through my head. How lucky we are. In five years of war, each of us has moved to the left, and then to the right, and not always at the same time. But in the end, we've always come back to a place more or less similar to each other's.

Not everyone's been so lucky. We know couples who haven't made it through the past five years and who have split up. We know families in which the wife desperately wants to go back to the States, but the husband won't budge. Or vice versa. We know couples in which one has moved way to the right, and one way to the left, and where, when you visit them at home, you can cut the air with a knife.

Somehow we've avoided all that. Despite our different visceral reactions to much of what's happened here, at the end of the day, we still dream about the same kind of country. About surviving with our kids intact. But with our souls intact, too. And today, with a bit of chutzpah, and a willingness to apologize when we inevitably get caught, each of us resolves to take the orange ribbon off.

Clearing the table, I look out the window and down the block to our car. From this angle, the two remaining ribbons are easily visible. Blue and white, hanging peacefully along the passenger's window.

I'd assumed we were going to have a rough moment or two if I took that ribbon off. Turns out I was wrong. Is it possible, just possible, I wonder, that this might happen across the country, too? Might it just possibly be that deep down, all the vitriol notwithstanding, there's still a shared dream here that might carry us through the weeks to come?

Reengagement

We returned to a country bereft of ribbons. When we'd left for England for our summer vacation with the kids, Israel was festooned in orange. And blue. And white. And the cataclysm of the disengagement loomed.

I'd wanted to be here for the disengagement, and we'd planned our trip accordingly. But then Sharon delayed the disengagement by a few weeks, and by that time, we had made our plans. We returned the day after the disengagement ended. And the first thing that I noticed in the car on the way back to Jerusalem was that the ribbons were gone. Almost completely. Overnight, it seemed (though it was longer than that), the orange had disappeared. The blue was gone. As was the white. It felt, climbing up the hills to Jerusalem, like a country in black and white. Like a state with its colors drained.

Where did all the ribbons go? They were just flimsy pieces of cloth, Elisheva said. After all, they'd been pretty ratty even when we'd left. Maybe they all just started falling off.

That didn't seem likely to me. No, I was certain that people had taken them off. But why? They were probably tired, I figured. It had been an exhausting two months.

Two weeks later, now that Israel has finished the pullout from Gaza, I think otherwise. It's not that the ribbons frayed and fell off. Nor was it that people are tired of arguing (turning on the radio is all the proof one needs of that). Rather, I think, it is because the morning-after reality is too painful for slogans. Or ribbons. Now that it's over, the only thing that matters is moving beyond it and dealing with the lives and the hearts that were broken. And recognizing, no matter how we feel about it, that we live in a shrinking country.

There is good news, of course. The state survived. In the long, hot, depressing summer that preceded the disengagement, the prevailing question was what would happen when the forces of the state confronted the forces of religion. In that age-old seesaw of Israel as a Jewish and a democratic state, what would happen when the Jewish and the democratic came head to head? Would someone blink, or would we end up with a civil war?

Democracy—battered and imperfect, for there never was a referendum, and to this day, we don't really know what percentage of the citizens really supported this withdrawal—won, or at least survived.

Remember rabbis like Rav Schapira and Rav Eliyahu? They were the rabbis who instructed their students and their adherents to disobey orders, and who appeared to have enormous power in the days before the retreat. Two weeks later, they're gone. Not silenced, perhaps. But not quoted, either. Because they overplayed their hand. Most Israelis simply didn't have it in them to bring the enterprise down. It's frail enough as it is. At the end of the day, the settlers (still a terrible term) obeyed the police. With tears and with dignity, but without violence, most simply bade their homes good-bye and walked away from the lives they'd built for decades. And their sons and daughters in the army, by and large, obeyed their orders.

Despite the pain that defies description, the loss of homes and businesses, schools and yeshivot, *batei midrash* and parks, playgrounds and friendships, despite the wounds that will take not weeks or months but many years to heal, the state won. It was, given what we had feared, an extraordinary statement by Israelis that despite everything—or because of everything—there's a bond between us all that has triumphed even over the deep divisions. At the end of the day, most people here recognized that what was at stake wasn't settlements, or homes, even people. What was at stake was the still fragile state we call home. The home we have is smaller and will get still smaller. And in the face of that, there was really no place for ribbons.

That is probably why it went as smoothly as it did. No shots were fired. Thousands of people were evicted from their homes. Their children would not return to the same schools and in many cases would have trouble finding schools to take them. They would never live in houses like those again, they would leave behind the cemeteries in which their children are buried (those graves were moved a few days later) . . . and they walked out peacefully.

Admittedly, the army and police handled it all magnificently, with very few exceptions. The soldiers sent in were not the eighteen- and nineteen-year-old kids who might have been hotter under the collar, but reservists, with wives and kids, who'd been around the block a few more times, and who would know how to handle the hurt and the hate. The police, who normally wear uniforms with the word "Police" on the front, were issued new hats and vests. The same color, the same shape. But instead of the word "Police," just the printed image of an Israeli flag, so that the settlers who saw the long columns of blue uniforms marching into their communities, saw police, yes, but they also saw a long line of bobbing Israeli flags. The flag they love. The flag they know is the only one the Jews will have as long as any of us are alive, and far beyond that. And in the end, the residents packed up, and with tear-stained faces and the sort of dignity that emerges only from hearts bursting with anguish, just walked away from it all.

Twenty percent of the IDF's officers are religious. And how many of them refused orders when it came down to it? Virtually none. True, the army didn't use most of the younger religious units. Why put those kids in such an impossible situation? But there were religious officers there, lots of them. You just had to watch the news and the videos to see.

What I did see, during and after, was some of the saddest footage I've ever seen. People who had survived the horrors of Europe in the last century, the numbers still tattooed on their arms, being displaced again. The old man who collapsed on the sidewalk and just couldn't go any farther. The soldiers and the police who, themselves, were crying. Some of the people being evicted screaming at the top of their lungs, hurling invectives at the soldiers. And the soldiers standing stoic, saying nothing in return—for what is there to say, and, of course, because they were ordered to say nothing—and then offering the people water.

It's a small gesture, in the face of the loss of a house and dream, a plastic bottle of chilled water. But in the heat of the Middle East summer, it's a ubiquitous, and often lifesaving, gesture. And its simple humanity made the scene even more horrific. And wondrous.

Indescribably painful footage, true, but also the kind that makes us proud to be part of this huge experiment called the Jewish state. No arms. I remember in May thinking that Rabbi Meidan's suggestion that the army forswear the use of weapons during the disengagement was naïve. After all, what kind of army doesn't use arms? This army, it turns out.

Tears, yes, but no violence. Disbelief. Soldiers knocking at the door and, when answered, cutting their own uniforms in the traditional sign of Jewish mourning. Because even for those on the left, there's nothing to celebrate about Jews being evicted from their homes. Because even for the blue ribbons, this was not a victory. Who can celebrate, as our borders close in around us? There was nothing else to do but mourn. And wipe the tears away.

That's why there was also no gloating. Talia was hesitantly in favor of the disengagement. Not without tremendous misgivings, both political and religious, but at the end of the day, she thought it was what we needed to do. She came home one day with a blue ribbon tied to her purse. Surprised, I asked her why, knowing that in her crowd, that couldn't be an easy thing to do. "If my friends who are opposed are willing to go to jail for what they believe in [by refusing orders, which a few did]," she said, "the least I can do is tie a ribbon to my purse."

Sometimes the simplest things your kids do just take your breath away.

And then we left for London without her. Her draft date was approaching, and the army wouldn't allow her out of the country. So I called her every day, to make sure she wasn't too lonely. "What are you doing?" I asked her one day. Watching the live coverage of the disengagement all day, she said. "It's horrible, Abba. There's no way to describe it. It's killing me, and still, I can't turn it off."

"Do something else," I told her. "Get out of the house. Go see some friends. Do anything." She said she would. When I called the next day, I asked her what she was doing. The answer? She and friends, some in favor and some opposed, were all going to spend the day at a hotel, packing food, toys, and other goods that were being collected in enormous quantities for the newly homeless families.

There were no sides anymore, these kids seemed to intuit. And no need for ribbons.

Avi, too, decided he was "blue" in the last days before the disengagement. Sixteen years old, he's impatient with ideologies in general, and
with a conflict that seems to have no end in sight. So he's decided that
someone has to break the cycle. And decided he was blue.

And then the school year began. A few days after school started, he
came home late, exhausted and filthy. Where were you, we asked him.
Working in greenhouses all day, he told us. His class went to a small
community just outside Gaza and spent the day hauling thousands of
plants, planters, equipment, and the like, trying to help a few families get
their greenhouse businesses up and running again.

No more ribbons, no more sides. Just trying to rebuild, in the shadow
of the destruction that was, and in the face of the knowledge that there's
probably more to come.

Avi brought a plant home with him. Hundreds of the plants were
dying already, he said, and the greenhouse owners were going to throw
them out. But the kids asked to take them home. Avi brought his into the
house and asked Elisheva, "Ema, do you think we can save it?" Now that
he'd confronted the human side of what this whole thing meant, one had
the sense that it was much more than the little plant he was hoping we
might save.

And then, this morning, Tali left for the army. Without regret, with no
sense that she's doing anything terribly extraordinary. Because she knows
that this little, and ever smaller, country is the only chance we're going to
get. So the kids have to defend it.

The orange kids and the blue kids are all olive-green kids today.

Israel finished pulling out of Gaza today. In the early hours of the
morning, the last tank crossed the line, and the gate was shut. Most of the
news coverage is about how the Palestinians burned the synagogues that
we'd left standing. For me, though, that story wasn't particularly interesting. We knew they'd desecrate the synagogues. What did we expect? A
disgusting sight to be sure, but not really news.

What struck me, instead, is how quickly it was all over. How in a
matter of weeks, any vestige of those thriving communities simply
disappeared. Erased. As if it never was. The towns and the houses, the

schools and the parks, the cemeteries and the factories, the gardens and
the synagogues, they're all gone. Those places that we took the kids to see
have been bulldozed. To see whole Jewish communities disappear like
that was more than sad—it was frightening, given the people who still
surround us on all sides.

Deep down, most people here know that the communities of
Gaza will not be the last to be erased. At dinner tonight, Avi, Micha, and
Elisheva were engaged in a heated discussion about whether Jerusalem
will ever be divided again. Interesting, I thought. They're not even
bothering to talk about the West Bank. Or of the Golan. To them, it was
obvious that we're going to give those back. Not tomorrow. Not next
month. But sometime.

I wonder what it feels like to be a kid who lives in a shrinking country. Sinai back to the Egyptians. A pullout from Lebanon in 2000 (a place
we never said we'd stay, of course). Gaza today. And tomorrow?

When I was a kid, I grew up with the image of Israel as a growing
country. The absurd borders of the 1947 UN partition plan expanded to
the borders of 1949 at the end of the war. The Sinai captured in 1956 and,
though returned, captured again in 1967, along with the Golan, Gaza,
the West Bank, and Jerusalem.

My kids are growing up in a very different world. The "Exodus" (biblical, or the boat) is no longer about leaving someplace else and coming
here. Exoduses are now about leaving the place we dreamt of coming to.
About contracting. And each one becomes more painful, more dangerous, and more controversial.

What do you do in the face of that? You can protest. You can vow to
get Sharon out of office (only to watch someone else retreat in his stead,
of course). You can tell your yeshiva students to ignore the orders they're
given. You can compare Sharon (as some did) to a Nazi. You can lose
hope. You can walk away in disgust (especially if you never lived here in
the first place).

Or you can roll up your sleeves and get to work. You can put on a uniform, hoist onto your back a knapsack that weighs almost as much as you
do, give your brothers and your parents a kiss, and head off to defend
what's left.

Because whether you were blue or orange during the summer that's passed, none of that matters anymore. Because you know that this place isn't about ribbons, but about chances. For a hot and horrid summer, we allowed ourselves to imagine that what mattered was the color of the ribbon on our car. And now we know we were wrong. What matters is something much simpler.

What matters is the clear and undeniable fact that this small, pain-wracked country is the last chance we have. And probably ever will.

There Are No Words

W ait till you see her in a uniform," my friend Asher says to me one Shabbat morning in shul, knowing that Talia's draft date is approaching. "You see your kid come home in that green, and there are no words."

Strangely though, when I see her all dressed in her uniform and ready to go, her brand new backpack stuffed to the limit, I'm proud of her, but for me, it's not one of those memorable moments. I give her a hug and watch her walk out the door, she and her mother heading for the car as Elisheva gets ready to drive her to the base and to the beginning of basic training. And I just hope she'll be OK.

A couple of days later, I have to go to the States for a very quick trip. About ten-thirty in the evening, as Nir is driving me to the airport, I call Talia's cell phone, figuring that by now, she's got to be done. I'll see how she is and say good-bye. Maybe she'll want something from America.

But there's no answer. Just her bubbly voice, in that Hebrew that sounds thoroughly Israeli, as native as can be. "Hi, you've reached Talia's voicemail. Leave me a message and I'll talk to you soon."

"Hi, it's Abba," I tell her. "I'm going to the States. Where are you? It's ten-thirty at night. Don't you get any time off? My flight's not until one in the morning, so I'll have my phone on until then. Call me. I love you."

But she doesn't call. I think about calling her again, but I know that the last thing she needs is a father to pester her. Maybe she's talking with friends. Maybe she's sleeping. Midnight passes, and one o'clock comes, but there's no call. The plane pushes back from the gate and starts the slow taxi to the runway. I turn the phone off.

Less than forty-eight hours later, I'm back. The plane touches down at Tel Aviv, and instinctively I turn on my phone. One message.

"Hi, Abba. Tali. Sorry I missed your call. We didn't get back to our barracks until after one in the morning. We were out at the firing range, practicing shooting at night. I'm tired now, exhausted. Hope you're having a safe trip. I guess you'll get this when you get back. Love ya."

Since then, she's come home and gone a few times, and now we've got a routine. Every couple of weeks, she comes home on Friday afternoon, tosses her filthy uniforms into the wash, takes a shower, and sleeps. And sleeps. Hangs out for a while with some friends and then sleeps some more.

It seems we hardly see her during her visits. She needs to sleep. To catch up with friends. And to get to bed before she has to head back to the base on Sunday morning.

She could take the bus from our house to the central Jerusalem bus station, and then another bus to Tel Aviv and yet another from there to the base in the center of Israel where she's stationed, but if I drive her to the bus station in Jerusalem, I can save her at least the first of the bus trips, and some time. She can sleep a few extra minutes. So that's what we do, each time.

"What time do you want to leave in the morning?" I ask her.

"I need to get the six-fifteen bus if I'm going to make it to the base on time, so can we leave the house at six?"

"Sure. Should I wake you?"

"I'll set an alarm for five-forty, but just poke your head in to make sure that I'm awake."

Five o'clock in the morning, I'm at my desk, grabbing some quiet time for work before the house comes to life. It's still dark outside, but the morning is crisp and beautiful, so I have the window open. Without many cars on the roads yet, it's virtually silent outside. After a few minutes, there's a distant sound, which I know is the muezzin chanting out his call to worship from one of the mosques in the Old City. And a short while later, the church bells from the Dormition Abbey on Mount Zion begin to chime. And a few minutes after that, it's the quiet chatter of the men making their way to *selichot*, the early-morning penitential prayers that are being recited each morning now that Rosh Hashanah is just days away.

Rosh Hashanah. I remember how quiet it was on Rosh Hashanah just five years ago, our first year in this house. How filled with promise everything seemed. Barak was going to get us out of Lebanon. And make peace with Syria. And then with the Palestinians. Listen up, he'd said to a nervous but hopeful country, everything's going to be OK. Everything's going to change.

And then everything did change. And spun completely out of control. Into years of bombings. Of everyone here being afraid to listen to the news, but being afraid not to listen to the news, too. Of wondering where our kids were every second of the day. And of wondering if it would ever end.

Now, on the eve of yet another Rosh Hashanah, it just might be ending. The summer of disengagement has passed, with a searing pain that abides and with jagged scars that have yet to heal, but without the civil war we'd once feared. True, the country has shrunk, and it's likely to shrink again before this is all over. With more pain. More dislocation. More risk. But we've made it through so far. That's a good sign.

And the third Intifada hasn't started, at least not yet. Maybe it won't. Who knows?

A first ray of light begins to creep over the rooftops and trees outside the window, and I look at the clock. It's time to make sure that Tali's awake.

I tiptoe up the stairs and quietly open her door. She's in bed, stirring, but not quite awake, the radio playing softly in the background. With her blanket pulled up to her chin, her face looks different, and I'm suddenly struck that she's all grown up. She is, after all, older than Elisheva and I were when we met. We brought her here seven years ago, a little girl, a few months shy of her Bat Mitzvah. She had two quiet years here, two glorious years to get used to a new life. And then, in the past five years, just as she was about to start high school, she and her brothers watched as we slid into war, as we managed to survive a war. Now, finally, we may be exiting a war. And my little girl is all grown up.

"You awake?" I whisper.

"Yeah, thanks," she says, and sits up. The blanket drops an inch or two. And there, peeking out of the top of the blanket, pressed against her shoulder, is her stuffed animal. It's Curious George, or "Curious," as we've called him since he joined the family when she got him nineteen years ago, the week she was born.

On the chair next to her, her uniform waits, ready for a new day. On the floor, her backpack ready to go. And in the closet, I know, is her gun.

Yet peering out from under her blanket, more than a bit worn but still soft, there he is. Curious.

I think about saying something funny, but there's nothing funny to say. There's an M-16 in the closet. And there's Curious. Asher was right. There are no words.

"See you downstairs in a few minutes?" I whisper, hoping she can't hear my voice beginning to crack, or see the tear beginning to well at the bottom of my eye.

"OK."

A few minutes later, she's downstairs in her uniform.

"Ready?"

"Yup," she says, slinging her gun over her shoulder. "Let's go."

It's not light yet in Jerusalem, and the city is still mostly asleep. Sitting next to me in the front seat, Tali leans her head back against the headrest and starts to doze. I turn the radio off, figuring she can use the quiet, and a few more minutes of shut-eye.

It's still a gorgeous city, Jerusalem. Wounded, to be sure, but recovering. The rising sun begins to reflect off the stone all around us, and there's a golden hue to the morning. It's the hue I used to love when we visited, the hue I hated to leave behind when we left. And now, it's the color of home.

I take the final left turn toward the bus station, and Tali's awake. There's a spot right next to the curb, and I slow the car to a stop.

"Thanks, Abba."

"Love you. Have a safe trip."

"Thanks. Love you, too."

And with that, she's out. She goes to the back of the car, takes out her pack, and swings the gun over her head. She closes the door, puts on the pack, and waves to me.

It's just a couple minutes shy of six-fifteen, and though the city is still quiet, the sidewalk is packed. Soldiers. Dozens of them, perhaps a hundred, all in green, are waiting in line to get into the bus station. Tall soldiers and short soldiers. Men and women. White skin and darker skin. Religious soldiers and secular soldiers. Soldiers who were probably orange, and soldiers who were probably blue, now all in green. Seasoned officers and brand-new recruits.

Tali walks toward the mass of green, and in a minute, I can't find her. I start to pull the car away, and turning my head, see her one last time as she walks through security and blends in with the rest of the crowd.

For the first time since she put that uniform on, I feel like crying. Because now, there really are no words. Because I miss her when she's not around. And maybe because I'm a little worried. About her. About all those kids who have to protect this still shrinking country.

And perhaps I'm feeling the way I do because of Curious, still lying there all alone on her bed at home, because there's something about Curious that means that she shouldn't have to be doing this.

But mostly, I think, the power of the moment stems from how easily, and how confidently, she blended into that crowd. Knowing what she has to do. Even wanting to do it. She knows that this country's in for a few more rough years, but she's willing, wholly without fanfare, to do her share, to tough it out.

And it's because she's totally comfortable here, comfortable in a way that Elisheva and I never will be.

I pull the car away from the curb, slide into traffic and into the left lane, beginning to make my way back to a house that I know will seem a little empty when I get there. As the bus station recedes in the rearview mirror, though, I reassure myself that it's OK. She hasn't really left home, I remind myself.

She *is* home, home in a way that she couldn't be anywhere else.

And so are we.

Acknowledgments

While working on this manuscript, I was reminded yet again how fortunate I have been to be associated with the Mandel Foundation since our family's arrival in Israel in 1998. I would not have met many of the people described in these pages or seen some of the sides of Israel described here were it not for the multifaceted dimensions of Israel with which the Foundation is engaged. The Mandel Foundation and its Mandel Leadership Institute are intellectually challenging, socially conscious, and culturally rich institutions, from which I have learned a great deal.

I am very grateful to Morton L. Mandel for the extraordinary vision for Jewish life in Israel and beyond that animates his work and that of the Foundation. To work with Mr. Mandel means to have an opportunity to grow and to learn with each conversation and with every exchange of ideas. It is a privilege and an honor to be associated with him and with his passion for the work that the Foundation does.

The very first time I met Professor Seymour Fox, in the summer of 1996, he asked me, almost at the start of our first conversation, "What can I do to help your career?" No one had ever asked me that question before, and no one else has done so much to introduce me to a new professional world, an environment in which the dialectic between theory and practice richly pervades each day's efforts. In the years that have passed, Professor Fox has become a cherished mentor, a teacher, and a friend, and Elisheva and I are deeply grateful to him for everything he has done to make our lives here possible.

Annette Hochstein, president of the Mandel Foundation, could not be more supportive or a more wonderful colleague, each and every day. Her guidance, wise counsel, prodigious knowledge, and personal warmth make my professional life both an exhilarating challenge and an ongoing pleasure. Annette has been a wonderful friend to our family; she is an extraordinary professional partner, and I look forward to working with her for many years to come.

To Vicky Bar-El and Nava Hatuel, my thanks for the devotion and talent that enable our office to run as smoothly as it does. Without their assistance and support, I cannot imagine having been able to complete this project.

To Stephen Kippur, president of the Trade Division at John Wiley & Sons, who initiated our correspondence and suggested this project, and to Kitt Allen, publisher at John Wiley, my thanks for their warmth and professionalism. Eric Nelson, senior editor at Wiley, has done much more than edit this book. He has helped to shape it and to give it focus, and he pushed me to think about the material in ways that I never would have had it not been for his guidance and insight. In the process, he has enriched this book immeasurably and has taught me a great deal about the craft of writing. I am deeply grateful.

Richard Pine, with whom I've had the pleasure of working for over ten years, is the consummate literary agent. One simply couldn't ask for more from an agent, a teacher, or a friend.

A number of colleagues either encouraged me to write some of the pieces that ultimately found their way into this volume or published selections in their journals once I'd written them. My thanks to Steven Bayme of the American Jewish Committee, Susan Berrin of *Sh'ma Magazine*, and Leo Haber of *Midstream Magazine* for their support and encouragement. To Stephen Flatow, my thanks for his generous permission to reprint his personal e-mail to me in this volume.

Throughout the years described in this volume, our family has been buoyed by the enduring friendship of many people from whom we're now separated by thousands of miles. They are too numerous to name here, but special thanks are due to Rabbi David Wolpe, who writes and speaks with an eloquence to which I dare not even aspire. For years David has faithfully kept us supplied with the *Atlantic Monthly*, the *New Yorker*, the *New York Times Magazine* and *Book Review*, TNR, and many more, concrete expressions of a friendship that only becomes more precious to us with time. And to Zion Ozeri, a world-renowned photo-journalist, my thanks not only for taking the author photo for this book but for a friendship that knows no geographical bounds. A tank commander during the Yom Kippur War and now an artist par excellence, Zion is one of those people whose insights and conversation about Israel, the Jewish people, and its destiny continuously leave me enriched and inspired.

Elisheva and I are also blessed to share our lives with a wonderfully supportive community in Jerusalem. Here, too, it would be foolhardy to attempt to mention all the friends who enrich our lives each day. But to our Bakk'a circle, and our friends beyond the 'hood, our thanks and our love for being the family that we don't have in Jerusalem. Particular thanks go, as always, to Pinchas and Sandy Lozowick, who when we first arrived, helped us make a home here in ways that no one else could, and to Levi Lauer, friend, colleague, and "sparring partner," whose love for this country and impatience with its imperfections constantly challenge me to think about what I'm seeing in new and deepened ways.

As I intimate in several places in these pages, my love for Israel and for the abiding miracle that this country is was first nurtured by my parents. Though Israel has changed a great deal since my parents first brought us here when I was a child, my parents' love for the Hebrew language, for the history of the Jewish people, and for the miracle of this country's very existence remains. Those qualities, along with their abiding and unconditional love, are but a few of the many extraordinary gifts they have given us.

My brothers and their wives, who live in the United States and in Canada, love this country no less than we do. It was Yonatan and his wife, Robbie, who first suggested many years ago, when they were living outside Jerusalem, that I consider preserving the letters I was writing so that they might be published. Elie and Avra offer boundless hospitality, H&H bagels, and a home away from home on my numerous work-related jaunts to New York. To all of them, and to my nieces and nephew, our thanks and love for their encouragement and all their support.

Our children have made our journey here all the more wondrous by adding three more sets of eyes through which to view this land and all that has transpired here over the past seven years. They've grown old enough that material that mentions them now has to be vetted, but they are lenient and tolerant censors and generous with their permission to have the story of their lives told a bit more widely than most kids their age have to endure.

Micha, our youngest, is our "most Israeli" child. He's the only one of the three who's lived here more than half his life, and yet he still marvels at this country and at his life here with the sort of insight one does not usually find in a twelve-year-old. I pray that he retains that awe about his adopted home for many years.

Avi, particularly of late, has brought to our conversations about Israel a passionate devotion to fairness and to understanding the "other," coupled with a commitment to the security, the Jewish character, and the legitimacy of the Jewish state that knows no bounds. I know very few people who combine those difficult-to-balance attributes in the elegant and honest way that he does. His intellectual acuity and moral integrity are, for Elisheva and for me, not only sources of pride, but standards to which we seek to hold ourselves accountable.

Talia, as the eldest, has had to do it all first. She was the first to go to high school here, the first to learn to drive on Israel's inimitable streets, the first to go to the army. But she's done more than do it first. She's done it all with aplomb and with her unique style. Whether debating in Singapore, Germany, or England, or speaking about Israel in Chicago, she's brought a remarkable savoir faire to doing it first. And most recently, to have her serve as the primary research assistant for this book—work that she did superbly—was a significant milestone, though probably more meaningful to me than to her!

To all of you, Ema and I love you and admire you, probably more than you can know. You have taught us infinitely more than we have taught you, and we pray that the love you now feel for Israel accompanies you for the rest of your lives.

From the day that we first met, Elisheva has loved Israel with a passion that has at times bemused me but that has always inspired me. We are here because of her, and she has embraced life here with a passion that has infected us all. We would not be part of the story that unfolds in this book were it not for her.

As she's done with every book I've written, Elisheva spent countless hours applying her editorial pen and her sensitive ear to every page of this manuscript, and she improved the text in countless ways. Now that she's also completed the tour guide course, her love for this country is matched by an encyclopedic knowledge of its nooks and crannies. Her erudition has enriched this book, but much more, her love and her devotion have enriched our family's collective lives beyond measure. Yehuda Amichai, one of Israel's greatest poets, wrote that "in a foreign country, you must love a girl who is a student of history," for "love is a serious matter." It is, and she is.

And I am, each and every day, ever more conscious of how richly blessed I am that our paths crossed one fine summer day, ten thousand miles from here, almost thirty years ago.

Jerusalem
Erev Rosh Hashanah 5766
October 2005

Credits

I am very grateful to the people and publications that afforded me an opportunity to share a portion of this material publicly in the past few years and thus to benefit from helpful responses, corrections, and suggestions. While I believe this list to be complete, because some of the material in this book first appeared in my letters published over the Internet, I am sometimes unaware of when that material is subsequently republished. My apologies to any publications that have been inadvertently omitted.

Chapters are referenced in the order in which they appear in this book.

"When Magical Thinking Will Not Suffice" first appeared, in different form, as "When Magical Thinking Will Not Suffice: Israeli Democracy, Israeli Arabs and the Kinneret Declaration," a contribution to the American Jewish Committee's *Symposium on the Kinneret Covenant*, January 2003.

"A Place Where Life Goes Through You" appeared in a slightly different form as "Why—Despite It All—We Stay," in the *Jerusalem Post*, June 13, 2004, p. A9, and was reprinted in a slightly altered version in *World Jewish Digest: Confronting Issues Facing Israel and World Jewry*, September 2003, pp. 20–23. It appeared, as well, as "Why We Stay," in *The Jewish Week*, June 27, 2003, pp. 34–35.

"Shattered" was published in a different form as "Questions Not Answered, Hopes Not Shattered" (Part 1 of 2), in the *Greater Des Moines Jewish Press*, October/November 2003, p. 13.

"Unacceptable, Unjust" appeared under that title in *The American Jewish World* (vol. 92, no. 30, April 9, 2004), p. 5.

"An Ode to Ambivalence" first appeared, in a very different form, under that title as part of a symposium on settlers and settlements, in *Sh'ma Magazine* (May 2004), p. 8.

"Even the Victors Ought to Mourn" first appeared as "Even the Victors Ought to Mourn: What the Left Owes the Settlers" in the *Jerusalem Post Up Front* (*Opinion*) section, October 29, 2004, p. 17, and was subsequently reprinted in the *Atlanta Jewish Times* as "In Gaza, a Sense of Betrayal" (November 12, 2004), p. 26.

"Lucky, Don't You Think?" was also published as "Daughters in Green: A Father Sends His Child to Arms," in *World Jewish Digest* (vol. 2, no. 7; March 2005), pp. 18–19.

"Exodus(es), Redux" was published as "A Last Look at Gaza," in the *National Jewish News* (vol. 32, no. 5; May 2005), pp. 1–7, and as "Goodbye to All That: A Family Takes a Final Road Trip Through Gaza," in *World Jewish Digest* (vol. 2, no. 11; July 2005), pp. 17ff.

Translations from the Hebrew Bible are taken from *Tanakh—The Holy Scriptures* (Philadelphia: Jewish Publication Society, 1988), often with minor modifications on my part.